Cultural Gerontology

Edited by Lars Andersson

AUBURN HOUSE
Westport, Connecticut • London

HQ1061 .C793 2002

0134110763833

Cultural gerontology

2002.

2008 05 26

Library of Congress Cataloging-in-Publication Data

Cultural gerontology / edited by Lars Andersson.
   p. cm.
  Includes bibliographical references and index.
  ISBN 0-86569-327-7 (alk. paper)
   1. Gerontology. 2. Ageism. 3. Culture. I. Andersson, Lars.

HQ1061 .C793 2002
305.26—dc21   2002023050

British Library Cataloguing in Publication Data is available.

Copyright © 2002 by Lars Andersson

All rights reserved. No portion of this book may be reproduced, by any process or technique, without the express written consent of the publisher.

Library of Congress Catalog Card Number: 2002023050
ISBN: 0-86569-327-7

First published in 2002

Auburn House, 88 Post Road West, Westport, CT 06881
An imprint of Greenwood Publishing Group, Inc.
www.greenwood.com

Printed in the United States of America

The paper used in this book complies with the Permanent Paper Standard issued by the National Information Standards Organization (Z39.48-1984).

10 9 8 7 6 5 4 3 2 1

Contents

Introduction   vii
   Lars Andersson

1 Time to Pay Back? Is There Something for Psychology
   and Sociology in Gerontology?   1
   Svein Olav Daatland

2 Utilization Patterns of Gerontology and the Dynamics
   of Knowledge Production   13
   Hans-Joachim von Kondratowitz

3 On the Possibilities of Spirituality and Religious Humanism
   in Gerontology or Reflections of One Aging American
   Cultural Historian   25
   Thomas R. Cole

4 Ageism and Globalization: Citizenship and Social Rights
   in Transnational Settings   45
   Chris Phillipson

Contents

5 Positioning Gerontology in an Ageist World 59
   Bill Bytheway

6 Involvement in Social Organizations in Later Life:
   Variations by Gender and Class 77
   Sara Arber, Kim Perren, and Kate Davidson

7 The Secret World of Subcultural Aging: What Unites and
   What Divides? 95
   Andrew Blaikie

8 Political Mobilization and Political Identity among
   Swedish Pensioners 1938–1945 111
   David Gaunt

9 The Making of Older Immigrants in Sweden: Identification,
   Categorization, and Discrimination 129
   Owe Ronström

10 Women Aging and Body Talk 139
    Chris Gilleard

11 Body Memories of Aging Women 161
    Marja Saarenheimo

12 The Bodywork of Care 173
    Julia Twigg

13 Going Concerns and Their Bodies 191
    Jaber F. Gubrium and James A. Holstein

14 Dis-Membered Bodies—Re-Membered Selves:
    The Discourse of the Institutionalized Old 207
    Haim Hazan

Index 221
About the Contributors 229

Introduction

Lars Andersson

During the past decades, the issue of culture has gained considerable attention within the humanities and social sciences, in general, as well as in the field of gerontology. Gerontology is a multidisciplinary science used to adopting new perspectives. The new perspectives certainly widen the scope of gerontology, but they diversify in different directions and can run the risk of being trivialized. Many disparate academic, political, and social issues fall under the overall umbrella of "cultural gerontology," making clear the need for a volume in which these issues are discussed.

The chapters cover a range of orientations from technical-instrumental to interpretive and emancipatory. The contributors examine the growth of gerontology as a discipline within an academic culture, the development of the concept of "ageism" as a sociocultural concept, identity politics in which older persons are perceived as belonging to a separate culture or subculture, and images of the older body in cultural perspective. They pay due attention to the impact of ageism, self-identity and self-image.

Svein Olav Daatland opens the introductory chapter with a bird's-eye view of the history of (social) gerontology and discusses its interchange with the mother disciplines of psychology and sociology. He notes that the trend from grand theories of aging to small-scale theorizing poses a number of dilemmas. For theoretical distinctiveness, gerontology on the one hand needs to view aging and old age as part of normal life to combat ageism; on the other hand, it needs a discontinuity. On the political or practical side, support has been given to problem-oriented research of a multidisciplinary type, where theorizing tends to become enervated. The increase in user-dominated multidisciplinary research and its effects is also discussed in the chapter by Hans-Joachim von Kondratowitz. The utilization of five types of gerontological knowledge and their different contexts are explored. The possible pathways of gerontology are taken further in Thomas Cole's chapter, which discusses the possibilities of spirituality and religious humanism in gerontology. He argues that the discourse of gerontology encourages a postmodern religious humanism, which accepts spiritual perspectives as necessary and constituent elements of the search for meaning.

Chapters 4 and 5 look more closely at the overriding concept of ageism. Chris Phillipson argues that the institutional factors influencing ageism are being transformed. In the twenty-first century, the sovereignty of nation-states will be challenged. It will be less appropriate to examine responses and solutions to ageism within national borders. While the possibilities for challenging ageism are pronounced, new sources of exclusion are also likely. Bill Bytheway, using articles from the years 1997–2000 in a gerontology journal as data, sets out to analyze how gerontologists relate their work not only to the concept of ageism, but also to gerontology in general and to older people.

The latter part of the book builds on two basic pillars of reality: politics and the body (Eagleton, 2000). Chapters 6 through 9 deal with identity politics. Since the 1980s, much of the politics of older people, especially older women and ethnic and minority aged, takes the form of an "identity politics" in which groups are mobilized to further their specific interests. This development follows the end of mass-utopia (Buck-Morss, 2000). Two key questions have been raised among scholars: the first addresses the absence of vision regarding the purpose of an extended life course; the second inquires into the sources of self-identity and self-image in higher ages. It has been suggested that spare-time activities can fulfill these functions. Sara Arber, Kim Perren, and Kate Davidson analyze involvement in social organizations in later life and how it varies as a function of gender and class. Andrew Blaikie discusses earlier attempts to view all people above, for instance, 65 years of age as a distinct subgroup with common interests and identity, as well as subdivisions such as young-olds versus old-olds and Third Age versus Fourth Age. Based on Merton's criteria for group membership, Blaikie suggests we might discern three paths in which older people maintain identity and self-esteem: cultures of resistance, cultures of incorporation, and cultures of consolation. David Gaunt relates the events in Sweden in the 1930s that led up to the formation of a pensioner organization critical to the government and the subsequent establishment of an organization loyal to the ruling Social Democratic party. Owe Ronström's chapter on the making of older immigrants in Sweden gives another example of how identity politics can also be imposed from above.

When people survive to old age, fear of death is often replaced by fears of disability or institutionalization, that is, fear of the so-called Fourth Age. In this context, what cultural meanings are ascribed to the gendered aging body in late modernity is a central question for ageism, social identity, and self-image. These questions become especially relevant in confrontations with bodily decline and negotiations of intimacy in institutions for older people.

In the last decades, there has been a growing interest in embodiment, focused especially on the material body. The five chapters on the aging body look specifically at the aging of women's bodies. Chris Gilleard outlines an approach toward viewing "body talk" as a means to expand the understanding of the actuality of aging, suggesting three main body practices through which women can talk about the subjective experiences of aging—body surfacing, body shaping, and body well-being. In Marja Saarenheimo's chapter, the relationship between body and memory is problematized by considering the autobiographical memory from the perspective of a mind that by necessity is situated in a body. The chapter illustrates the "search for the body" in empirical data from a reminiscence study. The search shows that talk about everyday life events has a strongly embodied nature.

Carework means working directly on the bodies of older people. In Chapter 12, Julia Twigg explores central dimensions of this activity. Taking a closer look at four features of bodywork, she examines how far and in what way they relate to the character of carework: the ambivalent, potentially negative nature of the work; its body-pleasing, body-pampering character; its potential as a form of Foucauldian biopower; and its location on the borders of sexuality. In the following chapter, Jaber Gubrium and James Holstein take a closer look at social institutions, for which they use the term "going concerns," and how they provide interactional resources and opportunities for assembling, altering, and sustaining our selves and identities. They illustrate how the body is used to signify the going concerns of various institutions, emphasizing how the construction of the body varies across institutions and over time.

In the final chapter, Haim Hazan focuses his interest in the symbolic position of older people and the cultural properties reflected by it. He suggests that the real position of older people can be identified in the residences meant for those who carry the cultural label "old" and that such places not only set boundaries between inside and outside in terms of social inclusion and exclusion, but also manifest a societal norm.

The chapters are based on invited presentations given at the Third International Symposium on Cultural Gerontology, held in June 2001 in Visby, Sweden. The symposium was arranged by the Swedish Gerontological Society and was sponsored by the Swedish Council for Social Research, KP's Jubileumsfond, and Senior 2005.

REFERENCES

Buck-Morss, S. (2000). *Dreamworld and catastrophe*. Cambridge, MA: MIT Press.
Eagleton, T. (2000). *The idea of culture*. Cambridge, MA: Blackwell.

Time to Pay Back? Is There Something for Psychology and Sociology in Gerontology?

Svein Olav Daatland

INTRODUCTION

It is nearly one century since Elie Metchnikoff coined the term *gerontology* for what he hoped would become a new scientific discipline and slightly more than one-half century since this field of research was institutionalized in the form of international associations, journals, and congresses. Hence, it is appropriate to reflect on the developments in the field to date, and indeed many have already done so. Full issues of the leading gerontology journals have been devoted to the theme, quite often in a slightly masochistic style, outlining the field's limitations and shortcomings. The main message has been the lack of theory and the bias toward applied issues.

Gerontology is said to be rich in data, but poor in explanations, and consequently has a low standard and status in the academic world (Achenbaum & Bengtson, 1994; Settersten & Dobransky, 2000). Correction of this weakness has been attempted, for example, by the recent publication of a separate handbook on the theories of aging (Bengtson & Schaie, 1999).

Let me add that as I myself have recently reached the half-century mark and spent half of this time in some association with gerontology, I have equally good personal reasons to pause and reflect. The low status of gerontology may help to explain the reaction I sometimes get when I present myself and my field of research, when others may look at me with some mix of surprise and pity: "What went wrong, dear?" Could this bittersweet question be directed also to gerontology?

Gerontology—and I here refer to social gerontology only—is indebted to the mother disciplines of psychology and sociology. What has (social) gerontology done with this loan? Have we managed the borrowed ideas and models well, or even refined them? Have we something to return to the basic disciplines, and are they interested in such a return from gerontology?

I begin with a retrospective glance at the formative years and sources of social gerontology. Second, what has come out of the effort? A third section covers the dilemmas of gerontology as an institution and as a field of research. From dilemmas I move briefly into the problems of exchange and communication between social gerontology and the basic disciplines. The concluding section faces the future: In what promising themes and issues may gerontology contribute positively to mainstream sociology and psychology?

THE FORMATIVE YEARS

We may date the scientific interest in aging to the emergence of modern medicine in the eighteenth century (Kirk, 1995). Some seeds for a *social* gerontology were planted in the nineteenth century in research and publications on mortality and demography, but the more immediate forerunners of social gerontology as we know it today can be dated to the 1920s and 1930s. A few articles on aging were published earlier in the century in psychology journals, but it was more of a breakthrough when Stanley Hall published his book *Senescence: The Second Half of Life* in 1922. He presented a psychologist's contribution "to the long desired, but long-delayed science of gerontology" (Birren & Birren, 1990). Stanley Hall probably had a self-interest in the theme, as he then was rather old, but for whatever reasons his initiative was important because of his status as a leading expert in developmental psychology. His book *Adolescence* was published in 1904. Developmental psychology was in these years restricted to childhood and adolescence. It was assumed that no psychological development took place in adulthood, at least not of a kind that deserved scientific interest.

Stanley Hall's *Senescence* did not open the blind eyes of developmental psychology to adult development, even though some well-known psychoanalysts like Else Frenkel Brunswik, Charlotte Bühler, and Carl Gustav Jung also wrote about maturity and indeed about aging in the 1930s. In contrast to Freud, they found adult development, even maturity and old age, to be of interest to psychology. In the 1950s, Erik Erikson followed suit and came to personify the developmental paradigm in social gerontology. Although Erikson himself did not identify with gerontology, one could use his model for such a purpose. The idea of a psychological development over the life course was useful in the construction of gerontology as a discipline.

Erikson represented what we may call a *normative change model*, in contrast to *the implicit stability model* of Freud and others, for example, that which is implied in trait psychology. We may also contrast the Erikson model to the *implicit decline model* of popular opinion. Continuity or change came to be the central issue within the psychology of aging; this issue has sailed under different labels over the years—from continuity theory in the 1960s and 1970s to various selectivity theories in the 1980s and 1990s. More is presented about this later.

The emergence of gerontology as a scientific field, a discipline in its own right, came in the years immediately following World War II. The leading persons and institutions were located in the United States, but Europe soon followed. The institutionalization of gerontology happened quickly, first with the establishment of national associations and soon after by international associations, congresses, and journals. The First World Congress of Gerontology was held in Liège, Belgium in 1950.

CLAIMING A SCIENTIFIC STATUS

A field with the ambition of claiming to be a scientific discipline needs its own distinct theories and methodologies. For social gerontology, one theory in particular came to symbolize this, namely, *disengagement theory*, outlined in Elaine Cumming and William Henry's book *Growing Old* in 1961. "This is an important book," wrote Talcott Parsons, the leading U.S. sociologist of the time, when he introduced the book in his foreword to the first edition. Parsons calls it "the most serious attempt so far to put forward a general theoretical interpretation of the social and psychological nature of the aging process." To be on the safe side he adds, "in American society," which is a reservation that Cumming and Henry themselves should have adopted. He also predicted that the book would serve "as the most important focus of discussion" of these issues for some time, as it did.

Parsons indicates that one reason that sociology, and indeed society in general, had failed to acknowledge the importance of gerontology is the value ascribed to youth and productivity, leading to the neglect of those who are seen as noncontributors, even burdens, to society. Parsons also praises the authors for their focus on the normal aging process, but he indicates his doubts about disengagement being the key process in question. He even suggests other mechanisms that might produce the same pattern, an unusual comment in a foreword to "an important book" and the first serious attempt to theorize "the social and psychological nature of the aging process." Parsons may have been praising the pioneering spirit and initiative of the authors more than their theory and conclusions.

The rest of the story is well known. Disengagement theory came to be in the center of the debate in the following years, not because it attracted support (it did not) but because it spurred debate and resistance. Gerontology needed a grand theory of aging in order to claim a position as a scientific discipline. Disengagement theory could serve such a purpose for several reasons: (1) it was a global theory on the aging process, (2) it included at least two disciplines—psychology and sociology, and (3) it presented old age as a qualitatively distinct phase of life and as a distinct piece of reality that needed a special theoretical and methodological approach, namely, gerontology. Arlie Hochschild (1975) has stated that a new discipline will often start out with a grand theory, followed by a period of critique with less ambitious theorizing, until new global theories may be developed. Gerontology has not produced a new wave of global theorizing and is seemingly still residing in the second phase, which may be taken as a proof in point: We are talking about a field of research—a paradigm or a perspective—rather than a scientific discipline in its own right.

Talcott Parsons may also have spoken highly about *Growing Old* because the authors' way of theorizing fit well into the structural-functionalist scheme of Parsons and the time. We should, however, notice that Cumming and Henry also refer in the introduction to their theory to David Riesman and Erik Erikson, two of the leading scholars of their time in sociology and psychology. Two researchers passing by in gerontology, as Elaine Cumming and William Henry did, were probably closer to the leading stars of psychology and sociology in their time than most others have been in the years that followed. One might have the impression that gerontology started on the top and has declined from grace ever since. If so, part of the reason may be that the first generation of gerontologists was recruited from mainstream psychology and sociology simply because it was the first. The relative emptiness in the new field attracted untraditional and bold scholars and invited grand theorizing. Later on, the field became dominated by followers and then regressed into details and small-range modeling.

VIRTUES AND VICES

A virtue of disengagement theory was its insistence on the discontinuity in the second half of life. Disengagement theory was based on common sense (the rocking-chair image), but it was also presented in contrast to another commonsense theory, what Cumming and Henry called the dominant but implicit theory of aging, whereby middle age was seen as the norm for successful and indeed normal aging. But why should 70- or 80-year-olds not have other needs and perspectives than those of 50-year-olds?

The true virtue of disengagement theory for gerontology was to give old age a status and quality (however problematic) as something different from earlier phases of life. The strategic advantage of this position was that such a distinct phase of life and living needed an equally distinct discipline. But when disengagement theory was discarded and proved wrong and was replaced by paradigms that trivialized the differences between old age and midlife, should not the idea of gerontology as a separate discipline also be discarded? It was not.

The alternative paradigm of the time, the so-called activity theory, came to be the dominant in the 1960s and 1970s, with an emphasis on the value of activity and continuity and the threats of social exclusion. This position was represented by such scholars as Robert Havighurst, Bernice Neugarten, Ernest Burgess, and others. Their virtue was to see aging in a societal context: how modern society might be a threat to activity and social integration in old age. They discussed differential aging, with many ways of aging and diversity in old age. But the insistence on continuity and the value ascribed to activity tended to make midlife the norm and to see decline in old age as a failure. This weakened the very reasoning and grounds for a distinct discipline. Indeed, Neugarten—in her older years—argued for "the end of gerontology" (Neugarten, 1994). This was a strong statement from a person who had spent most of her academic career in the field, although her interest had always been broader than aging as such and included changes over the whole life course. She now recommended basing research in the field on a broader life-course perspective.

DILEMMAS

The early years of gerontology were dominated at the macro level by functionalist thinking and role theory. The focus was first generally on the role and status of elders in society; later it divided into more specific studies of role transitions in the domains of work (and retirement) and the family. The roles and functions of social policies were also major issues. At the micro or individual level, the focus was on psychological adjustment—often in some form of stage theory—and life satisfaction. Later on, studies of coping and control and various forms of selectivity theories based on images of strategic adaptations, more than passive adjustments, became prominent. Among these were Paul and Margaret Baltes' (1990) model of selective optimization with compensation and Laura Carstensen's socioemotional selectivity theory (1991). The focus was in all years on the conditions and contents of so-called successful aging. This topic was also on the agenda for sociologists, but under other labels such as welfare and level of living.

From the bolder theorizing about the status and role of older people in modern society on the macro level (Burgess, 1960; Cowgill & Holmes, 1972) and from theorizing about human universals on the micro level (Cumming & Henry, 1961; Erikson, 1959), gerontology eventually retreated into small-scale modeling. Some would rather say that gerontology regressed into individualistic perspectives, with a focus on how the aging individual adapts and how one can assist and ameliorate the predicaments and problems of old age (Hagestad, 1999; Hagestad & Danefer, 2001). This position is what Peter Townsend (1981) criticized as "acquiescent functionalism," through which conventional gerontology, according to Townsend, contributed to reproducing the dependencies of old age and to legitimizing societal ageism. Gerontology in a sense needed and reinforced the very ageism it set out to combat. Therefore, Townsend and others called out for a new—and critical—gerontology.

The main trend in social gerontology had moved from more ambitious theories about aging and elders to a variety of smaller studies and data collections, at best with only small-scale theorizing and often so intimately connected to applied issues and problems that theories and theorizing suffered. This raised two types of dilemmas.

Theoretically, the dilemma concerned the distinctiveness of aging as a process and old age as a condition and thus the very argument for a distinct discipline. On the one hand, gerontology aimed to include aging and old age into the normal course of life in order to combat prejudice and ageism. On the other hand gerontology needed a difference—a discontinuity—that would justify a distinct treatment.

On the *practical* or *political* side, the dilemma was between theory and application, between the academy and the professional field. The best arguments for financial, moral, and political support concerned the immediate use of research in order to ameliorate problems among elders. Through this avenue one could also expand gerontology as an institution by including practitioners and could integrate people and perspectives from several disciplines and professions. Therefore, gerontology was presented as a multidisciplinary—even an interdisciplinary—science, whatever the latter might be. While problems and interventions may be multidisciplinary, theorizing may not—or may be so only at the expense of theoretical sophistication.

The attempt to include people and perspectives from a number of disciplines resulted in a tragic compromise, where each special flavor was lost in the general blend.

PROBLEMS OF EXCHANGE

The relative isolation of gerontology from basic disciplines like psychology and sociology—or for that matter, like economics, anthropology, and history—should not be blamed on gerontology alone. Vern Bengtson and Jim Dowd (1980) have outlined four major reasons for the poor exchange between social gerontology and sociology. The first is the preoccupation with applied issues or so-called ameliorative gerontology—practical knowledge that can be applied immediately instead of theory of more general relevance. The main problem may be not the lack of theories as such, but the low interest in theorizing among those with an inclination for practice, who were expanding to become dominant in the gerontological arena. A second reason is the lack of manpower and the low attractivity of the field. A third reason is the preoccupation with old people (patterns) instead of with aging and life-cycle changes (processes), another side of the story of prioritizing application over theory. The fourth reason is that the concept of age has been neglected in sociology as a parameter of social organization.

Sociology has been (relatively) blind to how age and aging is constructing—and is in turn constructed by—social organization. This theme has been the central issue in Mathilda White Riley's (1985) age-stratification paradigm, about whose value she insistently has tried to convince sociology, with mixed luck.

Riley is proof that a gerontologist may be highly regarded in a basic discipline. She was elected president of the American Sociological Association. Alice Rossi and Jill Quadagno, both of whom are active in aging studies, have also been elected president of this association. Hence, the sociology of aging has reached a certain level of respect, at least in the United States.

A brief glance through some major textbooks from the later years indicates that aging and gerontology have probably a stronger position in the United States than in Europe. Some European textbooks have hardly discovered that the life course and the population have changed dramatically over the last one hundred years.

Let me add a few other reasons for the problems of communication between gerontology and the basic disciplines. One is that gerontology may have been trapped in the cage of interdisciplinarity. Most established disciplines and universities resist such an effort, which, while it may be an advantage when you want to solve practical problems, may be a drawback when you develop theories. Theories are more or less by their nature discipline specific; in fact, they may even refer to sub-specialties within each discipline.

Resistance to gerontology may also come from gerontophobia (fear of aging) and ageism in modern society. In modernity the machine developed as an important metaphor and image of societies and individuals. Productivity and utility then became indicators of status and value, while older people and others who were seen as unproductive were conceived as burdens. Old age and orientation toward the past were given less value than youth and orientation toward the future. Features like these seem necessary to explain the strange lack of interest in research on aging in a period with more radical changes in life courses and populations than ever before—changes that have made aging more and more relevant both to individuals and societies.

FUTURE POTENTIALS

When we consider what gerontology has in fact contributed—whether as paybacks or as its own products—we need to refer not only to sophisticated constructs and theories, but also to good data and interesting research questions in a field that has been neglected by the basic disciplines. The development of designs and methods may be included among such contributions. The extension of developmental psychology to include adulthood, maturity, and old age is clearly an important achievement, although gerontology should not be the only field credited. Aging and old age may in fact be a particularly adequate "laboratory" for research on individual coping and adaptations, considering the many stresses associated with aging and the long lines of influences over the life course. The many selectivity, coping, and control models from the later decades prove the fact.

In the postmodern era, the modernist dream of unified and universal theories may be over (Cole, 1995), while the anti-order of postmodern life and experience may find a particular resonance in the experience of old age. According to Hazan (1995), there is a striking similarity between the lack of stable communities in postmodern society and the absence of community experienced by many elders. So also with the management of multiple selves and identities in postmodernity: Older people are models of postmodernist experience in their efforts to manage their inner and outer selves, their feelings of separation between mind and body, and their feelings of being strangers—immigrants—in time (Dowd, 1986). All these are promising areas for research.

Gerontology has been instrumental in the development of research designs through the separation of age, cohort, and period effects via various forms of longitudinal, time lag, and sequential studies. Among its contributions to sociology are family and intergenerational studies. Gerontologists ironically—and "ungratefully"—contradicted the Parson thesis on the isolated nuclear family and the loss of family functions. Intergenerational relationships are still strong in modern society, with frequent contacts and instrumental exchanges also beyond the nuclear family. The "modified extended family" seemed a better characteristic for the modern family (Connidis, 2001). Also important are the outlining of the life course as a socially constructed institution (Kohli, 1986) and the introduction of the age stratification paradigm (Riley, 1985), with age as a structuring principle of societies as well as individuals. Aging and old age may also be seen as one of the few relevant avenues to studies of human universals and the connections between nature and man. In old age we live at the edges of life and are constantly reminded of that.

Let me conclude by suggesting some directions for future inquiry. They refer to the old themes of continuity or discontinuity in psychology and to social inclusion or exclusion in sociology. The themes are not new, but they may be approached from new angles and will have increasing importance as lives are getting longer, as social distances between cohorts are expanding, and as solidarity between age groups is increasingly under pressure. We should study the continuities and discontinuities in individual lives—over individual time—including what are the needs and possibilities for seeing life as a whole. In so doing, we should focus on variability in styles and ways of aging and how differential aging is produced in interaction between societal structures and individual choices over the life course.

A second focus could be on continuities (and discontinuities) over *historical time*—across historical generations—which may become increasingly difficult as lives are getting longer and the social pulse is beating faster. The construction of continuity between past and present may then be threatened. While the young may experience problems of inclusion, elders may face increasing risks of exclusion from ever earlier ages. Elders need both a society that remembers the past and a stake in the future. The young may need the resonance and images from history and the space necessary to create new futures.

A third focus could be on social integration across generations within families and, at the macro level, between age groups, cohorts, and historical generations in society. The challenges of the expanding gap across age and ethnicity will in the future add to or go beyond the traditional divisions associated with class and gender. Age segregation may be the tune of the future, if we are not able to bridge the gap between age groups and historical generations.

One need not be a (social) gerontologist to look into these questions. We might do better if we could convince mainstream social science to adopt such perspectives, which should be possible in light of the radical changes we are now experiencing. The average life span in modern societies became 50 percent longer during the last century and is still expanding, in particular in the developing world. Populations have changed from a majority being young to a majority being middle-aged or older; again, the developing world is following at a more rapid pace. Aging and the second half of life should then be increasingly relevant for individuals, societies, and the sciences.

REFERENCES

Achenbaum, W. A., & Bengtson, V. L. (1994). Re-engaging the disengagement theory of aging: On the history and assessment of theory development in gerontology. *The Gerontologist, 34*(6), 756–763.

Baltes, P. B., & Baltes, M. M. (1990). Psychological perspectives on successful aging: The model of selective optimization with compensation. In P. B. Baltes & M. M. Baltes (Eds.), *Successful aging: Perspectives from the behavioral sciences*. Cambridge, U.K.: Cambridge University Press.

Bengtson, V. L., & Dowd, J. J. (1980). Sociological functionalism, exchange theory and life-cycle analysis: A call for more explicit theoretical bridges. *International Journal of Aging and Human Development, 12*(1), 55–73.

Bengtson, V. L., & Schaie, K. W. (Eds.). (1999). *Handbook of theories of aging*. New York: Springer.

Birren, J. E., & Birren, B. A. (1990). The concepts, models, and history of the psychology of aging. In J. E. Birren & K. W. Schaie (Eds.), *Handbook of the psychology of aging*. San Diego: Academic Press.

Burgess, E. W. (1960). Aging in Western culture. In E. W. Burgess (Ed.), *Aging in Western societies*. Chicago: University of Chicago Press.

Carstensen, L. (1991). Socioemotional selectivity theory: Social activity in life-span context. *Annual Review of Gerontology and Geriatrics, 11*, 195–217.

Cole, T. R. (1995). What have we "made" of aging? *Journal of Gerontology, 50B*(6), S341–343.

Connidis, I. A. (2001). Family ties and aging. Thousand Oaks, CA: Sage.

Cowgill, D. O., & Holmes, L. D. (1972). *Aging and modernization*. New York: Appleton-Century-Crofts.

Cumming, E., & Henry, W. E. (1961). *Growing old: The process of disengagement*. New York: Basic Books.

Dowd, J. J. (1986). The old person as a stranger. In V. W. Marshall (Ed.), *Later life: The social psychology of aging*. Beverly Hills, CA: Sage.

Erikson, E. (1959). *Identity and the life cycle*. New York: W. W. Norton.

Hagestad, G. O. (1999). A gray zone? Meetings between sociology and gerontology. *Contemporary Sociology: A Journal of Reviews, 28*(5), 514–517.

Hagestad, G. O., & Danefer, D. (2001). Concepts and theories of aging: Beyond microfication in social science approaches. Chapter 1 in R. H. Binstock & L. K. George (Eds.), *Handbook of aging and the social sciences* (5th ed.). New York: Academic Press.

Hazan, H. (1995). Lost horizons regained: Old age and the anthropology of contemporary society. In A. S. Ahmed & C. N. Shore (Eds.), *The future of anthropology*. London: Athlone.

Hochschild, A. R. (1975). Disengagement theory: A critique and a proposal. *American Sociological Review, 40*, 553–569.

Kirk, H. (1995). *Da alderen blev en diagnose*. København: Munksgaard.

Kohli, M. (1986). The world we forgot: A historical review of the life course. In V. W. Marshall (Ed.), *Later life: The social psychology of aging*. Beverly Hills, CA: Sage.

Neugarten, B. L. (1994). The end of gerontology. *Northwestern University Center on Aging Newsletter, 10*, 1.

Riley, M. W. (1985). Age strata in social systems. In R. H. Binstock & E. Shanas (Eds.), *Handbook of aging and the social sciences*. New York: Van Nostrand Reinhold.

Settersten, R. A., & Dobransky, L. M. (2000). On the unbearable lightness of theory in gerontology. *The Gerontologist, 40*(3), 367–373.

Townsend, P. (1981). The structured dependency of the elderly: A creation of social policy in the twentieth century. *Aging and Society, 1*, 5–28.

2

Utilization Patterns of Gerontology and the Dynamics of Knowledge Production

Hans-Joachim von Kondratowitz

INTRODUCTION

In this chapter, I draw attention to a range of effects on the bases and the structure of knowledge in our societies—effects that I perceive to be consequences of the growth and increasing importance of gerontology. I begin with a brief comment on the assertion that noticeable "growth" in gerontological impacts is exemplified in the research arena and by the influence research has had both on discourse within the discipline and on societal discourse in general. Second, I trace different diffusion patterns of gerontological knowledge in a practical work context. I then present a typology of modes of gerontological knowledge. Based on an empirical study conducted in Germany, it delineates an ambivalent development that requires further discussion: an increase in "user-dominated gerontological contexts of work" with their own logic of action. In a fourth section, I address further dimensions of these user-dominated contexts and, finally, attempt to show that these contexts might lead to the implementation of new approaches in cultural-gerontological research and projects.

GROWTH AND DIFFERENTIATION OF THE GERONTOLOGICAL DOMAIN

Is there remarkable *growth* in gerontology? I use the term here mainly in a social science perspective (including care and public health or social medicine, as well as social work). Considering the growth rates in gerontological research (publicly funded or supported and conducted by various foundations) and the increasing numbers of new institutional facilities providing counseling, expertise, and further (adult) education in gerontology, evidence of such growth is clear. Moreover, gerontological expertise now reaches developing countries through the agency of international research networks and educational facilities. The acquisition of gerontological expertise proceeds at different paces in these countries, depending on each nation's socioeconomic situation, but the overall trend is toward a relative increase in the societal significance of the field.

This increasing significance is most clearly demonstrated by the *differentiation* taking place in the discipline, in close and inextricable association with the growth process. In developing countries, gerontology seems increasingly to be abandoning the classical domains of demography, health policy, and sociopolitical research. It is beginning to establish itself with a sociogerontological approach in its own right, taking greater account of local project experience and practical contexts dominated by social work. But differentiation is also apparent in the industrialized countries of the "first world," within the spectrum of established academic gerontology, including cooperation with the natural and social sciences, and within the social sciences.

In the wider and cooperative gerontology spectrum, something of a stalemate has developed with regard to the old promise of supposedly genuine interdisciplinarity. The repeated evocation of interdisciplinarity over the years has not succeeded in making it a constituent factor in the self-definition of gerontology. It can be argued that disciplinary approaches still play the decisive role in the gerontology adventure. Sometimes, however, this promise of interdisciplinary research bears fruit, as in the case of the *Berlin Aging Study* by Paul Baltes and associates (Baltes & Mayer, 1999). But conditions for cooperation have been very specific, and they had to be carefully tended, monitored, and safeguarded throughout the duration of the project. Interdisciplinary contexts remain rare exceptions, needing constant renegotiation. Less well monitored and more casual, everyday "on the spot" research is not at the same level, nor can it compete. This often means that researchers fall back on the scientific stature and logic of their own original disciplines, thus showing suboptimizing behavior.

This brings us to the second dimension of differentiation. There appear to be attempts to confirm disciplinary definitions by reverting to and reintegrating the central discourses and theoretical premises of the social sciences from which gerontologists originally come. Such reintegration promises active participation in decisive and broader theoretical developments within these disciplines and may therefore serve at best as a deliberate external "transfusion" for the gerontological debate. On the other hand, it implies that "social gerontology" is too narrow in scope and too limited in intellectual challenge. Such a view has now materialized in Germany. The recent foundation of a special "Ageing and Society" (Altern und Gesellschaft) section within the German sociological association has also been justified as a deliberate challenge to the logic of professional gerontological associations, a move which could be seen almost as shifting sociological debate from gerontologically-defined contexts. To my knowledge there have been similar developments in the United States, where the renewal of disciplinary trammels is based on a more refined level of experience with the gerontological enterprise. The United States is still at a different, more advanced stage of development in the establishment of gerontology in the academic infrastructure and its presence in practical contexts.

However, a tendency to develop a relative distance between the social sciences and social gerontology appears to be only one line of disciplinary reaction. Gerontologists point to a second phenomenon. More than ever, gerontology appears to have become an inviting enterprise for sociologists who years ago would not have dreamed of engaging in the field, but who are now increasingly interested in actively participating in a specialization that, in an aging society, appears to be attracting increasing funds.

DIFFUSION AND EXTENSION OF GERONTOLOGICAL KNOWLEDGE

These diverse differentiation processes are also reflected in research practice and in the design of projects that are "gerontologically self-defined," and they have produced several characteristic developmental patterns in the gerontological discourse that can be followed at different levels of analysis.

First of all, an important but still substantially unresearched field, the *diffusion of gerontological knowledge,* should be mentioned. This pattern of diffusion could be operationalized as the use, incorporation, and distribution of single gerontological terms, comprehensive gerontological terminology, and far-reaching concepts in everyday language and their transfer to everyday conceptions about structuring the course of human life. Generally speaking, I will try to demonstrate this at the "longue durée" level (to use French historian Fernand Braudel's term) and at a "meso-level," but with the prospect of at least discovering areas that may prove important for the micro-level, as well. At the "longue durée" level, I see these everyday conceptions as shaped by *historical processes of expert dominance and administrative regulation* in the process of structuring and shaping the "risk of old age" in modern society (cf. von Kondratowitz, 2000). In Table 2.1, I try to show how these typologies of old age or types of social constructions are organized, processed, and negotiated at the societal level in Germany. The table shows a clear dividing line between—to use Anthony Glascock's terminology— "healthy" or "intact" age, as opposed to "increpit age." In its various representations, this dichotomization emphasizes the presence or absence of *orientation* toward *societal achievement* in the course of the phase of life termed "old age," while the associated need constellations (as representations of the developing and expanding welfare state) figure as the central elements in ascribing *societal inclusion* or *exclusion*.

THE DYNAMICS OF ORGANIZING TYPES OF KNOWLEDGE

While the empirical material offered by various studies demonstrates an impressive kind of long-term continuity, there is also considerable change over time; it is interesting to note that this change occurs in increasingly shorter spans of time as we approach the present. Growing emphasis is placed on the "healthy side," putting more pressure on the "increpit side," with a tendency almost to eliminate this less comforting part of old age. Indeed, one might ask whether more recent and powerful concepts like "successful aging" still have any counterpart on the "infirm side."

A process of societal acceleration is also apparent. Together with extension of the healthy side and contraction of the infirm side, models and concepts succeed at an ever faster pace—sometimes in competition and with much overlapping—as we approach the present situation. German old-age policy design and implementation at the local authority level is more than ever characterized by competition and interaction between differing concepts of old age. The emphasis is on the healthy side of age. Even the concepts for long-term care—with their explicit concentration on rehabilitation and prevention—which on the surface appear to differentiate "infirm age," are in fact heavily committed to

TABLE 2.1. Expert Dichotomizations of Old Age in Modern Society

Dichotomizations of Old Age	Essential content of the dichotomously organized social constructions	Dominance of the dichotomous models over time
1. "High of Age" vs. "Worn Out Age" ("Hohes Alter" vs. "Abgelebtes Alter")	Discourse of "veneration" as a reflection of an age-related power structure—Gradual disappearance of "vital force" over the lifetime	18 century to the first half of 20 century
2. "Still hale and hearty age" vs. "Infirm/Decrepit Age" ("Rüstiges Alter" vs. "Gebrechliches Alter")	Remaining ability to show cooperative societal achievements—Body images accentuate signs of weakening capabilities (by using the metaphor of fragile bones)	Turn of 19/20 century to mid-century
3. "Normal Age" vs. "Pathological Age" ("Normales Alter" vs. "Pathologisches Alter")	"Majority" definitions of social adequacy of old age developments—"Minority" definitions of old age as "unproductive" (Quetelet) or as a social burden	Late 19 cent. into the fifties of 20 century
4. "Age in Need" vs. "Frail Age" ("Bedürftiges Alter" vs. "Hinfälliges Alter")	Old age as increasingly exposing material and emotional needs—Old age as being dominated by the need to take care (by using the metaphor of the fall syndrome)	Late forties to the early seventies
5. "Active Age" vs. "Age in Need of Care" ("Aktives Alter" vs. "Pflegebedürftiges Alter")	Construction of old age as participating in offers of local social policy and as increasing competence—Health-impaired older people as potential clients of the service sector	In the seventies
6. "Young Old" vs. "Old Old" ("Junge Alte" vs. "Alte Alte")	Adopting the Anglo-American distinction between two different need constellations	In the eighties
7. "Third Age" vs. "Fourth Age" ("Drittes Lebensalter" vs. "Viertes Lebensalter")	Adopting the Anglo-American/French distinction between two complex and highly differentiated life situations in old age (explicitly "value neutral")	In the late eighties and early nineties
8. "Autonomous Age" vs. "Dependent Age" ("Autonomes Alter" vs. "Abhängiges Alter")	Emphasis on the degree of freedom to organize life in old age as a self-determined process—Emphasis on the increasing necessity to negotiate service packages according to the relative status of health	In the early nineties

the vision of a prolonged activity pattern. This now extends even to the highest age groups, which medical science used to term "incurable chronically ill."

AMBIVALENCES IN THE UTILIZATION OF KNOWLEDGE

Such a broad frame of reference indicates how comprehensive the field of normative structures is in which everyday perceptions of old age are formed and shows that there are experts and specialists who serve as "gatekeepers of meaning." Indeed, this points to a long-term research program, for there are clear indications that the current competing concepts of aging just mentioned and their verbal expression and connotations are slowly entering a wider public domain and even being accepted as legitimizing models by self-help groups and social movements among the aged. If we therefore address the subject of how and to what extent they will be integrated at the everyday level, certain important questions—which I can do no more than raise at this point—will need to be answered.

From a sociological point of view, we are dealing with the much broader problem of how scientific (or, more modestly, systematically organized) knowledge is adopted and integrated in everyday life. According to a well-known thesis, the successful integration of such structured knowledge would paradoxically increase its invisibility and cause its consequent oblivion. The utilization of knowledge ought therefore to be considered a process of reinterpretation in given contexts of action and praxis.

Elements of knowledge collected and contemplated free from the pressure of specific action are now confronted by constraints, perceptions, and situational factors that tend to divest this knowledge of its scientific roots, transforming and translating it into modes of everyday conversation and rules of action. Such transformation would also markedly increase the autonomy of those using the transformed knowledge. "Split utilization" of knowledge in terms of user definition is conceivable, which means that the knowledge in question could be rejected in one context and accepted in another, giving the framing of the context a decisive function. Some authors, including Ulrich Beck, have termed this process *trivialization* (cf. Beck & Bonss, 1989). But they have been justifiably criticized for tacitly assuming a hierarchy in which a still identifiable "scientific knowledge" has a higher-quality standing from the outset and therefore confronts and even competes with "lower-level knowledge" in everyday life.

This point of criticism alone makes it clear that the theoretical perspective just elaborated raises several controversial issues. Is "everyday consciousness" the objective of scientific investigation, or should it be? Is social science knowledge really so exclusively enriched by interpretations as these observers claim? Is there not a wide range of sociological information that could be qualified as technical, data-specific, or at least relational in quality? Are contexts of utilization not rather confronted by existing institutional structures, by "systems of utilization" (in the words of Niklas Luhmann), rather than by individuals pursuing different strategies for gaining possession of scientific knowledge? These ineluctable questions impose scrutiny of these implicit "hierarchizations" of knowledge and their societal perception.

EMPIRICAL DECIPHERMENT OF THE USE OF GERONTOLOGICAL KNOWLEDGE

Without a doubt, the notion of a hierarchy of knowledge that renders the development of "trivial transformations" necessary leaves several questions unanswered. The inability to conceptualize sociological knowledge in a nonessential manner is one of the main reasons why interactionist approaches are now attracting attention. The issue is how users of sociological knowledge define this type of knowledge for themselves. Whether such a perspective can reflect long-term societal influences as described earlier rather than merely mirroring what users attribute to organizational sources as "knowledge" remains to be seen and would make further empirical investigation imperative. However, any further analysis requires the introduction of a "meso" level in order to trace negotiations on the implementation of sociological expertise about old age. While this level would mirror the increasing autonomization of users with the consequence of an increase in *user-dominated contexts*, it would also have to reflect the existence of institutional contexts that shape the use of knowledge if it is to be able to describe these new contexts of user-domination more appropriately.

In order to analyze this in the case of gerontological knowledge, I therefore undertook a three-city comparative study (in Berlin, Munich, and Wiesbaden) dealing with discourses and negotiations relating to the development of projects on supportive counseling for home care delivery in Germany (von Kondratowitz, 1993). The research was conducted during the restructuring of national policy on care in Germany, which began with the 1989 Health Reform Act and ended with implementation of the new Long Term Care Insurance (LTCI) in 1995/1996. The field of research was thus strongly influenced by the discussion and turbulence arising from these radical changes in service delivery and the accompanying changes in language and perceptions, while proving to be highly dynamic, flexible, and open for contrasting experiences. Besides a thorough sociopolitical analysis of welfare strategies for the aged within the "local welfare state," I also conducted qualitative interviews on these problems within the three municipal settings with different groups of knowledge users from different levels of expertise. I cannot go into too great detail at this point, but suffice it to say that I took an ethnomethodological approach in that I tried to relate the routine practices of everyday men and women to knowledge production, which was justified scientifically in order to let them share a common construction of reality.

My approach to "practical gerontological knowledge" was threefold. The first assumption was that such knowledge is formed by rules, propositions, and specialized terms that reveal a certain intimacy with discipline-specific findings of social science–oriented research on aging, but which are nevertheless translated into a different language and flexibly adapted to the given situation (e.g., critique of the "deficit model of aging," the role of "independent living," and "active aging"). A second aspect was concerned with patterns of interpretation at the everyday level as expressed in proverbs, governing principles of aging, recipe-type recommendations, and so on, which tend to be independent of scientific knowledge but most of which relate to "body images" of age, as shown in Table 2.1, and are of early modern origin. The third perspective could be summed up as the process of "dealing with knowledge," as pointing to a more self-reflexive and critical way of handling information, depending on the given situation and needs. My interview material yielded five new and differing types of gerontological knowledge, rendered utilitarian through attribution to and

TABLE 2.2. Gerontological Knowledge and Utilization Contexts

Types of Knowledge Contexts of Utilization	Gerontologial knowledge of justification and legitimation	Gerontological knowledge of (nonjuridical) competence	Gerontological knowledge of production	Gerontological knowledge of negotiation	Gerontological knowledge of everyday experience
Administrative action and activities	dominant	strong	balanced	dominant	weak
Professional cultures	moderate	weak	balanced	strong	balanced
Public domain	moderate	weak	balanced	strong	balanced
Organized interests	moderate	balanced	dominant	strong	moderate
Micropolitical processes	balanced	weak	moderate	balanced	strong

processing in different settings, which I refer to as "contexts of utilization." Table 2.2 tries to categorize them by presence and degree of intensity. It should be stressed that these contexts are to be considered as prearranging and framing conditions for visualizing knowledge for the user.

While different loadings are apparent, as well as the concentration of certain types across most contexts (knowledge of production; knowledge of negotiation), it is clear that Table 2.2 cannot adequately reflect change in following the implementation of home care programs and the gerontological knowledge types used. It would be highly interesting to know whether there are "coalitions" between different contexts—the concentration just referred to seems to point in this direction. Change over time is also not adequately reflected. I am sure the picture would be different now that Long Term Care Insurance has been fully implemented and specific networks of new initiatives and of negotiatory constraints have developed, as we are now aware some six years after the legislation came into effect.

I conclude this section with Table 2.3, which shows the presence or absence of the three perspectives on gerontological knowledge in the five types of knowledge identified in the context of practical, local home care programs.

TABLE 2.3. Presence of Types of Gerontological Knowledge

Perspectives Types of Knowledge	First perspective: reinterpreted adaptations of science; concepts; terms	Second perspective: everyday life patterns of interpretation; recipe-type knowledge	Third perspective: "dealing with" knowledge; self-reflexive modes
Gerontological knowledge of justification and legitimation	present	not present	not present
Gerontological knowledge of (nonjuridical) competence	present	not present	not present
Gerontological knowledge of production	present	present	present
Gerontological knowledge of negotiation	not present	present	present
Gerontological knowledge of everyday experience	not present	present	present

THE COMPLEXITY OF KNOWLEDGE AUTONOMIZATION

The increasing autonomization of demand vis-à-vis the offerings of social science knowledge is not specific to social gerontology, as we have seen in the preceding sections. In fact, the common basis for the discourse is not a particular knowledge type but social science knowledge and its transformation rules in general. But it is obvious that a scientific endeavor like gerontology with weak theoretical ties and intellectual traditions is subject to particular pressure. Here the long-deplored poor theoretical base of gerontological reasoning produces ambivalent results. On the one hand, the existing dominance of practical contexts, which the insistence on more theoretical work was intended to offset, is now even stronger and potentially more difficult to counterbalance. On the other hand—and this complicates the situation even more— a clear pattern of increasing diversification in gerontological research is apparent beyond the already implicit autonomization of knowledge production in the social sciences, due to important changes in welfare regimes, at least in Germany.

While this diversification proceeded at a slower pace in the early 1990s, it received marked impetus from the introduction of new provisions on care (LTCI) and the considerable changes they brought. They included an enormous increase in new organizational units for home care (e.g., private and nonprofit care service organizations) as well as institutional care. The old image of Germany presented by comparative welfare state research as typically low on social services and high on informal family work in the area of care for the aged began to crumble and cautiously change. At the same time, the boundaries between institutional and home care have become more and more flexible, now allowing the design and implementation of a multiplicity of new care arrangements between home and institution at the local level. This differentiation has in turn produced a greater need for coordination and cooperation and for accompanying scientific expertise among care providers and their support structures at several older and more recent levels. The trend is toward more user-dominated research contexts, and the resulting short- and long-term consequences for research strategies are now the subject of debate. In any case, the research outlook seems more than ever to be governed by the requirements of practical contexts rather than the discourses of theoretically-refined gerontological reasoning. It remains to be seen whether this is necessarily detrimental to the attempts of critical gerontologists to urge the theoretical reassessment of gerontology in general, but such a development cannot be disregarded and may make the project even more difficult. The strong trend toward more practical and user-dominated gerontological research contexts may therefore prove a two-edged blessing with unbidden consequences.

Another clear trend in the development of gerontological research is somewhat related to the topics just mentioned. The now acute awareness of the social consequences of aging societies has engendered a strong desire to take over "best practices" from other countries as functioning examples of policy-driven solutions. This is fostered by the growing sense of interconnectedness among national societies, with particular urgency in a united Europe, where a wide range of long-term adaptations and structural changes have to be adopted by parliaments and a commission. In the face of this pressure, the perspective of *comparing* welfare states and their achievements has been an increasingly important topic for gerontological research. The debate goes far beyond the classical procedure of comparing organizational arrangements or service networks. The attention of gerontological research is focusing more and more on the *embedded cultural prerequisites* and *normative foundations* of welfare states (e.g., as manifested in family cultures and care cultures). Recent British publications offer excellent examples of work being done in this direction. *User domination* as an expression of the ongoing *autonomization* of social science, together with this *cultural-gerontological* outlook on *comparative work* on the changing normative foundations of our welfare delivery, seems to constitute one important line of research in a future cultural gerontology in Europe.

REFERENCES

Baltes, P. B., & Mayer, K. U. (1999). *The Berlin Aging Study: Aging from 70 to 100.* Cambridge, U.K.: Cambridge University Press.

Beck, U., & Bonss, W. (1989). *Weder Sozialtechnologie noch Aufklärung? Analysen zur Verwendung sozialwissenschaftlichen Wissens.* Frankfurt a.M.: Suhrkamp Verlag.

von Kondratowitz, H-J. (2000). *Konjunkturen des Alters: Die Ausdifferenzierung der Konstruktion des "höheren Lebensalters" zu einem sozialpolitischen Problem.* Regensburg: Transfer-Verlag.

von Kondratowitz, H-J. (1993). *Verwendung gerontologischen Wissens in der Kommune.* Berlin: Deutsches Zentrum für Altersfragen.

On the Possibilities of Spirituality and Religious Humanism in Gerontology or Reflections of One Aging American Cultural Historian

Thomas R. Cole

INTRODUCTION

In this chapter, I try to articulate some ideas about science, humanism, religion, and aging that have been trying to form themselves in my mind over the last few years. What follows is a speculative, often deliberately provocative line of thinking about how a postmodern religious humanism might contribute to gerontology.

To begin this task, I undertake an intellectually reflexive account of my own thought, which I hope will not appear too self-indulgent. Specifically, I need to pick up a line of thinking that originated in my work on the history of aging in America. I realize that my remarks emerge from and are limited by my specific location in early twenty-first century American culture, and I offer them not as monological truths but as contributions to an ongoing dialogue about meaning in later life. This chapter, we might say, takes the form of intellectual autobiography as a means of pursuing humanistic or critical or cultural gerontology. (We need more theorizing about these terms and their interrelationship.) I have come to believe that gerontology—whose dominant forms of inquiry and practice are naturalistic, instrumental, and quantitative—needs to be infused with what Lionel Trilling called the "humanistic educational ideal,"[1] which originates in the ancient Greek and Roman educational and spiritual ideals of *paideia* and *humanitas*.[2]

The humanistic educational ideal is not exclusively based in intellectual content from humanities disciplines; instead, it involves an elusive blend of feeling, knowledge, and compassionate action. Whether scientists or humanities scholars, we who hold this ideal can never pretend to transcend or evade our own lived humanity—our vulnerability, our failures, our feelings, our worldviews, our responses to suffering, our reactions to injustice or cruelty.[3]

I am arguing on behalf of an exclusively secular and modern humanism, which sets itself above or against religion. Instead, I suggest that the discourse of gerontology encourage what we might call a postmodern religious humanism, which welcomes pluralistic religious and spiritual perspectives not as instruments of universal truth and techniques of control, but as necessary and constituent elements of the never-ending human search for meaning.

THE SCIENTIFIC MANAGEMENT OF AGING AND ITS MYTHOLOGY

In 1991, I published a book entitled *The Journey of Life: A Cultural History of Aging in America*. *The Journey of Life* tried to accomplish several things at once: (1) a general overview of the dominant cultural meanings of aging in Europe and the United States from antiquity to the late twentieth century, (2) a specific historical analysis and critique of the transition from religious to scientific meanings in American middle-class culture, (3) a critique of the dominance of science in gerontology, and (4) a call for renewal of the moral and spiritual possibilities of aging in postmodern culture. This book was the culmination of 15 years of work, during which I gradually realized that although I am formally licensed to "practice history," I am fundamentally interested in what might be called the problematic of "aging and meaning."[4]

The Journey of Life argued that the vast gerontological literature that has appeared since World War II is dominated by a kind of instrumental reasoning that ignores (or presupposes answers to) the essential moral and spiritual questions that arise in the second half of life. The dominant forces in American culture have little or no interest in why we grow old, how we ought to grow old, or what it means to grow old. Like other aspects of our biological and social existence, aging has fallen under the dominion of scientific management, which is primarily interested in how we age in order to explain and control the aging process. American culture thrives on the mythology that aging is not a fated aspect of our individual and social existence but rather one of life's problems to be solved through willpower, science, medicine, and the accumulation of wealth. The most recent evidence for this claim is the dramatic rise of "antiaging" in American medicine and consumer culture.[5]

The problem with this mythology of scientific management is not that it is altogether false, but that it is only half true. The scientific management of aging fundamentally misconstrues the "problem" of aging. As T. S. Eliot once remarked, there are two kinds of problems in life. One kind requires the question, "What are we going to do about it?" and the other provokes other questions, "What does it mean? How does one relate to it?"

The first kind of problem is like a puzzle that can be solved with appropriate technical resources and pragmatic responses. The second kind of problem is really a mystery rather than a puzzle. It poses a deeper range of challenges, which no particular policy, strategy, or technique will overcome. Faced with a mystery, the human heart cries out for meaning. Born of viable cultural symbols and rituals, moral commitment, spiritual practices, and personal reflection, the experience of meaning helps individuals to understand, accept, and imaginatively transform the unmanageable, ambiguous aspects of existence.

Clearly, growing old involves both puzzles and mysteries. Yet people do not face life with the clear light of reason alone. We are always informed (for better or for worse) by beliefs, values, and symbols that are embedded in history and society. Whether we are aware of them or not, cultural beliefs and values always shape our understanding of life's big questions.

A RATIONALE FOR HUMANISTIC GERONTOLOGY

During the 1980s, it became clear that the time was ripe to formulate a rationale for and to map the boundaries of the emerging interdisciplinary field that became known as humanistic gerontology or "age studies,"[6] among feminist and cultural studies thinkers. I belonged to a small band of renegade humanities scholars and humanistically-oriented scientists who had operated at the interstices of the Gerontological Society of America since the mid-1970s.[7] We decided to pool our intellectual resources and—with awareness of the inherent irony—join the ranks of authoritative "handbooks" of gerontology.[8]

Bob Kastenbaum initiated the idea of a *Handbook of Humanities and Aging*. In November 1984, at a Wendy's in New Orleans between Gerontological Society sessions, Bob, Rick Moody, and I began sketching a table of contents. It fell to me to try to formulate a rationale for humanistic gerontology. That rationale, outlined in the introduction to the first edition, went roughly like this: Something important is missing in a purely scientific and professional gerontology. Highly technical and instrumental, avowedly objective and value-neutral gerontology lacks an appropriate language for addressing basic moral and spiritual issues in our aging society. Researchers, teachers, students, professionals, patients, clients, administrators, and policymakers have no ready way to speak to one another about fundamental questions of human existence.

The predicament of gerontology mirrors a larger historical tendency. Since the late nineteenth century, the decline of widely shared religious and philosophical frameworks, the growth of experimental science and technology, the culture of professionalism, and the emergence of the modern university have all contributed to the erosion of a common language for discussing questions of meaning and value, justice, virtue, wisdom, or the common good. In the contemporary world of postmodern culture, where exploding communications technology both saturates personal experience and undermines traditional assumptions of the self's unity, it has become increasingly important to identify and talk about moral and spiritual concerns.

The crisis of meaning in later life is not simply an academic issue; it is a historical-cultural situation[9] increasingly experienced by our aging selves and our aging societies. The theoretical and practical value of life review and reminiscence, the revival of narrative as a way of knowing, and the rapid growth of life-story groups among American elders all respond to the growing need for personal and sacred narratives that craft meaning and orient identity.[10]

In American society at least, the accelerating speed of communication and social change and the continuing extension of longevity leave many people feeling like Washington Irving's character Rip van Winkle, who fell asleep one night before the American revolution and awoke 20 years later to an alien world: "God knows ... I'm not myself—I'm somebody else. ... I was myself last night, but I fell asleep ... and every thing's changed, and I'm changed, and I can't tell what's my name, or who I am."

The crisis of meaning may take its most exaggerated form in the United States, but it seems to pervade Western societies. As Chris Phillipson suggests, "modern living undercuts the construction of a viable identity for living in old age."[11]

Humanism and the Postmodern Challenge

This rationale (formulated in collaboration with many colleagues) was based on my sense of the limitations of the "human values and aging" approach, which offered neither a critique of power nor a substantive orientation to fundamental existential issues confronting all of us who (not being gods or God) are inescapably social, temporal, and mortal. While I felt the inadequacy of a cafeteria-style interdisciplinary humanities framework, I was not yet prepared to look into the humanist tradition itself for guidance. I was aware that the humanities and social sciences had emerged from the humanist tradition as separate disciplines by declaring their specialized knowledge claims.[12] But I did not yet understand that in doing so they were in large measure creating a new form of scholastisicm.

During the 1980s, as graduate program director for a curriculum in the medical humanities, I became responsible for teaching graduate seminars in the history and theory of humanism and the humanities. Virtual ignorant of early modern European history, I began reading seriously in the historiography, literature, and philosophy of humanism. I found myself attracted not to any particular "doctrine of man" but to the practical modesty of Renaissance humanists, who accepted the uncertainty, ambiguity, and plurality in all human knowledge but who nevertheless sought wisdom, virtue, goodness, and human fulfillment through the critical exploration of their cultural heritage.[13] As a humanities teacher and a gerontologist, I came to embrace the "humanistic educational ideal"—the ideal of self-development, of cultivating of one's full humanity—and I saw that it held great promise for guiding late-life development and encouraging the pursuit of meaning and identity in old age.

I was drawn to the work of the philosopher Charles Taylor, who argues that one's full identity, or self, is a complex ontological accretion, formed in response to external value frameworks that provide the self with a place to stand in "moral space." "The full definition of someone's identity," writes Taylor, "usually involves not only his stand on moral and spiritual matters but also some reference to a defining community."[14] Taylor does not directly address issues of aging. But his view that modern culture's crisis of meaning is caused by the loss of widely shared religious or philosophical frameworks prodded me to think not only about secularization but also about the loss of humanism as a viable tradition.

As I began learning about the contested tradition of humanism in the 1980s, I also struggled to come to terms with the postmodern deluge that had crossed the Atlantic and first upset business-as-usual in American academic departments of literature a decade earlier. I grappled with the antihumanism embedded in Heidegger[15] (ironically in his "Letter on Humanism"), Althusser, Lyotard, and the early Foucault.[16] I could see the liberating power of the idea that "man," or "humanity," or "the subject" are not universal truths but social fictions rooted in historical relations of power and knowledge.[17] But I was not prepared to surrender the idea of existential truths that can only be represented by *yet are not reducible to* specific cultural constructions. As I learned more about humanism, I became convinced that much of the postmodern attack on "humanism" was based on a inaccurate reading of the humanist tradition.

In my view, it is a mistake to think of humanism as a fixed philosophy of "man." Humanism is better understood as a contested educational tradition in which imagination and the arts of language (rhetoric) compete with (and complement) the search for rational conclusive knowledge (philosophy as a science).[18] Renaissance humanism (which emerged in fourteenth century Italy and spread to other parts of Europe) was primarily an educational movement opposing the then-dominant scholastic curriculum of the medieval university, with its emphasis on logic, natural philosophy, and metaphysics.[19] Petrarch, Leonardo Bruni, and Lorenzo Valla, for example, laid special emphasis on rhetoric—the art of graceful, persuasive, and effective verbal communication, both orally and in writing. Based on the study, translation, and imitation of Roman orators (primarily Cicero and Quintillian), rhetoric aimed to help laymen make sense of and act in the ambiguous, practical world of law, commerce, and public life. Its goal was not to discover eternal truth but to develop an "articulate, broadly effective personality adequate to any situation."[20]

From the perspective of these early Italian humanists, the medieval schoolmen overvalued abstract rationality as the defining characteristic of "man." Instead, humanists addressed real flesh-and-blood individuals, understood as unpredictable bundles of passion, intellect, and spirit. The humanists wanted "to address man, every man, at the vital center of his being."[21] They were not, as is commonly thought, liberating "man" from the superstitions of religion. Grief-stricken by the mass death brought to Europe by the plague and confused by social and cultural change in the fourteenth century, they looked to "the ancients" for models of knowledge, virtue, and behavior.[22] They remained Christians who insisted on the value of experience in *this world* and whose awareness of the limitations of all human knowledge led them toward tolerance and dialogue, which required educating men and women in the arts of language.[23] Renaissance humanists aimed at educating active, responsible individuals by cultivating a more reflective human consciousness.

Once we grasp the "postmodern" insight inherent in Renaissance humanism (i.e., that formalized systems of rational knowledge do not address "man at the vital center of his being"), the critique of humanism as metaphysical and naively anthropocentric loses its force. We can understand, for example, that Protagoras' famous dictum "man is the measure of all things" implies not that a unified humankind is capable of objective knowledge but rather the opposite—that individuals are limited by their experience yet entitled to measure their own experience.[24] Postmodernism, then, has reiterated what the premodern humanist tradition already understood—all efforts to find an Archimedean point or a God's-eye view from which to observe ourselves are vain attempts, as Hannah Arendt put it, to "jump over our own shadows."[25]

Humanism is no longer intellectually viable as an "ism" in the modern philosophical and political sense. That is, there can be no single, unified theory of human being or human nature that requires our allegiance because it is universally true. But this does not mean there can be no humanisms after postmodernism. Acknowledging that all truths are "man-made" does not require that we disdain them for being "merely" human and strive to recover the false idol of Being. The alternative to standing outside the hermeneutic circle or transcending merely human consciousness is to strive to enlarge both. We need to overcome the moral and political paralysis induced by the stance of permanent skepticism toward all ideals and by the assumption that race, gender, ethnicity, religion, or nationality creates incommensurable worlds of difference. We need to reappropriate humanism not as any particular "philosophy of man" but as an educational ideal that explores and promotes personal growth and public action regarding two key questions: What does it mean to be human?, and How do we promote human flourishing?

The humanist task today is not to find our way back to a forgotten Greek origin (the way of Heidegger and Arendt), or to preserve the values of heroic Western civilization (the way of Bloom and Bennett), or to recover timeless truths from the corrosion of historical contingency (Arnold, Eliot, and Kermode). Rather, the goals are: (1) to recover our bearings through a critical interrogation of the humanist past (the way of Gadamer), (2) to build on this tradition through education and scholarship aimed at expanding human consciousness through continuous dialogical engagement with plurality and alterity (Buber, Bahktin, and Habermas), and (3) to publicly address real human problems (Dewey) by personal engagement in various scholarly, educational, professional, and political practices.

Human beings who are morally equal and distinct cannot be adequately understood or properly educated through the monologic, disembodied, decontextualized rationality of modern philosophy and science. But the critique of rationalism need not lead to relativism or thoughtless pluralism. Instead, we need a rationality that is engaged, dialogic, fallible, and open-ended.[26] Summarizing Gadamer's approach to the human sciences, Bernstein has aptly captured this kind of dialogical rationality.

> The basic condition for all understanding requires one to test and risk one's basic convictions and prejudgements in and through an encounter with what is radically "other" and alien. To do this requires imagination and hermeneutical sensitivity. . . . Critical engaged dialogue requires opening of oneself to the full power of what the "other" is saying. Such an opening does not entail agreement but rather the to-and-fro play of dialogue.[27]

Humanism as an Educational Ideal, Humanistic Gerontology, and Religion

So what does this have to do with gerontology, religion, and spirituality? I believe that the contested tradition of humanism has a great deal to offer gerontology: sensitivity to the formative power of language, an emphasis on historical and contextual thinking, a commitment to imagination as a way of knowing, a tradition of moral and spiritual reflection, and a primary insistence on dialogue. A postmodern humanism does not set religion and science against each other. Rather, it recognizes religion and spirituality as constituent elements of human identity and development.

This recognition is already present in the work of Giambattista Vico (1688–1744), an ambivalent believer, a humanist professor of rhetoric, and an author of the first major work of interpretive social science, *Scienza Nuova* (1725). Vico thought that religion originated historically in the terrorized imagination of ancient peoples. He argued that all societies everywhere invent sacred stories based on three core principles: divine providence (which requires a fable of the gods or God), marriage (which requires a fable of the passions restrained), and burial (which requires a fable of the body decaying and of the soul's fate). For Vico, as Stephen Greenblatt points out, "the fact that the whole enormous structure of belief is based on a universal poetic invention is not a source of disillusionment. Instead it underwrites the very possibility of scientific understanding."[28] Vico placed human poetic invention at the core of his basic axiom: "[T]he world of civil society has certainly been made by men, and . . . its principles are therefore to be found within the modifications of our own human mind."[29]

The words "Know Thyself," inscribed above the entrance to the ancient oracle at Delphi, might be considered the basic mantra of humanistic thought and practice. But what makes knowledge or practice "humanistic"? By using the term *humanistic*, I refer to knowledge (not necessarily in the humanities) and practice that is informed by or conforms to the ancient Roman ideal of *humanitas*—a term that originally meant "human feeling" and later came to encompass a wholistic blend of feeling, knowledge, and compassionate action in the world.

Humanistic knowledge is more difficult to achieve than cognitive knowledge alone, because (in contemporary terms) it demands heightened awareness that all knowledge resides in particular individuals who are embodied, embedded in social relationships, and limited. Humanistic knowledge requires attention to the context of knowledge-making and to the practical needs and problems of any given situation. It requires a depth of self-understanding that allows both detached discernment and personal engagement, depending on the human needs of any given situation and the scholarly, practical, or pedagogical aims of the knower. The personal integration essential to humanistic knowledge is a fluid, wholistic ideal that can occasionally be achieved and exemplified but cannot be taught directly or didactically. It is a spiritual ideal, an ongoing personal and interpersonal practice. Humanistic education seeks, as Erasmus put it, "nourishment for the soul instead of a mere scratching of the intellect."[30]

Humanism's basic commitment to cultivating personal integration, its concern with self-knowledge and the conditions of human flourishing, can bring a rich variety of perspectives (and practices) to bear on the basic question of humanistic gerontology: What does it mean to grow old? This question, of course, has no single or universal answer—at least not one that finite, historical beings can provide. Indeed, the question itself is abstracted from other innumerable questions that arise in historically and culturally specific forms—What is a "good" old age? Is there anything important to be done after children are raised and careers completed? Is old age the fulfillment of life? What happens after we die? What does God require of us? What are the possibilities of flourishing in old age? What kind of elders do we want to be? What are the paths to wisdom? What are the vices and virtues of the elderly? What kinds of support and care does society "owe" its old? What do the elderly owe their society?

In the last few years, I have come to believe that these questions are unanswerable without culturally viable religions and/or worldviews, that is, without cosmological maps and ultimate meanings that give us reasons and guidance for living with the flow of time rather than against it.[31] Religions and worldviews (for better and for worse) authorize ideals of old age. They provide cultural cognitive maps that chart a way into the unknown territory of later life. They illuminate the moral and spiritual work of aging. They require not only cognitive answers but human practices that cultivate living answers in communities and in individuals.

I am evolving into a (not-yet-fully formed) religious humanist. Perhaps I exemplify a movement that Robert Wuthnow has identified in

American spirituality since 1950—from a spirituality of "dwelling" to a spirituality of "seeking" and on to a spirituality of "practice."[32] (As a practicing Jew influenced by contemporary Buddhist spiritual teachings, I am learning to rebalance and integrate what Matthew Arnold called "Hellenism" and "Hebraism."[33])

As a scholar, I am still recovering from an overdose of the "positive" (or "exclusive") secularism built into American university education. A few words about this issue. In *The Soul of the American University: From Protestant Establishment to Established Nonbelief* (1994), historian George Marsden recently argued that over the last century, the American academy has essentially replaced one domineering, totalizing orthodoxy with another. In place of the old Protestant Christian orthodoxy, Marsden claims that universities now operate under the aegis of a strictly secular understanding of human existence, which suppresses explicit religious discourse and is intolerant of religious perspectives in scholarly discourse.[34] If Marsden's view is basically convincing (and I think it is), we need to think more carefully about the meaning of secularism in scholarship and society.

The last 20 years have witnessed a growing reaction to the dominance of the secular in the United States. My own thinking about these subjects has been influenced by Wilfred McClay, who notes that the god of Scientific Rationality and the Comtean religion of Humanity are now on the defensive.[35] Renewed interest in spirituality, which may or may not take explicitly religious forms,[36] is evident in popular culture. In religious, academic, and theological circles, fundamentalists and postmodernists alike are supported by a new wave of interest in the sacred. In gerontology there is new interest in spirituality, in personal narrative in the creation and recreation of identity, in the effects of religion on health, and in the place of religious beliefs and practices in caring for the elderly.

Wilfred McClay asks a central question: Is there a way to enjoy the fruits of secularism, without making it into a substitute orthodoxy, an establishment of irreligion? He suggests that we begin by distinguishing two basic concepts of secularism, analogous to Isaiah Berlin's "Two Concepts of Liberty": (1) a "negative" concept, which opposes established belief—including a *nonreligious* establishment—and protects the rights of free exercise and free association; and (2) a "positive" secular ideal, which is a proponent of established *unbelief* and a protector of strictly individual expressive rights, including the right of religious expression.[37] A "negative" secularism allows the possibility of a non-established secular order that is equally respectful of religionists and nonreligionists. "Such an order," writes McClay, "preserves a core insistence upon the freedom of the uncoerced individual conscience. But it has a capacious understanding of the religious needs of humanity, and therefore does not presume that the religious impulse should be understood as a merely individual matter."[38]

A "positive" secularism, on the other hand, affirms the secular ideal as an ultimate and alternative comprehensive faith, undergirded by a modernist view of science that supposedly competes with and ultimately triumphs over traditional religion. Actually, "positive" secularism relies on scientism—an inflated view of science whose claims to metaphysical and cosmological certitude are unsupportable by scientific methodology alone. On the other hand, a more modest and defensible view of science sees it as an "inherently tentative and provisional form of knowledge, defined by strict adherence to certain procedural norms involving the formulation of hypotheses, and the careful conduct of observable and replicable experiments to test those hypotheses."[39]

We can, in other words, celebrate the enormous accomplishments of Western science, modestly construed, while also denying its authority to serve as a substitute metaphysics or an alternate faith.[40] In these terms, one might say that my earlier work in the cultural history of aging demonstrated the emergence of a "positive" secularist and scientific approach to aging in American culture, emerging full-blown by the middle of the twentieth century. Only in the last 30 years have theologians, religious communities, physicians, and scholars[41] begun to chip away at the cultural dominance of "scientific management of aging."[42] Even now, the primary emphasis in the academic literature of religion and aging revolves around an effort to show that religion is good for your health.[43] This is fine as far as it goes, but promoting health is the business of medicine, not the primary business of religion—except for the secular religion of health that seems to reign in contemporary America. Before what Philip Rieff calls "the triumph of the therapeutic," health was a means toward living well, living according to a vision of the good life. Today, health has become an end in itself; capitalism's medicalized consumer culture responds to all qualitative questions with the quantitative answer "more." Longevity has eclipsed eternity in the hierarchy of cultural values.

I think my point of view might be characterized as postmodern religious humanism.[44] That is, my humanism belongs neither to the camp of the exclusive or "positive" secular humanists (who look to science as the demystifying power that can expose and dissolve the fears and illusions that support human irrationality) nor to the camp of traditional religionists unaware of the irreparable damage done to modern conceptions of self, the unity of knowledge, and the eternal truths of fixed sacred texts.[45]

I write as a "negative" secularist and a strong supporter of science modestly construed. I have no wish to return to ancient and medieval social structures or worldviews, in which aging is understood as a fixed element in the eternal order of things. But I think we are culturally impoverished by modernity's tendency to remove old age from its place as a way station along life's spiritual journey and to redefine it as a problem to be solved by science and medicine. We need to reconceive and resymbolize aging as a spiritual journey, as an opportunity to fulfill one's own humanity, to continuing learning, developing, creating, and serving in a pluralistic world where nonfundamentalist religious views are an essential part of public dialogue as well as of scientific and professional discourse.

I support modernity's affirmation of everyday life, its commitment to relief of pain and suffering, its dedication to social justice and universal human rights. I agree with liberal pluralism that human freedom is best served when no particular view is in charge, but this does not by itself accredit the view that human life is better off without transcendental vision altogether. We tend to identify modern freedom with an exclusive secular humanism, that is, one based entirely on the notion of human flourishing, which recognizes no aim beyond itself. As Charles Taylor puts it, "the strong sense that continually arises that there is something more, that human life aims beyond itself, is stamped as an illusion and judged to be dangerous . . . because the peaceful coexistence of people in freedom has already been identified as the fruit of waning transcendental visions." Exclusive humanism, as Charles Taylor says, "closes the transcendent window, as though there were nothing beyond—more, as though it weren't a crying need of the human heart to open that window, gaze, and then go beyond; as though feeling this need were the result of a mistake, an erroneous worldview, bad conditioning, or, worse, some pathology."[46]

I think that gerontology cannot afford to rely either on an overweening scientism or an exclusive humanism. Both thought styles tend to study religion by reducing it to a mere primary variable or by trying to show that religion is good for you—or bad for you, depending on one's point of view. Gerontology will continue to be impoverished if it excludes metaphysical, spiritual, and religious perspectives as genuine contributions to knowledge. At the same time, gerontology will remain impoverished if it grants exclusive authority over religious issues to ordained clergy, professional theologians, or other religious/spiritual teachers who have a vested interest in an established religion.

I applaud gerontology's recent narrative turn, in which reminiscence, life-story writing, oral history, fiction, and the arts are understood as vehicles for individuals to craft some kind of coherence in their lives.[47] I have been teaching life-story writing and spiritual autobiography to older people for the last five years. It is a rich and rewarding experience.

I find that many people come with unexplained gaps in their stories, unresolved conflicts in their lives, and unexplored memories in search of a storyline. People often arrive at these workshops with the implicit question, "What is the meaning of my life?" Answers tend to come when they ask, "What story am I part of?"

But as essential as it is, the individual search for meaning cannot manufacture the symbols, images, and rituals that offer consolation or explanation in the face of gross iniquity, intense pain, or undeserved suffering. Religious belief, as the anthropologist Clifford Geertz puts it, does not emerge via a "Baconian induction from everyday experience—for then we should all be agnostics—but rather from a prior acceptance of authority," which transforms those experiences.

> Religion tunes human actions to an envisaged cosmic order and projects images of cosmic order onto the plane of human existence.... What any particular religion affirms about the fundamental nature of reality may be obscure, shallow, or all too often, perverse; but it must, if it is not to consist of the mere collection of received practices and conventional sentiments we usually refer to as moralism, affirm something.[48]

What can gerontology—not being a religion—affirm? Certainly not the truth or untruth of any religious claim or tradition. It can, however, affirm that human beings are symbolic/spiritual animals who need love and meaning as well as food, clothing, and shelter. This affirmation carries with it a fundamental principle of interpretive social science: we do not adequately understand people of any age without viable interpretations of how they understand themselves.[49]

Secular, scientific gerontologists need to understand that philosophical and theological perspectives do not attempt to provide rational and conclusive answers to specific questions, but rather general value orientations that guide the search for specific answers and solutions. They need to make a more serious effort to understand and respect (not agree with) religious perspectives on their own terms, which in turn will encourage them to respect religious contributions to gerontology.

From a religious perspective, for example,

> the problem of suffering is paradoxically, not how to avoid suffering but how to suffer, how to make of physical pain, personal loss, worldly defeat, or the helpless contemplation of others' agony something bearable, supportable—something, as we say, sufferable.... For those able to embrace them, and for so long as they are able to embrace them, religious symbols provide a cosmic guarantee not only of their ability to comprehend the world, but also, comprehending it, to give a precision to their feeling, a definition to their emotions which enables them, morosely or joyfully, grimly or cavalierly, to endure it.[50]

The world's religions came into existence when "aging" itself was not a prominent feature of human experience. As far as I can tell, there is little fully developed speculation, say in Christianity, Judaism, Islam, Hinduism, or Buddhism. What was written in the founding sacred texts of these traditions could afford to idealize the aged, to authorize the wisdom of elders in support of existing social and ideological regimes. There were not enough old people around to demand careful thinking about how to care for them, how to promote their well-being, how to balance the claims of youth against the prerogatives of age. In the Hebrew bible, for example, the primary injunction to care for the vulnerable specifies "the widow, the stranger, and the orphan," not the elderly per se. I think we need a great deal more careful mining, critique, and reinterpretation of the world's classic sacred texts as we examine their resonance, guidance, and limitations in today's world of mass longevity.

Most of the work in religion and aging falls under two rubrics: the study of health outcomes among practitioners of religion and the use of religion in care giving, most often among clergy or hospital chaplains who need moral and spiritual resources in caring for the frail, demented, or dying elderly. But gerontology can also encourage theologies of aging. Theology was long ago dethroned as the queen of the sciences, but she should be welcomed back as an equal partner in the human search for self-knowledge. Theological traditions today must acknowledge their own plurality and ambiguity. But they need not feel or think defensively in relation to science. As science in any field gets closer to completing its task of explanation, all the questions that God was an answer to will still be waiting. (What was there before the Big Bang? Why were human beings designed to live a certain maximum life span? Should we try and intervene genetically to alter the aging process or the maximum life span?)

I am not a theologian or a scholar of religion per se; I have no systematic thoughts on these issues to offer. But here are some thoughts about encouraging a much-needed partnership between gerontology and theology. We need more gerontologists to become accomplished in the study of religion, and we need more theologians and religious studies scholars to become accomplished gerontologists. What are some of the issues that might be tackled?

Take wisdom. I am personally skeptical of the idea that wisdom emerges naturally in old age. I am more impressed by the Talmudic saying that a person who is a fool in his youth will also be a fool in his old age and a person who is wise in his youth will grow in wisdom as he gets older. Robert Atchley's notion of "everyday mysticism," Charles Reich's idea in *America the Wise*, and Lars Tornstam's studies of gerotranscendence (if I read him correctly) imply that wisdom is somehow a natural developmental feature that accompanies aging. This perspective leaves out the formative roles of culture and education in human development. I suspect (and this could be empirically investigated) that people who become wise or reach higher levels of consciousness are either consciously doing what we might call the "moral and spiritual work" of aging[51] or they are living off their cultural inheritance, (whether they are believers and churchgoers or not.) I worry that a scientific, secular society is squandering that inheritance by not renewing sacred canopies to guide, motivate, inspire, and console us in what Ronald Blythe calls "the long, late afternoon of life."

Postmodern critics have done excellent work in deconstructing old age and in demonstrating the extent to which aging is a cultural construction, which gerontology itself helps shape.[52] Images of health, vigor, successful aging, and leisure activities in consumer culture tend to trivialize the moral responsibilities, existential issues, and spiritual possibilities inherent in later life. But the political and cultural deconstruction of gerontological knowledge and the popular culture of aging is only half the battle. I think that there is an equally important place for constructing theological and cultural ideals of aging, as partial and limited as they will be.

Here are some questions that might aid in resymbolizing and culturally reconfiguring old age.[53] What might it mean to reconvert aging from a solvable problem into a fated mystery that brings unique challenges and opportunities? What would happen if we viewed long life not as a reward for proper behavior or the result of good genes but as a sign of God's ongoing interest in us, who might think of ourselves not in terms of recreation or procreation but in terms of cocreation, as God's partners in the ongoing work of Creation? What would it mean if we were to imagine longevity from the perspective of eternity, rather than from the perspective of mortality? What would it mean if gerontology took seriously (not as universally true) various religious symbols and beliefs of Ultimate Reality and helped us in the work of aiming toward and aligning ourselves with the "Ground of all Being"?

What would happen if we stopped using scientific methodology as an excuse for not raising questions that it cannot answer? "Is there any reason," asks Huston Smith, "for thinking that consciousness, or sentience, or awareness—all of these being names for the point where Spirit first comes to attention—is any less fundamental than matter?" If we no longer assume (as science assumes) that "consciousness is not simply an emergent property of life but is instead the initial glimpse we have of Spirit, perhaps we can stop wasting our time trying to explain how it derives from matter and turn our attention to consciousness itself."[54]

In one way or another, the world's major religions all insist on the paradox of physical decline and spiritual growth, not as a testable hypothesis but as an existential possibility. It is time to think more deeply about the "ageless self"—not at the level of ego or individual identity but at the level of pure consciousness or pure awareness, with no content or images imposed on it.

Huston Smith suggests that we think about pure consciousness as both as infinite potential (as opposed to God's consciousness, which is actual infinitude) and as the common property of all of us. Conscious human beings have an innate tendency to ask ultimate, unanswerable questions: What is the meaning of existence? Why are human bodies built to decline and die? Why, in the end, is life worth living? What is "real" after all?[55]

The growth of the infinite potentiality of the human spirit requires that we wrestle with these great mysteries and how to live our lives in relation to them. When confronted with such questions, I do not follow the pragmatist Richard Rorty, who advises us to "change the subject," nor should we allow science to rule these questions out of bounds because all answers are tentative and involve a leap of faith.[56] We need gerontological theologies today that are radically pluralistic, that speak to universal concerns from within specific traditions that involve texts, symbols, gestures, and beliefs that are not universally shared. "We have long been," writes George Steiner, "I believe that we still are, guests of creation. We owe to our host the courtesy of questioning."[57]

NOTES

1. Lionel Trilling, The uncertain future of the humanistic educational ideal. *American Scholar,* 44(1) (1974); 52–67.

2. See John Stephens, *The Italian Renaissance: The origins of intellectual and artistic change before the Reformation* (New York: Longman, 1990), especially the preface, xi–xvii.

3. Jonathan Glover, *Humanity: A moral history of the twentieth century* (New Haven, CT: Yale University Press, 2000), chapter 43, "Ethics Humanized."

4. In the early 1980s, I began talking with Harry R. Moody about this topic, which we both wrote about in a collection I edited with Sally Gadow, *What does it mean to grow old? Reflections from the humanities* (Durham, NC: Duke University Press, 1986).

5. The American Academy of Anti-Aging Medicine, founded in 1992, is dedicated to addressing "the phenomenon of aging as a treatable condition." See T. Cole and B. Thompson (Eds.), Anti-Aging: Hype or hope, *Generations* (Winter 2002), for a collection of articles on this topic.

6. See for example, Margaret Morganroth Gullette, Age-studies as cultural studies, chapter 11 in Cole, T., Ray, R. and Kastenbaum, R. (Eds.), *Handbook of the humanities and aging* (2nd ed.) (New York: Springer, 2000).

7. The major force behind this intellectual movement was the historian David Van Tassel. During the mid-1970s, Van Tassel organized the first two American conferences at which professionally trained humanists addressed questions of aging and old age. These conferences revolved around the theme of "aging and

human values" and resulted in two path-breaking volumes: S. Spicker, D. Van Tassel, and K. Woodward (Eds.), *Aging and the elderly: Humanistic perspectives in gerontology* (Atlantic Highlands, NJ: Humanities Press, 1978); David Van Tassel (Ed.), *Aging, death, and the completion of being* (Philadelphia: University of Pennsylvania Press, 1979). My formulation of the problem of "aging and meaning" grew out of appreciation for and a critique of the "human values" approach.

8. For a fascinating analysis of gerontological handbooks, see Stephen Katz, Reflections on the gerontological handbook, in Cole, Ray, and Kastenbaum.

9. See Jugen Habermas (Ed.), *Observations on the spiritual situation of the age* (Andrew Buchwalter, trans.) (Cambridge, MA: MIT Press, 1984).

10. See, for example, James E. Birren and Donna E. Deutchman, *Guiding autobiography groups for older adults: Exploring the fabric of life* (Baltimore: Johns Hopkins University Press, 1991); Ruth Ray, *Beyond nostalgia: Aging and life-story writing* (Charlottesville: University Press of Virginia, 2000).

11. Chris Phillipson, *Reconstructing old age* (London: Sage Publications, 1998), 53–54.

12. See Robert Proctor, *Education's great amnesia* (Bloomington: Indiana University Press, 1988).

13. For a philosophical account, see Stephen Toulmin, *Cosmopolis: The hidden agenda of modernity* (New York: Free Press, 1990).

14. Charles Taylor, *Sources of the self: The making of modern identity* (Cambridge, MA: Harvard University Press, 1989).

15. See Tom Rockmore, *Heidegger and French philosophy: Humanism, anti-humanism, and being* (New York: Routledge, 1995).

16. See Jean-Francois Lyotard, *The postmodern condition: A report on knowledge* (Geoff Bennington and Brian Massumi, trans.) (Minneapolis: University of Minnesota Press, 1993); Michel Foucault, *The order of things: An archaeology of the human sciences* (New York: Vintage, 1973).

17. For an excellent Foucauldian critique of gerontology, see Stephen Katz, *Disciplining old age: The formation of gerontological knowledge* (Charlottesville: University Press of Virginia, 1996).

18. P. O. Kristeller, *Classics and Renaissance thought* (San Francisco: Harper and Row, 1963); W. Bouwsma, *Culture of Renaissance humanism* (Richmond, VA: William Byrd Press, 1973); Bruce Kimball, *Orators and philosophers: A history of the idea of liberal education* (expanded ed.) (New York: College Entrance Examination Board, 1995); and Chaim Perelman, *The new rhetoric and the humanities* (Dordrecht, Holland: D. Reidel Publishing Company, 1979).

19. This approach was first worked out by Paul Oskar Kristeller. See *Classics and Renaissance thought* (San Francisco: Harper and Row, 1963) 11; W. Bouwsma, *Culture of Renaissance humanism* (Richmond, VA: William Byrd Press, 1973), 7; and John Stephens, *The Italian Renaissance: The origins of intellectual and artistic change before the Reformation* (New York: Longman, 1990), especially the preface, xi–xviii.

20. Bouwsma, *Culture of Renaissance humanism*, 15.

21. Bouwsma, Changing assumptions in later Renaissance culture. In *A useable past: Essays in European cultural history* (Berkeley: University of California Press, 1990), 76, 77.

22. See Robert Proctor, *Education's great amnesia* (Bloomington: Indiana University Press, 1988).

23. Gary Remer, *Humanism and the rhetoric of toleration* (College Park: The Pennsylvania State University Press, 1997).

24. Renato Barilli, *Rhetoric* (Giuliana Menozzi, trans.) (Minneapolis: University of Minnesota Press, 1989), 4.

25. Hannah Arendt, *The human condition* (Chicago: University of Chicago Press, 1958), 10.

26. See David Tracy, *Plurality and ambiguity: Hermeneutics, religion, hope* (San Francisco: Harper and Row, 1987).

27. Bernstein, *The new constellation: The ethical-political horizons of modernity/postmodernity* (Cambridge, MA: MIT Press, 1992).

28. Stephen Greenblatt, *Hamlet in Purgatory* (Princeton, NJ: Princeton University Press, 2001), 48–49.

29. *The new science of Giambattista Vico* (1744) (3rd ed.) (Thomas Goddard Bergin and Max Harold Fisch, trans.) (Ithaca, NY: Cornell University Press, 1968), 48–49.

30. Cited by James D. Tracy, Ad fontes: The humanist understanding of scripture as nourishment for the soul. In Jill Raitt (Ed.), *Christian spirituality: High Middle Ages and Reformation* (New York: Crossroad, 1987), 254.

31. See Reasons to grow old: Meaning in later life, *Generations* (Winter 1999–2000), Ronald Manheimer, guest editor, for a collection of essays that addresses meaning without the consolations or inspirations of religion.

32. Robert Wuthnow, *After Heaven* (Princeton, NJ: Princeton University Press, 1998), chapter 1.

33. See the classic essay of this title in Matthew Arnold, *Culture and anarchy* (J. Dover Wilson, Ed.) (Cambridge, U.K.: Cambridge University Press, 1996).

34. George Marsden, *The soul of the American university* (New York: Oxford University Press, 1994).

35. Wilfred M. McClay, Two concepts of secularism. *Journal of Policy History*, 13(1) (2001), 47–72.

36. Robert Wuthnow, *After Heaven: Spirituality in America since the 1950s* (Berkeley: University of California Press, 1998).

37. McClay, Two concepts of secularism.

38. McClay, 60.

39. McClay, 61.

40. Stephen Jay Gould, *Rocks of ages* (New York: Ballantine, 1999); Huston Smith, *Why religion matters* (New York: Harper, 2001).

41. See, for example, Seward Hiltner (Ed.), *Toward a theology of aging* (New York: Human Sciences Press, 1975); Melvin Kimble, et al. (Eds.), *Aging, spirituality and religion* (Minneapolis: Fortress Press, 1995); Harold Koenig, *Aging and God* (New York: Haworth Press, 1994).

42. Thomas R. Cole, *The journey of life: A cultural history of aging in America* (New York: Cambridge University Press, 1991), chapter 9.

43. See, for example, Jeffrey Levin (Ed.), *Religion in aging and health: Theoretical foundations and methodological frontiers* (Thousand Oaks, CA: Sage, 1994).

44. I am particularly influenced by the postmodern theology of David Tracy, in particular his *Plurality and ambiguity: Hermeneutics, religion, hope* (New York: Harper and Row, 1987), and by Charles Taylor, *Sources of the self* (Cambridge, MA: Harvard University Press, 1989) and *A Catholic Modernity?* (New York: Oxford University Press, 1999).

45. See, for example, David Tracy, *Plurality and ambiguity*, John Milbank, *Theology and social theory: Beyond secular reason* (Oxford, UK: Blackwell, 1990); Susan A. Handelman, *The slayers of Moses: The emergence of rabbinic thinking in modern literary theory* (Albany: SUNY Press, 1982).

46. Taylor, *A Catholic Modernity?*, 26–27.

47. See, for example, Marc Kaminsky (Ed.), *The uses of reminiscence* (New York: Haworth Press, 1984); Ruth Ray, *Beyond Nostalgia*; Jaber Gubrium and James Holstein, *The self we live by* (New York: Oxford University Press, 2000).

48. Clifford Geertz, Religion as a cultural system, in his *The interpretation of cultures* (New York: Basic Books, 1973), 90, 98–99, 109.

49. Charles Taylor, Interpretation and the sciences of man, in Paul Rabinow and William M. Sullivan (Eds.), *Interpretive social science* (Berkeley: University of California Press, 1979), 25–71.

50. Geertz, 104.

51. See Harry R. Moody, Conscious aging: The future of religion in later life, forthcoming in M. Kimble, S. McFadden, J. Ellor, and J. Seeber (Eds.), *Aging, spirituality and religion* (2nd ed.) (Minneapolis: Fortress Press, in press).

52. See, for example, Andrew Blaikie, *Ageing and popular culture* (Cambridge, UK: Cambridge University Press, 1999); Margaret Gullette, *Declining to decline* (Charlottesville: University Press of Virginia, 1997); Stephen Katz, *Disciplining old age* (Charlottesville: University Press of Virginia, 1996); Haim Hazan, *Old age: Constructions and deconstructions* (Cambridge, U.K.: Cambridge University Press, 1994).

53. In the United States, this reconfiguration is being initiated in popular culture by groups like Earth Elders, Spiritual Eldering, the conscious aging movement, creative retirement, lifelong learning, and volunteerism. For related scholarship and performance art, see A. Basting, *The stages of age* (Ann Arbor: University of Michigan Press, 1998); R. Kastenbaum, *Defining acts: Aging as drama* (Amityville, NY: Baywood, 1994); A. Wyatt-Brown and J. Rossen (Eds.), *Aging and gender in literature: Studies in creativity* (Charlottesville: University Press of Virginia, 1993); Kathleen Woodward (Ed.), *Figuring age: Women, bodies, generations* (Bloomington: Indiana University Press, 1999); Margaret Urban Walker (Ed.), *Mother time: Women, aging, and ethics* (Lanham, MD: Rowman and Littlefield Publishers, 1999).

54. Smith, *Why religion matters*, 261, 264.

55. Smith, *Why religion matters*, 274.

56. Rather, I am influenced on these issues by the pragmatist William James, especially the essays What Makes a Life Significant? and The Will to Believe, in Giles Gunn, ed., *Pragmatism and other writings* (New York: Penguin, 2001), 286–304, 198–218).

57. George Steiner, *Grammars of creation* (New Haven, CT: Yale University Press, 2001), 338.

REFERENCES

Armstrong, K. (2000). *The battle for God*. New York: Alfred A. Knopf.

Chopra, Deepak. (1993). *Ageless body, timeless mind*. New York: Harmony Books.

Cole, Thomas R. (1991) *The journey of life: A cultural history of aging in America*. New York: Cambridge University Press.

Cole, Thomas R., Ray, Ruth, & Kastenbaum, Robert (Eds.). (2000). *Handbook of the humanities and aging* (2nd ed.). New York: Springer.

Geertz, C. (1973). Religion as a cultural system. In *The interpretation of cultures* (pp. 67–72). New York: Basic Books.

Gillman, N. (1990). *Sacred fragments: Recovering theology for the modern Jew*. Philadelphia: Jewish Publication Society.

Gould, S. J. (1999). *Rocks of ages: Science and religion in the fullness of life*. New York: Ballantine.

Gullette, Margaret. (1997). *Declining to decline*. Charlottesville: University Press of Virginia.

Hiltner, S. (1975). *Toward a theology of aging*. New York: Human Sciences Press.
Katz, Stephen. (1996). *Disciplining old age*. Charlottesville, University Press of Virginia.
Kimble, Melvin A., McFadden, Susan H., et al. (Eds.). (1995). *Aging, spirituality, and religion: A handbook*. Minneapolis: Fortress Press.
Lawler, P. A. (1999). *Postmodernism rightly understood: The return to realism in American thought*. New York: Rowman and Littlefield.
Levin, J. S. (1994). *Religion in aging and health: Theoretical foundations and methodological frontiers*. Thousand Oaks, CA: Sage.
Marsden, G. M. (1994). *The soul of the American university: From Protestant establishment to established nonbelief*. New York: Oxford University Press.
Marsden, G. M. (1997). *The outrageous idea of Christian scholarship*. New York: Oxford University Press.
McClay, Wilfred. (2001). Two Concepts of Secularism. *Journal of Policy History* 13(1), 47–72.
Milbank, J. (1990). *Theology and social theory: Beyond secular reason*. Oxford: Blackwell.
Milbank, J., Pitstock, R., & Ward, J. (Eds.). (1999). *Radical orthodoxy: A new theology*. London: Routledge.
Moody, H. R. (1993). What is critical gerontology and why is it important? In Thomas R. Cole, et al. (Eds.), *Voices and visions: Toward a critical gerontology* (pp. xv–xli). New York: Springer.
Moody, H. R., & Carroll, David. (1997). *The five stages of the soul*. New York: Anchor Books.
Reich, T. (1998). *America the wise*. Boston: Houghton Mifflin.
Santner, E. L. (2001). *On the psychotheology of everyday life: Reflections on Freud and Rosenzweig*. Chicago: University of Chicago Press.
Schacter, Z., & Brown, R. (1995). *From age-ing to sage-ing*. New York: Ballantine Books.
Smith, H. (2001). *Why religion matters: The fate of the human spirit in an age of disbelief*. San Francisco: Harper and Row.
Smith, H., & Griffin, D. (2001). *Primordial truth and postmodern theology*. San Francisco: Harper and Row.
Steiner, G. (2001). *Grammars of creation*. New Haven, CT: Yale University Press.
Taylor, C. (1989). *Sources of the self: The making of modern identity*. Cambridge, MA: Harvard University Press.
Taylor, C. (1999). *A Catholic modernity?* New York: Oxford University Press.
Tracy, D. (1981). *The analogical imagination: Christian theology and the culture of pluralism*. New York: Crossroad.
Tracy, D. (1987). *Plurality and ambiguity: Hermeneutics, religion, hope*. San Francisco: Harper and Row.
Tracy, D., (1989). Theology, public discourse, and the American tradition. In M. Lacy (Ed.), *Religion and twentieth-century American intellectual life* (pp. 193–203). Cambridge, U.K.: Cambridge University Press.
Turner, J. (1985). *Without God, without creed: The origins of unbelief in America*. Baltimore: Johns Hopkins Press.
Ward, G. (Ed.). (1997). *The postmodern God: A theological reader*. London: Blackwell.

4

Ageism and Globalization: Citizenship and Social Rights in Transnational Settings

Chris Phillipson

INTRODUCTION

The purpose of this chapter is to reassess the scope and utility of the idea of ageism, some three decades on from when the concept first appeared in the 1960s (Butler, 1969). The gerontological world was substantially different then from how it appears now at the beginning of the twenty-first century. Moreover, the intellectual framework underpinning discussions about ageism has undergone significant change. Ideas about globalization, identity, and the nature of risk have, for example, had considerable influence on debates within and beyond the social sciences (Hutton & Giddens, 2000; Giddens, 2001; Phillipson, 1998). The purpose of this chapter is to use these ideas to provide a fresh interpretation of the uses as well as the limitations of ageism, building upon the critical reviews of the concept developed during the 1990s (Cole, 1992; Biggs, 1993; Bytheway & Johnson, 1993; Bytheway, 1995; Vincent, 1999).

The chapter divides into four main parts: (1) a brief summary of the background to the concept of ageism, (2) a review of the development of ideas about ageism, (3) an assessment of the impact of ageism on the changes associated with globalization, and (4) a summary of the main argument.

AGEISM: SOME BACKGROUND

Ageism, defined as the systematic stereotyping of and discrimination against people because they are old, has been widely debated since first formulated by Robert Butler in the late 1960s (Butler, 1969; Butler 1975). Initially, as Simon Biggs (1993) notes, the concept provided impetus to social movements (such as the Gray Panthers) that sought to challenge age-based discrimination (Butler, 1975; Kuhn, 1991). But the idea of ageism helped, in some measure, to raise the profile of social gerontology and was part of a broader critical agenda introduced by feminist and Marxist perspectives as applied to the study of old age (Phillipson, 1982; Minkler & Estes, 1999). Debates about ageism brought together a number of concerns about the position of older people, notably issues regarding "structured dependency" (Townsend, 1981; Walker, 1981), the power of the "aging enterprise" and the "biomedical complex" (Estes, 1979; Estes, et al., 2001), and problems of age segregation accompanying, for example, the growth of specialized housing and retirement communities (Kuhn, 1991).

Arguments about ageism have typically divided into two main camps: structural on the one side and cultural on the other. The former focuses upon institutionalized ageism as a problem arising from the management of the economy in capitalist societies. This perspective gives particular emphasis to the role of the state both in distributing resources in old age and in regulating the institution of retirement (Macnicol, 1998). Townsend (1986, p. 43), for example, argues that "twentieth century processes of retirement, [the] establishment of minimum pensions, residential care and delivery of community services have created forms of social dependency among the old which are artificial. Forms of institutionalised ageism have been developed to suit the management of industry and the economy in capitalist . . . societies . . . and have come to be reinforced by the shifting distribution of power." Discrimination and low status are further regarded as characteristic of a public sphere devoted to the pursuit of profit and the maintenance of capital. New forms of ageism may emerge in periods of economic upheaval (for example, with the labelling of the old as an economic burden), this forming part of what Carroll Estes (1999, p. 23) identifies as "the broader phenomenon of crisis construction and management in advanced capitalism."

In respect to the cultural dimension, emphasis has been laid upon the internalization of negative images about aging, especially in relation to changes to the body. This is illustrated through the work of Norbert Elias (1978) and the idea of a heightened sensitivity toward bodily demeanor and functions as part of what the author termed "civilising processes." Age is particularly associated with changes to the physical appearance and functioning of the human body. These are the most obvious means of identifying old age and a source of discrimination and oppression. Biggs (1993) discusses the way in which writers such as Simon de Beauvoir and Susan Sontag highlight the increasing disjunction between a personal sense of continuity in old age and the discontinuity of the aging body. The self may continue to grow and develop, but it is likely to be compromised by what Featherstone and Hepworth (1991) refer to as "bodily betrayals." This type of analysis raises important issues about the treatment of the body within specific cultural contexts, as well as the ability of individuals to modify some of the negative attributes associated with growing old.

Bytheway and Johnson (1993) have emphasised three key aspects to definitions of ageism: first, the stigmatization of older people; second, the use of chronological age to deny resources and opportunities that those who are not old would enjoy; and third, the interpersonal consequences of denigration by society. Bytheway and Johnson (1993, p. 28) cite the view of Alex Comfort that ageism is "the notion that people cease to be people, cease to be the same people or become people of a distinct and inferior kind, by virtue of having lived a specified number of years." Accepting this as a broad statement about ageism, this chapter now considers the way in which the concept was developed through the 1980s and 1990s, highlighting some of the questions and problems it was seeking to address.

AGEISM AND THE WELFARE STATE

The starting point for these observations concerns the question: What were the factors that encouraged debates about discrimination against older people? One answer might be that they reflected the sense of disappointment (and for some, disenchantment) with particular features of social protection and support for older people. At one level, social welfare, viewed from the perspective of critical gerontology, was failing to deliver financial security, notably for groups such as elderly women and ethnic minorities (Minkler & Estes, 1999; Phillipson, 1998; Vincent, 1995). At another level, there seemed to be an absence of vision, as the writings of Harry Moody (1988) and Thomas Cole (1992) suggest, about the purpose of an extended life course. Older people appeared at best as partial rather than full citizens, estranged in significant ways from other age groups. From this perspective, the concept of ageism was used to open a debate on the issue of divisions between generations and the activities and values of professional groups involved with older people.

At the same time, critical perspectives on the application of ageism had been developed by a number of researchers. In Britain, Bytheway (1995) and Bytheway and Johnson (1993) reviewed some of the conceptual problems and challenged in particular what they saw as the limitations of viewing ageism as a conflict between "society" on the one side and "elderly people" on the other.

> It is not... sufficient to define ageism solely in terms of the systematic mistreatment of individuals as members of groups, reinforced by the "structures of society" or as "a new type of schism in society." As we have argued, the essence of ageism is much more subtle than a simple conflict between one group and another. This it would seem is the special character of ageism. Indeed it seems to us to be fundamentally ageist to presume uncritically that it is possible to identify a group and label it "old people." (Bytheway & Johnson 1993, p. 34)

This insight reflects what might be described as a "narrative turn" in discussions about ageism, with the use of insights and methodologies drawn from the broad field of cultural sociology. Andrew Blaikie (1999), in his study *Aging and Popular Culture,* reviews some of the advantages of a cultural studies perspective, identifying discussions relating to questions of self and identity, the use of the Gramscian concept of hegemony, and the focus on diversity and difference. Blaikie (1999, p. 18) points to the way in which a cultural sociology of aging indicates how "people make their own cultures," producing patterns of "resistance and rituals" to the institutional pressures leading to age discrimination and stereotyping. Simon Biggs (1999), in *The Mature Imagination,* illustrated some of the ways of achieving this through the idea of the "persona" and the use of personal strategies to protect the self from an ageist world. Biggs outlines what he terms the emergence of the "mature identity," one that he sees as leading to the fashioning of a coherent sense of selfhood, one integrated with the past but also in accord with the demands of present and future change.

Cultural historians such as Thomas Cole (1992) continued to develop a critical approach to the concept of ageism, arguing that it maintained the tradition of splitting aging into positive and negative poles: the "good old age" of health and self-reliance versus the "bad old age" of disease and decay. Cole (1992, p. 229) also raised concerns (along with other researchers) about analogies between ageism, racism, and sexism, suggesting that

> we must be sceptical of the liberal assumption underlying these analogies—that age is irrelevant, that old people differ from young people only in their chronological age . . . traditional thought about the ages of life presupposed the opposite. In age, as in race and sex, the Scylla of prejudice is never far from the Charybdis of denial of human differences—differences that need to be acknowledged, and cherished.

This view was also supported by Featherstone and Wernick (1995, p. 8), wherein they highlighted the dangers of overemphasizing the parallels between ageism and other forms of discrimination.

> While gender and race continue to be constituted as relatively unambiguous social categories which entail discrimination and power deficits for the outside group, this division is by no means as clear cut with reference to the elderly and its relation to the young and middle-aged. Unlike the other social oppositions, youth and old age, and indeed all positions in the life course, are transitional statuses within a universal process. Unlike the other opposition, provided we live long enough we will experience a movement into the opposite status. Without effort we will move from youth to old age and what was from the point of view of youth the distant "unrealizability" of old age, becomes a haunting possibility for people in mid life once they have reached a "certain age." Of course there is the growing popularity of gender bending and cross-dressing, of wanting to experience the forms of embodiment of the opposite sex, yet this is largely a matter of choice and effort: with aging all we need do is stick around, time will do the rest.

There are other reasons that the initial debate around ageism now appears somewhat limited. In outline form, the argument may be presented as follows: The concept of ageism that developed in the 1960s and 1970s was rooted, at least in part, in the idea of aging as a response to national circumstances and conditions. The initial formulation of ageism was reinforced by accounts from social and cultural historians about the way in which the status of older people varied across time, with different explanations adopted for the emergence of age-based discrimination. The strength of these histories was precisely their location within clearly-defined national settings, this leading to powerful stories that combined a nation's history with that of the emergence of older people as a social group. Examples here include Fischer's (1977) *Growing Old in America,* Cole's (1992) *The Journey of Life,* Graebner's (1980) *A History of Retirement,* Achenbaum's (1978) *Old Age in the New Land,* and Thane's (2000) *Old Age in English History.*

This historical work was complemented by research examining the development of social citizenship, with particular emphasis on the contribution of T. H. Marshall (1992). The main focus of Marshall's work was the association that he described between the nation-state on the one hand and citizenship on the other. In this tradition, as Delanty (2000, p. 51) notes, citizenship was viewed as "the internal or domestic face of nationality." In the case of old age, the provision of care and support was viewed as an example of the way in which the state sought to modify class-based inequalities operating within national borders.

This tradition of work in social history and social policy has, it might be argued, created difficulties both in adjusting to new sources of ageism and in finding new solutions to the problems it brings. The twentieth century story about aging concerned national aspirations to build institutions to service the needs of older people. Ageism arose along the way as a concept used to express some of the frustrations about the limitations and inadequacies of these institutions. In the new century, however, a contrasting story about aging is beginning to emerge. It is now less appropriate to examine responses and solutions to aging issues exclusively within national borders. John Urry's (2000) analysis of the new mobilities affecting the twentieth-first century and Castells' (1996) focus on the role of networks, rather than countries, in providing the architecture for the global economy come to the same conclusion in highlighting the various pressures facing nation-states. Increasingly, the sovereignty of nation-states is influenced—to a greater or lesser degree—by transnational organizations and communities of different kinds. Older people live in a global society even more than in their own national society, and they contribute to, as well as depend upon, transnational chains of paid and unpaid labor. Along with this, their rights as citizens are moving away from the Marshallian world of rights evolving within particular societies or citizenship as an emblem of nationality. Urry (2000, p. 166) summarizes these developments as follows:

> This post-national citizenship is especially connected with the extensive growth of guest-working across many different societies. It is also related to greater global interdependence, increasingly overlapping memberships of different kinds of citizenship, and the emergence of universalistic rules and conceptions regarding human rights formalised by various international codes and laws.... Overall, there is an increasing contradiction between rights, which are universal, uniform and globally-defined, and social identities, which are particularistic and territorially specified.

This global context is creating new agendas for ageism in at least three respects: first, through the rise of transnational organizations; second, through the development of transnational communities; and third, through different approaches to the issue of citizenship. I shall deal briefly with each of these areas before summarizing the main themes of this chapter.

TRANSNATIONAL ORGANIZATIONS AND COMMUNITIES

Transnational bodies of different kinds are increasingly setting the agenda for shaping responses to issues around aging and ageism. Of particular importance is the way in which globalization has created restrictions on the development of social welfare, a significant by-product of the influence of transnational organizations (Deacon, 2000). Financial globalization, to take one example, while not a direct cause of the erosion of welfare states, nonetheless sets significant boundaries around their development. David Held and his colleagues (1999, p. 232) make the point that a distinctive feature of the present period is the extent to which "financial globalisation has imposed an external financial discipline on governments that has contributed to both the emergence of a more market-friendly state and a shift in the balance of power between financial markets." In this respect, they suggest, the political agenda of advanced capitalist states reflects in part the constraints of global finance, even though the specific impact of financial globalization will vary greatly among states.

The emergence of a global social policy has had a mix of negative and positive outcomes where older people are concerned. On the negative side, bodies such as the World Bank, IMF, and OECD have fed into the crisis construction of aging, with warnings about the cost of public pension systems and the adverse affects of earlier retirement (Yeates, 2001). Policies to raise retirement ages and reduce the role of state pay-as-you-go (PAYG) pension schemes now dominate the global discourse on pensions, one that few countries can seriously challenge (Mishra, 1999). Also influential is the role of the World Trade Organization's (WTO) General Agreement on Trade in Services, which calls upon member governments to "reconsider the breadth and depth of their commitments on health and social services" (Yeates, 2001, p. 74). This will almost certainly place enormous pressure on countries to move further in the opening-up of public services to competition from global (and especially U.S.) corporate providers. Pollock and Price (2000) argue that

> To extend rights of access for private firms, the WTO, with the backing of powerful trading blocs, multinational corporations, and U.S. and European governments, is attempting to use regulatory reform to challenge limitations on private sector involvement. But this amounts to a challenge

which lies at the heart of social welfare systems in Europe. The new criteria proposed at the WTO threaten some of the key mechanisms that allow governments to guarantee health care for their populations by requiring governments to demonstrate that their pursuit of social policy goals are least restrictive and least costly to trade.

On the one hand, therefore, there is the danger of a new ageism driven by the agendas of transnational forums seeking to enhance private markets. This may be reinforced by the desire of multinational corporations to limit their responsibilities toward current and future generations of retirees. The globalization of capital in fact raises major concerns about the ease with which corporations can undermine the rights of older employees. Naomi Klein (2000) shows the extent to which some of the most successful corporations are built around anti–older adult employment strategies that target older workers for harassment.

On a more positive note, the ability of corporations or other organizations to evade their responsibilities may be constrained by various forms of transnational governance. For example, avoidance by successive U.K. governments of age discrimination legislation has finally been challenged by a European Union directive outlawing discrimination in the workplace on grounds of age, race, disability, or sexual orientation (Hall, 2001). Similarly, national legislation following the European Convention on Human Rights also has the potential to be used to challenge age discrimination in areas such as service provision and employment, as well as fundamental issues relating to the right to life, the right not to be subject to inhuman treatment, and the right to a fair hearing.

Both examples illustrate the way in which international law may be used to shape national discourses on issues relevant to ageism. However, this has also come about through the influence of transnational communities in creating a situation of cultural pluralism in respect to responses to aging. Perspectives from cultural studies have emphasized issues about diversity and difference that are challenging traditional approaches to ageism (Blaikie, 1999). But the roots of these need to be more firmly located in the influence of transnational communities and the role of migration in reshaping nation-states. In this context, if the first phase of aging (for much of the twentieth century at least) was about growing old as a reinforcement of national identity and citizenship, the second phase will involve to a far greater extent the development of hybrid identities. Growing old in the first phase was partly a celebration of community or of lives lived within particular communities with particular histories. In the second phase, however, belonging and identity become detached from particular places. Ulrich Beck (2000, p. 169) argues that "people are expected to live their lives with the most diverse and contradictory transnational and personal identities and risks." Martin Albrow (1996, p. 151) makes the important point that "under globalised conditions it becomes less easy for individuals to affirm their identity within the strict confines of nation, gender, age or any other categorical distinctions."

One conclusion from this debate is that experiences of ageism will reflect a much greater diversity of experiences and identities than was the case when the concept was first conceived. In this context, it may make more sense to talk about varieties of global aging and the mix of national, local, and ethnic-based cultures shaping reactions and responses to age-based discrimination. In practice, this leads to a different discourse than that which characterized early debates in the field. Challenging ageist language and limiting the attachment to chronological age are both still important elements in the work that needs to be done, but transnational populations are bringing new challenges to the field of discrimination. Indeed, the most pernicious forms of ageism today might be said to be those affecting the migrants who service the global economy and those deprived of its benefits. For the latter, talk of "aging societies" does indeed seem hollow where, as in sub-Saharan Africa, life expectancy remained lower than 60 years in 41 of the 53 countries during the period 1995–2000 (World Health Organization, 2000). For the former, the new ageism concerns migrants who struggle with care responsibilities that may span continents, who may be denied pensions and other benefits for their old age, and who may be allotted quasi rather than full citizenship in their new homeland (Castles, 2000).

Arlie Hochschild (2000) argues that most writing about globalization focuses on money, markets, and labor flows, with scant attention to women, children, and the care of one for the other. But older people might be added to this list. Elderly people are part of the global flow: they grow old as migrants; are part of the care chain, receiving or giving care; or go back and forth from one home to the other. Above all, they contribute to more diverse images of growing old, reflecting the phenomenon of transnational migration as well as hybrid identities. Recognition of these global dimensions will be important in developing effective responses to contemporary ageism.

CITIZENSHIP AND AGEISM

Debates around ageism will also be influenced by new views about the nature of citizenship, these responding to the different pressures shaping the emergence of transnational organizations and communities. At the center of current debates in this area is the break between nationality and citizenship referred to earlier. Delanty (2000, p. 19) argues that in this global age such a linkage can no longer be taken for granted.

> The state is no longer in command of all the forces that shape it and sovereignty has been eroded both downwards to subnational units, such as cities and regions, and upwards to transnational agencies, such as the European Union. With respect to citizenship what this means is that the marriage between citizenship and nationality is broken. At least there is no perfect equivalence between nationality, as membership of the political community of the state, and citizenship, as membership of the political community of civil society.

Yasemin Soysal (1994, p. 142) has argued the case for a "postnational" model of citizenship that recognizes the variety of attachments that characterize modern nation-states. The implications of this are as follows:

> In the postnational model, universal personhood replaces nationhood; and universal human rights replace national rights. . . . The rights and claims of individuals are legitimated by ideologies grounded in a transnational community, through international codes, conventions and laws on human rights, independent of their citizenship in a nation-state. Hence the individual transcends the citizen.

Debates about the changing nature of citizenship raise important issues for work in the area of aging. In the first place, the human rights focus may be a more productive field for challenging age-based discrimination than that associated with discussions around citizenship. Some of the implications of this approach have been developed by Bryan Turner (1993, 2001), who argues that a rights-based approach is necessary precisely because individuals are ontologically frail rather than autonomous beings, this arising partly through the affects of aging and decay, but also because life is inherently risky. Turner (1993, p. 180) concludes,

> to be precise, the argument is that, from sociological presuppositions about the frailty of the body and the precarious or risky character of social institutions, it is possible to offer a sociologically plausible account of human rights as a supplement to citizenship or as an institution which goes beyond citizenship because human rights are not necessarily tied to the nation-state.

This approach offers a broader perspective on some of the questions running through discussions about ageism and may offer a coherent long-term challenge to the recurring moral panics about "too many elderly and too few younger people" to which citizenship models have proved only intermittently effective. The model developed by Turner (1993, p. 185) is based on the view that "human beings will want their own rights to be recognised because they see in the plight of others their own (potential) misery." He goes on to note the importance of developing a theory of sympathy to underpin the connection between frailty and human rights, which would seem to be an important project to consider for those who may be especially vulnerable to ageism, for example, people with dementia, those with advanced physical disabilities, and those experiencing intense forms of social exclusion.

Another approach to "postnational citizenship" is to view older people as a group likely to benefit from what Delanty (2000) refers to as "cosmopolitan citizenship." Cosmopolitanism is an important philosophical idea for us to consider in that it offers the basis for combining concerns about social exclusion with ideas about new social roles for older people. Andrew Linklater (1998) cites Beitz's view that the essence of cosmopolitan lies in the belief that all human beings possess equal moral standing. Linklater argues that cosmopolitanism suggests that political communities should widen their ethical horizons until the point is reached where no individual or group interest is systematically excluded from moral consideration. Such an approach would challenge the construction of old age as a form of "otherness," a central feature behind ageist stereotyping. It would also consider the basis for older people to embrace active social roles as a consequence of the duties and obligations associated with membership of a multiplicity of communities. Developing a cosmopolitan view of aging may be significant as well in challenging linkages between aging and economic and cultural decline. For cosmopolitan citizens, age is of secondary consideration behind their responsibilities within civic society. This contrasts with national citizenship, where chronological age may continue to be important in determining access to a range of resources and responsibilities. Clarifying the basis for a new form of "civic citizenship" in later life would seem an important goal to consider for those involved in challenging the problem of ageism.

CONCLUSION

The argument of this chapter has been that the institutional factors influencing ageism are being transformed. The twentieth century story of aging concerned national aspirations to build old-age institutions. In the twenty-first century, however, a contrasting story about aging is beginning to emerge. The dominant actors over the past 50 years, while not receding from view, are being influenced by new, mostly transnational institutions: corporations, agencies, and communities. What sort of aging will emerge from this process is as yet unclear, but it will almost certainly have very different characteristics from that of the preceding 50 years. In the first place, the dominant actors are likely to be at one remove from the individual's national location. Corporations will shape aging as much as governments—indirectly through their influence on taxation and revenue and directly through their "branding" of graying societies. In the second place, transnational governance on issues such as age discrimination will exert a powerful influence on national governments and may accelerate the drive to establish equal treatment for older people in employment and related sectors. Third, the uncoupling of nationality from citizenship promises a more vibrant discussion about rights and responsibilities through the life course, one that will need to reflect the greater mobility of populations in the twenty-first century.

But what is most apparent from this analysis is that while the possibilities for challenging ageism are pronounced, so also is the likelihood of new sources of inequality and exclusion: Most people in the world lack the hope of a decent pension and proper health care; for many, expectations have receded over the past ten years. Global aging and global ageism both raise major new concerns and challenges for gerontologists to consider in their research and policy analysis. Ageism remains a useful concept for gerontologists to utilize in their work, but it will also require adaptation and refinement, given a more fluid and globalized social world.

REFERENCES

Achenbaum, A. (1978). *Old age in the new land*. Baltimore: Johns Hopkins.
Albrow, M. (1996). *The global age*. Cambridge, U.K.: Polity Press.
Beck, U. (2000). Living your own life in a runaway world: Individualisation, globalization and politics. In W. Hutton & A. Giddens (Eds.), *On the edge* (pp. 164–175). London: Jonathan Cape.
Biggs, S. (1993). *Understanding aging*. Buckingham, U.K.: Open University Press.
Biggs, S. (1999). *The mature imagination*. Buckingham, U.K.: Open University Press.
Blaikie, A. (1999). *Aging and popular culture*. Cambridge, U.K.: Cambridge University Press.
Butler, R. (1969). Ageism: Another form of bigotry. *The Gerontologist, 9*, 243–246.
Butler, R. (1975). *Why survive being old in America?* New York: Harper, Row.
Bytheway, B. (1995). *Ageism*. Buckingham: Open University Press.
Bytheway, B., & Johnson, J. (1993). On defining ageism. *Critical Social Policy, 29*, 27–39.
Castells, M. (1996). *The rise of the network society*. Oxford: Blackwell Publishers.
Castles, S. (2000). *Ethnicity and globalization*. London: Sage.

Cole, T. (1992). *The journey of life*. New York: Cambridge University Press.
Deacon, B. (2000). *Globalization and social policy: The threat to equitable welfare*. Occasional Paper no. 5, Globalism and Social Policy Programme (GASPP), UNRISD.
Delanty, G. (2000). *Citizenship in a global age*. Buckingham, U.K.: Open University Press.
Elias, N. (1978 [1939]). *The civilizing process, Vol. 1: The history of manners*. New York: Pantheon.
Estes, C. (1979). *The aging enterprise*. San Francisco: Jossey-Bass.
Estes, C. (1999). Critical gerontology and the new political economy of aging. In *Political and moral economy* (pp. 17–36). New York: Baywood Press.
Estes, C., et al. (2001). *Social policy and aging*. Thousand Oaks, CA: Sage.
Featherstone, M., & Hepworth, M. (1991). The mask of aging and the postmodern life course. In M. Featherstone, M. Hepworth, & B. Turner (Eds.), *The body: Social process and cultural theory* (pp. 371–390). London: Sage.
Featherstone, M., & Wernick, A. (1995). Introduction. In M. Featherstone & A. Werwick (Eds.), *Images of aging*. London: Routledge.
Fischer, D. J. (1977). *Growing old in America*. New York: Oxford University Press.
Giddens, A. (2001). *Sociology* (4th ed.). Cambridge, U.K.: Polity Press.
Graebner, W. (1980). *A history of retirement: The meaning and function of an American institution*. New Haven, CT: Yale University Press.
Hall, S. (2001, February 13). End to upper age limit on work. *The Guardian*.
Held, D., McGrew, A., Goldblatt, D., & Perration, J. (1999). *Global Transformations*. Oxford: Polity Press.
Hochschild, A. (2000). Global care chains and emotional surplus value. In W. Hutton & A. Giddens, *On the edge* (pp. 130–147). London: Jonathon Cape.
Hutton, W., & Giddens, A. (2000). *On the edge: Living with global capitalism*. London. Jonathan Cape.
Klein, N. (2000). *No logo: Taking aim at the brand bullies*. London: Flamingo.
Kuhn, M. (1991). *No stone unturned: The life and times of Maggie Kuhn*. New York: Ballantine Books.
Linklater, A. (1998). *The transformation of political community*. Cambridge, U.K.: Cambridge University Press.
Macnicol, J. (1998). *The politics of retirement in Britain: 1870–1948*. Cambridge: Cambridge University Press.
Marshall, T. H. (1992). *Citizenship and social class*. London: Pluto.
Minkler, M., & Estes, C. (Eds.). (1999). *Critical gerontology*. New York: Baywood Press.
Mishra, R. (1999). *Globalization and the welfare state*. Cheltenham, U.K.: Edward Elgar.
Moody, H. (1988). *Abundance of life: Human development policies for & aging society*. New York: Columbia Press.
Phillipson, C. (1982). *Capitalism and the construction of old age*. New York: Macmillan.
Phillipson, C. (1998). *Reconstructing old age*. London: Sage.
Pollock, A., & Price, D. (2000). Rewriting the regulations: How the World Trade Organization could accelerate privatisation in health care systems. *The Lancet, 356*, 1995–2000.
Soysal, Y. (1994). *Limits of citizenship: Migrants and postnational membership in Europe*. Chicago: University of Chicago Press.
Thane, P. (2000). *Old age in English history: Past experiences, present issues*. Oxford: Oxford University Press.

Townsend, P. (1981). The structured dependency of the elderly: The creation of policy in the twentieth century. *Ageing and Society, 1*(1), 5–28.

Townsend, P. (1986). Ageism and social policy. In C. Phillipson & A. Walker (Eds.), *Aging and social policy* (pp. 15–44). Aldershot, U.K.: Gower.

Turner, B. (1993). Outline of the theory of human rights. In B. Turner (Ed.), *Citizenship and social theory.* London: Sage Books.

Turner, B. (2001). The erosion of citizenship. *British Journal of Sociology, 52*(2), 189–209.

Urry, J. (2000). *Sociology beyond societies.* London: Routledge.

Vincent, J. (1995). *Inequality and old age.* London: UCL Press.

Vincent, J. (1999). *Politics, power and old age.* Buckingham, U.K.: Open University Press.

Walker, A. (1981). Towards a political economy of old age. *Ageing and Society, 1*(1), 73–94.

World Health Organization. (2000). Life expectancy rankings. Press release. Geneva: WHO.

Yeates, N. (2001). *Globalization and social policy.* London: Sage.

5

Positioning Gerontology in an Ageist World

Bill Bytheway

There is a growing interest in the history of gerontology and an increasing appreciation that this history is connected to much broader social, political, and cultural trends (Katz, 1996; Phillipson, 1998). Despite the fact that gerontology is a comparatively new discipline, there is much to be learned from the study of how people and organizations have established the discipline and endeavored to position it, both in relation to other disciplines and in the wider world.

On the face of it, gerontology is an academic discipline, characterized by studying and learning, teaching and research. It is represented by a literature, by individuals identifying themselves as gerontologists, and by a variety of organizations promoting its development. For example, the objectives of the International Association of Gerontology include the promotion of (1) gerontological research in the biological, medical, behavioral, and social fields, (2) training in the fields of aging, and (3) the interests of gerontological organizations. It is notable that these objectives do not include any reference to particular age groups (such as "people over 75 years of age" or "the elderly") or to age-specific organizations (such as those associated with pensioners or retired people). Rather, there is a simple equation of gerontology with research and training in aging.

Pension policies, employment practices, and health care in later life are political, and issues of disadvantage and prejudice inevitably arise. There is not space here to enter into a discussion of ageism (see Bytheway, 1995), but I would like to suggest that the wider worlds in which gerontologists undertake their work are essentially ageist in the sense that people are regularly classified according to age and then either privileged or denied what are deemed to be "appropriate" opportunities or services. Whether such prejudices are thought to operate against or in favor of their interests is a secondary issue. What is essentially ageist is the simple fact that all people located within a particular range of ages are judged to be characterized in a particular way. It is in this context that gerontologists have to address the question of how they relate their activities to the interests of the subjects of their studies.

THE JOURNAL

As editor over the last few years of the journal *Ageing and Society*, I have gained some insight into the production of gerontology, how knowledge is generated and disseminated, and how gerontologists relate their work to older people. For this chapter, I decided I would revisit the 117 articles that have been published in volumes 17 to 20 of the journal (published between 1997 and 2000). My objective was to consider how each article contributes to a sense of what gerontology is and where it is placed on the broader maps of academic, social, political, and cultural activities. In particular, I wanted to analyze how authors relate their work (1) to gerontology, (2) to the concept of ageism, and (3) to older people.

The formal aim that is published in every edition of *Ageing and Society* reads as follows:

> *Ageing and Society* is an international journal devoted to publishing contributions to the understanding of human aging, particularly from the social and behavioural sciences and humanities. Its interpretation of aging is wide and includes all aspects of the human condition whether they relate to individuals, groups, institutions or societies.

It is significant that this statement does not include the word "gerontology." Rather, it issues an open invitation to a wide range of "sciences and humanities" in relation to "all aspects of the human condition." The only formal constraint is that articles are submitted in the English language.

Ageing and Society is the journal of the British Society of Gerontology and the Centre for Policy on Aging (based in London). It has an editorial board that, broadly speaking, is intended to represent all aspects of gerontology. There is an "open" policy of accepting submissions from all relevant disciplines and from other countries as well as the United Kingdom. The primary criterion for publication is the independent recommendation of two referees. What the deliberations of the editorial board and the process of peer review achieve, apart from a degree of quality control, is a certain coherence and continuity regarding what is regarded as gerontology. In this way, the journal directly and routinely contributes to the accumulation of gerontological literature. On this basis, I feel able to claim that the 117 articles are a sample that adequately represents the work of "English-writing gerontologists" in the last decade of the twentieth century.

WHO ARE THE AUTHORS?

The 117 articles were the work of 244 authors, of whom 139 (57%) were based in the United Kingdom, 31 based elsewhere in Europe, 28 based in Australia, 18 based in the United States, 16 based in Canada, and 12 in other countries. With only a few exceptions, the research they report was undertaken in their own country, and so the cultural base of *Ageing and Society* is fairly limited. Although international in aspiration, it is heavily biased toward those countries where English is the primary language and to the United Kingdom in particular.

Regarding the personal characteristics of the 244 authors, little information is readily available. On the basis of first names, it would appear that approximately 57% are women. Only four authors provide any information that indicates they might think of themselves as "retired" or "older" people. Only one makes explicit reference to his age; the other three refer not to age but to their many years in research. Twenty others cite work that they had published ten or more years previously. It seems probable that the large majority of authors are aged between 30 and 60 years.

Three authors work in the health services, and another author works in private medical practice. Two are affiliated to private research companies, and four describe themselves as "freelance" or "consultants." Three indicate that they were "formerly" at a university. The remaining 231 (94.7%) are based in universities or linked research institutes: This is striking confirmation that *Ageing and Society* is an "academic" journal.

Regarding the disciplines from which they come, a rigorous classification is not possible since a large number are located in university departments with catchall titles such as "social relations." It is perhaps worth noting, however, that only 65 of the 244 were affiliated to departments or institutes explicitly connected to gerontology or research on aging.

Of the 117 papers, a total of 68 are based on fieldwork undertaken (or supervised) by the authors. Of these, 59 involved gaining access to older people: 43 entailed direct contact with older people, typically through interviews, ten were focused upon age-specific settings (such as observational fieldwork or interviews with staff), and six drew upon interviews with carers for older people. This leaves nine that drew on fieldwork that was not linked to older people in these ways. Rather, they drew upon samples of the general population or families, for example, studying attitudes to age and intergenerational relations.

For most of the 59, the research was dependent upon the cooperation of other agencies. Eighteen drew upon large sample surveys (defining these as entailing 200 or more interviews) where collaboration with other organizations is almost always essential. Of the other 41, 24 involved agencies providing services to older people: residential homes, day centers, community organizations, welfare agencies, local authorities, and hospitals. Fifteen of the 59 (25%) include at the end of their articles an acknowledgment to their sources of research funds. It is safe to presume that most of the others were also funded. Overall, about one-third were funded by health service agencies, one-third by government sources (specifically for social science), and another one-third by independent foundations. Perhaps half the contributions to the journal draw directly upon research, where the aims and methods have been agreed upon with the funding agency and where publications (such as the article published in the journal) have drawn upon research reports that have been accepted by these agencies and where dissemination has been actively encouraged. In this way, many of the published articles are an integral part of the process of maintaining and developing services for older people in what I have described earlier as an ageist world (Estes, 1979).

There are acknowledgments at the end of 54 of the articles. In addition to the 15 that refer to funding agencies, 16 acknowledge interviewees, and 31 acknowledge the contribution of colleagues. This suggests that overall there is a much more conscious appreciation of the contribution of colleagues (in contrast with interviewees), thereby suggesting that authors see themselves as contributing to the collective academic endeavor. Be that as it may, the majority of the sample were reporting research in which they were in contact with older people, having previously gained the support of some external agency. Although some of these agencies (funds for social science, for example) are not specifically directed toward particular objectives regarding policy or practice with older people, there has been an increasing trend, in the United Kingdom at least, toward directing all funded research toward specific utilitarian ends.

WHAT DO THE AUTHORS SAY ABOUT GERONTOLOGY?

It is interesting to note that 40 of the 117 articles make some explicit reference to gerontology or gerontologists. Most commonly (characterizing about two out of three of these references), these authors simply draw upon or refer to a review of "gerontological literature" or a specific section of it. For example, McColgan and associates (2000), referring to the recent challenge to the biomedical approach to dementia, comment: "These critical gerontologists are more concerned with the subjective experience of dementia" (p. 100). Several refer to the growth of gerontology and to the contribution that the particular article is making. Mehta (1997, p. 272), for example, modestly describes her article as offering "a small contribution to the present state of cross-cultural gerontology." A more specific objective relates to an apparent gap in gerontology, one that the authors believe should be filled. So Teo (1997, p. 649) refers to "the blind spots of gender in gerontological research." Similarly, Cheal and Kampen (1998, p. 147) conclude that more attention "in gerontology" should be given to the 55 to 64-year-old age group. Regarding the recent histories of international migration, Blakemore (1999, p. 765) writes "arguably academic gerontology has paid little attention to these realities."

This process also requires attention to the relationship between gerontology and adjacent disciplines and literatures. Robertson (1997, p. 433), for example, puts forward the argument that "moral economy has much to offer as an analytic framework for gerontology." Similarly, Biggs (1998, p. 423) considers the particular value of psychoanalysis for social gerontology, and Ylanne-McEwen (1999, p. 417) puts the case for a greater use of discourse analysis.

There is little evidence that authors think of gerontology as having an impact on the wider society even though, as Kastenbaum (1997, p. 21) recognizes, many conclude with recommendations. Biggs and associates (2000, p. 658), for example, regarding the residents of a retirement community, comment that "it appears that they have taken to heart many of the active-aging and antiageist messages from contemporary gerontological thinking," but they recognize that their evidence may reflect the antiageist policies of the community's management, rather than the direct impact of gerontology on the residents.

For all these authors, gerontological literature is identifiable and accessible and, in organizing their research and producing their articles, they have drawn upon it. Predictable though this might be, it confirms the identity of this literature as "gerontological" and its availability as such to contributors to the journal. They see themselves as contributing to the steady expansion and consolidation of gerontology as its knowledge base is more clearly defined, agreed upon, and consolidated.

No matter whether it is cultural, social, critical, or just plain "gerontology," the name exists, to use the powerful phrase of Gubrium and Holstein (1999, p. 520), as a "discursive anchor": a point of reference in positioning their own work. This social reality—with its political implications—is clearly articulated by Tulle-Winton (1999) when she writes that gerontology is "well placed to engage itself and its audience in the production of a new discourse on aging and old age" (p. 284). Clearly, in her view, gerontology is in a position to take action. In relation to ageism, for example, a new discourse on aging might successfully discredit negative images of older people. She goes on to comment, however, that "gerontology is normative in its pronouncements, embedded as it is in what Katz (1992) has referred to as power/knowledge relations which prevail in the wider society".(Tulle-Winton, 1999, p. 284).

Have gerontologists been "normative" in their pronouncements? Do they attempt to engage themselves in the production of new discourses? The analysis I have undertaken for this chapter is intended to address these questions.

WHAT DO THE AUTHORS SAY ABOUT AGEISM?

It is surprising to find that only 28 of the 117 articles make any explicit reference to ageism, and the word appears in the titles of only two articles. At least 12 other articles tackle issues associated with ageism (such as deprivation and being perceived to be "a burden"), and it is interesting that these authors did not make use of the concept. Given that many conclude with forceful recommendations regarding policies and practices, it is strange that they appear reluctant to use a concept that now has a wide currency in the popular media (Bytheway, 1995, p. 10).

Among the 28, the use of the concept varies. Some make only passing reference; for example, four briefly link ageism with sexism, noting the double jeopardy experienced by older women. In contrast, in 17 articles the concept of ageism is much more central, a few including a brief history of the concept (sometimes beginning with a reference to Butler, 1975). Several overlapping themes are clearly apparent. First, a number have studied structural issues concerning employment practices, commerce, and media images.

Employment, Business, and Media

Taylor and Walker (1998, p. 642) address the question of "institutional ageism" in employment practices. They found evidence of the social exclusion of older workers based on negative stereotypes (p. 654). Similarly, Irwin (1999) comments that "the recent trend to early retirement is both a consequence and a cause of a more entrenched ageist perception of the workforce" (p. 706). In reviewing the recent history of antiageist initiatives in employment practice, Loretto and associates (2000) note (with some skepticism) that the aim of these has been to persuade employers that discrimination against older employees is "not only irrational but also commercially damaging" (p. 283).

Carrigan and Szmigin (2000) provide a vivid critique of ageism in the advertising industry, and in another commercial context, Ylanne-McEwen (1999) analyzes in detail an exchange between the staff of a travel agency and an older couple. She concludes that "by linking the task of the assistants in this encounter . . . to the images portrayed in the brochures, it has been possible to illustrate institutional ageism at work" (p. 437). Hanlon and associates (1997) undertook a study of comic strips, assessing the extent to which they convey negative stereotypes of older people. They concluded that the many negative portrayals of older people "lend support to the thesis that this form of communication supports ageism and has the potential to promote stereotypes of ageing" (pp. 302–303). In a similar study of American images, Markson and Taylor (2000, p. 138) note ageism and sexism in the appearance and roles of film stars once they had passed the age of 60.

All these studies focus on institutional rather than individual ageism. Even though Carrigan and Szmigin, for example, feature the prejudices of individual executives, their primary concern is the ageism that permeates the advertising industry. Whether the focus is on practices in engaging older people as workers, advertising models, or film stars, the common concern is to expose and confront institutional ageism.

Public Attitudes

Ageism is often associated with the attitudes of the general public, and so it is no surprise to find studies focused on popular attitudes and organized attempts to change these.

Scott and associates (1998) report on the effectiveness of an intervention study to change the attitudes of adolescent schoolchildren. They believed in the potential of educational interventions: "It is now increasingly recognised that if we are to combat ageism the attitudes of young people need to be more positively constructed so that they do not hold stereotypic views of ageing" (p. 167). Their research, however, failed to provide any evidence that such intervention can have a significant impact. In their concluding discussion, they identify a number of obstacles: the lack of teacher training in gerontology and the roles of parents and of older people themselves. Significantly, in their view, older people are not necessarily "passive victims in the production of ageist behaviour and stereotyped attitudes" (p. 181).

In a comparable study, Loretto and associates (2000) surveyed the attitudes of university students of business studies. They found that their sample had experienced prejudice against younger people and were in favor of outlawing age discrimination. In addressing the question whether these young people are ageist, their findings are equivocal: "On the one hand, there is evidence of ageist attitudes. On the other, the students appear to hold more altruistic attitudes compared to practising managers" (p. 298).

Minichiello and associates (2000) examined the views of older people. They noted that few studies have researched how older people may recognize and give meaning to "ageism" (p. 254). Their aim was "to add new knowledge to the concept of ageism from the point of view of older people" (p. 255). In their concluding discussion, they recognize that some older people will not react against ageism, believing that "older people do not have the social power to change their situation." In contrast, others will work in both subtle and direct ways to change "ageist stereotypes and discriminatory practices." They see the latter as making a contribution to changing the image of older people and the climate in which ageism exists (p. 277).

Only these three articles among the 117 tackle individual ageism, and it seems significant that none of them focuses on evidence of intolerable attitudes toward older people. Rather, there appears to be a common assumption that relatively benign ageist attitudes exist in all groups (including older people) and that the role of gerontologists is to assess interventions intended to change these attitudes and to encourage, monitor, and predict continuing change toward less-ageist attitudes.

Practice

Many articles focus on practice, and several of these address aspects of ageism. Carter and Everitt (1998), for example, undertook a comparative analysis of two projects involving work with older people: one concerned community arts, and the other concerned health promotion. In their view, ageism is one issue that needs to be explored in relation to practice; in this context, they are particularly concerned about age differences.

Ageism and the age difference between practitioners and older people produce similarities with other dimensions of inequality but also differences.... Ageing belongs to everyone and, although the dynamics of ageism mean that many people try to reject this knowledge, progressive practice whether by younger or older workers demands recognition of the intricacies of difference and commonality. (Carter & Everitt, 1998, pp. 91–92)

Bernard and Phillips (2000), in developing "an integrated social policy" for an aging society, identify values in four key areas. One of these is the importance of "combatting all forms of discrimination" (p. 43). They argue that "The insidious impact of ageism ... is something which must be countered at every available opportunity" (p. 44) and conclude that the solution lies in "critically reflective practice" (p. 48).

Three other articles (Lewis, 1998; Twigg, 2000; Biggs, et al., 2000) address the questions of how ageism might affect practice and how changes in practice might challenge "ageist narratives of dependency and decline" (Biggs, et al., 2000, p. 669). The common theme here is how ageism can underpin bad practice and, conversely, how good practice can combat ageism. Only Carter and Everitt (1998), however, consider the potential of practitioners forging an antiageist alliance with older people. To what extent do gerontologists support this strategy?

The Antiageist Alliance between Gerontologists and Older People

Overall, the evidence of these 117 articles is not encouraging. Minichiello and associates (2000) found that many older people feel they have only limited power to change their circumstances. The study of Scott and associates (1998) revealed the potential of older people, unintentionally perhaps, to reinforce ageism rather than to challenge it. For Bender and Cheston (1997), drawing on their work in clinical psychology, ageism is an "important determinant of the behaviour and feelings of older people" (p. 515). With this kind of experience, the belief appears to be strong among gerontologists that older people, the victims of ageism, have been disempowered and that what they need is the support of gerontologists and other professionals.

The results reveal the importance for researchers to understand and articulate the real experiences of older people and to recognise that for older people to understand ageism is dependent upon them developing an awareness of being treated as old. (Minichiello, et al., 2000, p. 276)

Unfortunately, gerontologists can be dubious allies. Oldman and Quilgars (1999), in mounting a critique of the literature concerning residential care, raise two issues. First, they address the question of how residents are viewed prospectively by researchers.

> It has also been noted that although ageism is often offered as an explanatory construct, paradoxically, "not-old" researchers themselves are ageist. The very frailty, physical weakness and failing memories of "subjects" can discourage in-depth interviewing. (p. 370)

Second, they question the powerful impact of the structured dependency paradigm in understanding "the processes of ageism and alienation which continue to characterise life in a residential home" (1999, pp. 381–382). They argue that the determinism of this paradigm needs to be supplemented by "a humanist perspective." What they imply here is first that some residents may be able to resist the development of structured dependency and second that the paradigms of gerontologists can be oppressive.

The potential for professional allies to take the lead and set the agenda is also apparent when Milne and Williams (2000) argue that independence-promoting forms of intervention by mental health services "can be expected to have mental health value in that ageism is challenged, isolation reduced" (p. 707). In this context, Harbison and Morrow (1998) recognize the dangers of older people forming alliances with professionals: "Where older people do take up the issue of mistreatment and neglect, they usually do so in partnership with professionals rather than alone, perhaps reflecting internalised as well as societal ageism" (p. 704).

Apart from dependence, however, Minichiello and associates (2000) (as indicated earlier) also discovered evidence of resistance to "ageist stereotypes and discriminatory practices." Conway and Hockey (1998) similarly undertook a study of lay beliefs in later life and became interested in the potential of older people to resist the medical model of decline.

> If older people's beliefs and practices are at odds with the ways in which medicine frames health in later life, we can therefore ask if they constitute a form of resistance not just to discriminatory medical frameworks, but also to the wider set of ageist beliefs and practices through which the category "old age" has been constructed. (p. 470–471)

They argue that the decline model was being reinforced by the way health care services were provided "for the elderly" (p. 483) and by cuts in health service resources (p. 491). Nevertheless, they note that, in the face of marginalization, older people "are challenging ageism," and in support, they cite the impact of age-based political action in Europe and the United States (p. 483). Harbison and Morrow (1998) similarly discuss potential resistance. Their main argument concerns the potential for policies against elder abuse to be ageist; in this context, they argue that "avoiding a connection with elder abuse and neglect may, for many older people, be part of their struggle to retain a positive social identity in an increasingly ageist society" (p. 696).

Insofar as authors have addressed the potential alliance between gerontologists and older people in challenging ageism, this analysis suggests that there has been considerable diffidence. Gerontologists are perceived to have knowledge and answers, and older people are perceived to be dependent as a result of being subject to ageism over many years. On only rare occasions are they resistant to the strategies of their allies. The cultural gulf is well described in the following:

> The findings suggest that the words used within the gerontological literature to talk about how older people are treated and perceived are not the words that older people use to describe their own experiences. (Minichiello, et al., 2000, p. 275)

THE RELATIONSHIP BETWEEN RESEARCHERS AND OLDER PEOPLE

Many of the contributors to *Ageing and Society* are concerned that their research should help to change and improve policies and practices regarding the circumstances of older people. Many, for example, focus specifically on questions of care in later life. But it is clear from the preceding discussion that gerontologists feel uncomfortable with the concept of ageism. Possibly many recognize that they occupy a compromised position and so prefer a less politicized relationship with the subjects of their research. How then do these authors present those older people who have been interviewed and studied?

Of the 117 articles, 29 do not draw specifically on any empirical base. Another 14 draw on large surveys in which the authors had, at most, limited involvement and certainly did not engage directly with any of those who were interviewed. Another nine analyze the content of books, magazines, and similar material. This leaves 65 where the authors (most probably) had some direct involvement with the subjects of their research. Of these, five interviewed only managers, owners, or workers in care facilities, eight interviewed only carers for older people (some of whom were of a similar age to those they cared for), and six interviewed samples drawn from the general population or younger people such as schoolchildren. This leaves 46 articles in which the authors were reporting on "firsthand" research with older people.

Most of these—34—included samples limited to people over a certain age. In every case, the criterion age was at least 50 years. In a statistical sense, these samples were intended to represent "the older population." Some, however, were of more narrowly-defined age groups. Four, for example, were limited to groups approaching retirement or recently retired, and four were the survivors of samples drawn from specific birth cohorts. Where ages or dates of birth were not specified, studies were confined to people in a particular age-specific setting.

It is perhaps worth recording at this point that, including the large surveys (but excluding national census data), the 117 articles draw upon interviews with approximately 22,500 older people and quote the spoken words of about 490, many of whom are given pseudonyms and introduced with detailed descriptions.

For the purposes of this analysis, an important question is: To what extent did the authors maintain a clear us/them distinction with these older people? In scientific studies, even in nonscientific studies, this distinction is inevitable where the authors are providing an account of what they, as researchers, did and what their interviewees told them. As several authors stated, their objective was to provide older people with the opportunity to describe some aspect of their experiences "in their own words." The questions of *who we are* and *who they are* become pertinent however, when such accounting moves into more general discussions about the authors' conclusions. Who do their interviewees represent: us as we grow older, or themselves who are now old; older people in general, or specific groups?

First-person pronouns are used almost exclusively in these articles in references to the authors, either as authors or as researchers. Occasionally, they are used rhetorically or nonspecifically, for example, in discussions of the concept of self. Sometimes, in opening paragraphs, the use is autobiographical. For example, van den Hoonaard (1997) begins her article: "This source first aroused my interest when a student lent me . . . a journal consisting of the author's first year as a widow" (p. 533).

When the first-person pronoun is used to describe the author's role as researcher, this leads logically to possessive pronouns and the third person being used to refer to the subjects of their research. Ahmad and Walker (1997), for example, comment that without any prompting several of our respondents . . . spoke of this [families divided by immigration policies] affecting their current circumstances" (p. 162). Sometimes the third-person pronoun (along with the continuous present) is also used when authors draw out generalizations to other research settings. For example, Conway and Hockey (1998) conclude that "when older people lay claim to 'good health' during a research interview, they may also be engaging in an act of resistance to a stigmatising social identity"

(p. 471). Complementing this, Bender (1997) draws on the first-person pronoun in commenting on the objectives of clinicians and researchers in the search for understanding: "Whether as social scientists trying to make sense of people's experiences, or as mental health workers trying to treat people with emotional difficulties, we all need to have a clearer understanding of past experience" (p. 347).

In drawing conclusions, most authors maintain this simple distinction in the use of pronouns. Coleman and associates (1998), for example, conclude their article with the important generalized comment that "not all older people have a past with which they wish to connect. That does not mean that they cannot develop major themes for the latter part of their life which may have quite a different character from that which has preceded it" (p. 415). This kind of conclusion about older people, drawing as it does on a representative sample, contrasts with those of articles by authors with a more individualistic orientation to personal experience. Freeman (1997), for example, addressing a similar issue about past biography, concludes his analysis of Tolstoy's *Death of Ivan Ilych* with the following comment:

> Self-understanding, therefore, is an act of submitting oneself to one's history, of standing before oneself, in the interest of discerning what the life in question has been. Perhaps the "results" of the process, in turn, can help us identify more clearly the substance of well-lived lives. (p. 394)

Similarly, Bluck and Levine (1998) define reminiscence in the following way:

> Our view is that while autobiographical memory is a system that encodes, stores and guides retrieval of all episodic information related to our personal experiences, reminiscence is one way in which we access this information for our use. (p. 188)

The primary concern here is to describe the experience of and human response to aging rather than to being old, matters that these authors feel to be of immediate relevance to themselves and the readers of their articles. They draw heavily upon personal and clinical experience and upon the study of biographical literature. Research that might engage gerontologists with representative samples of people and that focuses on the experience of aging across many years is of course expensive and difficult to sustain, as anyone with experience of longitudinal research will confirm. The consequence is that gerontology is informed primarily by a complex mixture of personal experience and interviews with cross-sectional samples of older people.

CONCLUSION

In drawing together the implications of this review, I want to finally make some reference to Andrews' (1999) article "The Seductiveness of Agelessness" and to the debate that has followed involving her, me, and H. B. Gibson. I will not attempt to summarize this debate here, but the implications for the relationship between gerontologists and older people are important. In the opening sentence of the abstract of the original article, Molly Andrews neatly summarizes her view as follows:

> In recent years, many researchers in the study of aging have adopted a terminology of "agelessness." They argue that old age is nothing more than a social construct and that until it is eliminated as a conceptual category, ageism will continue to flourish. This article challenges this view, stating that the current tendency towards "agelessness" is itself a form of ageism, depriving the old of one of their most hard-earned resources: their age. (p. 301)

I am one of several researchers who are cited as denying the reality of old age. Two years later, Gibson (2000) submitted an article in which he applauds Andrews and consolidates the attack, drawing in part on his own experience of ageism in his mid-eighties. He comments:

> This ageist attitude [i.e., valuing youth] however is unintentionally reinforced by those academics and professionals who insist that, although people must become "old" in years, the youthful ghost can remain untainted, as it were, by the passage of years. Many gerontologists write as though they accepted the existence of the young ghost inhabiting an elderly machine. Others appear to think that the ghost is ageless but the machine goes on aging. (p. 777)

Both Andrews and Gibson were claiming that gerontology had shifted its focus away from the distinct experience of old age toward an ageist denial of the realities of age. They would argue, for example, that the age differences noted by Carter and Everitt (1998) and the embarrassments of younger gerontologists noted by Oldman and Quilgars (1999) in interviewing very old people and coping with frailty and failing memories had led to a denial of age. Andrews (1999, 2000) and Gibson (2000) sensed that the mask of age and the potential for an alternative, more active, old age were more attractive issues, enabling gerontologists to construct and focus upon more positive images of later life. In this context, they felt that the time had come to reposition gerontology.

Naturally I took up their challenge and disputed every aspect of their argument. In particular, I suggested that "as gerontologists, we were vulnerable to seeing ourselves and those we study entirely in terms of age ... ageful rather than ageless" (Bytheway, 2000, pp. 785–786), but my main concern was to dispute the us/them dichotomy. While I would continue to do this, I recognize that this can be interpreted as a denial of age, a denial of difference, and that it might foster in gerontologists a lack of interest in the lives of those of older generations. I accept that a growing interest in gerontology in the lifelong processes and experiences of aging might reflect an ageist distaste for extreme old age and that it might be accompanied by a growing neglect at every level of those issues that affect the lives of very old people.

To try to summarize my current views about the positioning of gerontology, I would make the following points. First, it would appear that, overall, gerontological fieldwork research is more heavily dependent upon the sponsorship of funding and facilitating organizations than many gerontologists might appreciate. For example, although there is widespread recognition that midlife issues are legitimate subjects for gerontological research, only a few articles among the 117 touch on such "pre-old" subjects—preparation for retirement, intergenerational relations—and that is about as close as you get. In practice it would appear that gerontologists as a whole are willing to go along with the popular perception that the proper subject of gerontology is the state of dependency in late life. All too often there has been an implicit equation of old age with need, and the focus has mostly been upon solving problems and achieving positive outcomes rather than on documenting and analyzing the realities of growing older. No matter how often we might protest, much of our research is embedded within ageist assumptions about the societal implications of an aging population. Even in the year 2002, it would be difficult to dispute Townsend's (1981) famous accusation of acquiescent functionalism.

It is significant that none of the 117 articles is based on research undertaken in collaboration with the campaigning organizations of older people. This, together with an apparent reluctance to use the concept of ageism, suggests that gerontologists hesitate before taking on the more politically-charged issues of age. I know that many contributors do align themselves with the pensioners' movement and similar campaigns, publishing their views in journals that might be thought more appropriate than the academic *Ageing and Society*. I find it interesting that the insights into the experience of later life gained through such involvement rarely surface on the pages of *Ageing and Society*.

In short, although I have learned much for the 117 articles reviewed here, recognizing that most gerontologists work "in good conscience," I would welcome the following three shifts in a repositioning of gerontology:

- away from a focus on "the elderly" and toward (1) aging in general and (2) extreme age in particular;
- away from the planning, management, and delivery of age-specific services and toward the detail and routines of everyday (and every-year) life; and
- away from idealized models and processes of aging and toward an interest in how people talk about and act upon their age.

REFERENCES

Ahmad, W. I. U., & Walker, R. (1997). Asian older people: Housing, health and access to services. *Ageing and Society*, 17(2), 141–165.

Andrews, M. (1999). The seductiveness of agelessness. *Ageing and Society*, 19(3), 301–318.

Andrews, M. (2000). Ageful and proud. *Ageing and Society*, 20(6), 791–795.

Bender, M. P. (1997). Bitter harvest: The implications of continuing war-related stress on reminiscence theory and practice. *Ageing and Society*, 17(3), 337–348.

Bender, M. P., & Cheston, R. (1997). Inhabitants of a lost kingdom: A model of the subjective experiences of dementia. *Ageing and Society*, 17(5), 513–532.

Bernard, M., & Phillips, J. (2000). The challenge of aging in tomorrow's Britain. *Ageing and Society*, 20(1), 33–54.

Biggs, S. (1998). Mature imaginations: Ageing and the psychodynamic tradition. *Ageing and Society*, 18(4), 421–439.

Biggs, S., Bernard, M., Kingston, P., & Nettleton, H. (2000). Lifestyles of belief: Narrative and culture in a retirement community. *Ageing and Society*, 20(6), 649–672.

Blakemore, K. (1999). International migration in later life: Social care and policy implications. *Ageing and Society*, 19(6), 761–774.

Bluck, S., & Levine, L. J. (1998). Reminiscence as autobiographical memory: A catalyst for reminiscence theory development. *Ageing and Society*, 18(2), 185–208.

Butler, R. N. (1975). *Why survive? Being old in America.* New York: Harper and Row.

Bytheway, B. (1995). *Ageism.* Buckingham, U.K.: Open University Press.

Bytheway, B. (2000). Youthfulness and agelessness: A comment. *Ageing and Society*, 20(6), 781–789.

Carrigan, M., & Szmigin, I. (2000). Advertising in an aging society. *Ageing and Society*, 20(2), 217–233.

Carter, P., & Everitt, A. (1998). Conceptualising practice with older people: Friendship and conversation. *Ageing and Society*, 18(1), 79–99.

Cheal, D., & Kampen, K. (1998). Poor and dependent seniors in Canada. *Ageing and Society*, 18(2), 147–166.

Coleman, P., Ivani-Chalian, C., & Robinson, M. (1998). The story continues: Persistence of life themes in old age. *Ageing and Society*, 18(4), 389–419.

Conway, S., and Hockey, J. (1998). Resisting the "mask" of old age? The social meaning of lay health beliefs in later life. *Ageing and Society*, 18(4), 469–494.

Estes, C. (1979). *The aging enterprise.* San Francisco: Jossey Bass.

Freeman, M. (1997). Death, narrative integrity and the radical challenge of self-understanding: A reading of Tolstoy's Death of Ivan Ilych. *Ageing and Society*, 17(4), 373–398.

Gibson, H. B. (2000). It keeps us young. *Ageing and Society, 20*(6), 773–779.
Gubrium, J. F., & Holstein, J. A. (1999). The nursing home as a discursive anchor for the aging body. *Ageing and Society, 19*(5), 519–538.
Hanlon, H., Gfarnsworth, J., & Murray, J. (1997). Ageing in American comic strips. *Ageing and Society, 17*(3), 293–304.
Harbison, J., & Morrow, M. (1998). Re-examining the social construction of "elder abuse and neglect": A Canadian perspective. *Ageing and Society, 18*(6), 691–711.
Irwin, S. (1999). Later life, inequality and sociological theory. *Ageing and Society, 19*(6), 691–715.
Kastenbaum, R. (1997). Lasting words as a channel for intergenerational communication. *Ageing and Society, 17*(1), 21–39.
Katz, S. (1992). Alarmist demography: Power, knowledge and the elderly population. *Journal of Aging Studies, 6*(3), 203–225.
Katz, S. (1996). *Disciplining old age: The formation of gerontological knowledge.* Charlottesville, VA: University of Virginia Press.
Lewis, R. D. H. (1998). The impact of the marital relationship on the experience of caring for an elderly spouse with dementia. *Ageing and Society, 18*(2), 219–231.
Loretto, W., Duncan, C., & White, P. J. (2000). Ageism and employment: Controversies, ambiguities and younger people's perceptions, *Ageing and Society, 20*(3), 279–302.
Markson, E. W., & Taylor, C. A. (2000). The mirror has two faces. *Ageing and Society, 20*(2), 137–160.
McColgan, G., Valentine, J., & Downs, M. (2000). Concluding narratives of a career with dementia: Accounts of Iris Murdoch at her death. *Ageing and Society, 20*(1), 97–109.
Mehta, K. (1997). Cultural scripts and the social integration of older people. *Ageing and Society, 17*(3), 253–275.
Milne, A., & Willians, J. (2000). Meeting the mental health needs of older women: Taking social inequality into account. *Ageing and Society, 20*(6), 699–723.
Minichiello, V., Browne, J., & Kendig, H. (2000). Perceptions and consequences of ageism: Views of older people. *Ageing and Society, 20*(3), 253–278.
Oldman, C., & Quilgars, D. (1999). The last resort? Revisiting ideas about older people's living arrangements. *Ageing and Society, 19*(3), 363–384.
Phillipson, C. (1998). *Reconstructing old age.* London: Sage.
Phillipson, C., Bernard, M., Phillips, J., & Ogg, J. (1998). The family and community life of older people: Household composition and social networks in three urban areas. *Ageing and Society, 18*(3), 259–289.
Robertson, A. (1997). Beyond apocalyptic demography: Towards a moral economy of independence. *Ageing and Society, 17*(4), 425–446.
Scott, T., Minichiello, V., & Browning, C. (1998). Secondary school students' knowledge of and attitudes towards older people: Does an education intervention program make a difference? *Ageing and Society, 18*(2), 167–183.
Taylor, P., & Walker, A. (1998). Employers and older workers: Attitudes and employment practices. *Ageing and Society, 18*(6), 641–658.
Teo, P. (1997). Older women and leisure in Singapore. *Ageing and Society, 17*(6), 649–672.
Townsend, P. (1981). The structured dependency of the elderly: The creation of social policy in the twentieth century. *Ageing and Society, 1*(1), 5–28.
Tulle-Winton, E. (1999). Growing old and resistance: Towards a new cultural economy of old age? *Ageing and Society, 19*(3), 281–299.

Twigg, J. (2000). Carework as a form of bodywork. *Ageing and Society, 20*(4), 389–411.

van den Hoonaard, D. (1997). Identity foreclosure: Women's experiences of widowhood as expressed in autobiographical accounts. *Ageing and Society, 17*(5), 533–551.

Ylanne-McEwen, V. (1999). "Young at Heart": Discourse of age identity in travel agency interaction. *Ageing and Society, 19*(4), 417–440.

6

Involvement in Social Organizations in Later Life: Variations by Gender and Class

Sara Arber, Kim Perren, and Kate Davidson

INTRODUCTION

This chapter examines older men's and women's membership in different types of social organizations in Britain. There is extensive research on the social networks of older people, particularly in relation to contacts with family and friends (Wenger et al., 1996), but a lack of research on the involvement of older people in leisure, community, and religious organizations. Involvement in different types of social organizations might help augment an older person's social network and reduce social isolation, as well as providing sources of self-identity and self-esteem.

Several factors highlight the need to consider older people in studies of social organizational involvement: first, the growth in the proportion of the population above the pension age and the decline in the age of leaving paid employment (Kohli et al., 1991). In Britain, as the expectation of life for women is 79 years and for men is 74 (Ghee, 2001), the time between labor market exit and death is increasing. Membership in social organizations may be particularly critical as a source of well-being for this age group, compared to earlier stages of the life course. Laslett (1989) argued that the Third Age offered opportunities for self-fulfillment and agency, especially relating to leisure activities, education, and social productivity. One aspect of this is involvement in social organizations. However, a lack of socioeconomic resources in later life may hinder the possibility that many older people can engage in certain types of social activity (Carnegie, 1993).

A significant major transition for many older people is the experience of widowhood. Widowhood often represents the loss of a partner of 40 to 50 years, who may have been a prime source of companionship and support, especially for men, who frequently see their wives as their primary confidante and support (Askham, 1994; Davidson, 1999). Widowhood is normative for older women, since half of women over age 65 in Britain are widowed, and on average women can expect to be widowed for 9 years. The normative nature of widowhood for women contrasts with the norm that men will still be married at the time of their death. However, the majority status of marriage for men may blind us to specific issues that face the minority of older widowed men and the small but growing proportion who are divorced. Therefore, an important issue is to what extent widowhood leads to an increase in social organizational activity that might be seen as compensating for the loss of a marital partner (Ferraro, 1984).

Gilleard and Higgs (2000) point to a growth of leisure and self-fulfillment as an orientation of older people, but a key question is to what extent this Third Age of potential self-direction and self-development is one that is primarily available to a subset of older people with sufficient resources and cultural capital to enable participation. Thus, a goal of this chapter is to examine the extent to which older people who are already advantaged in terms of socioeconomic resources and education are also advantaged in terms of membership in certain types of social organizations. We consider the ways in which structural disadvantage among older people may be further perpetuated through differential involvement in social organizations.

GENDER, AGING, AND SOCIAL ACTIVITY

It is important to distinguish chronological age from physiological age (Arber & Ginn, 1995). In most research, age is included only as a control variable; however, in this chapter it is a focus of conceptual interest. Age represents a marker for several distinctive processes within older people's lives. First, age reflects the physiological aging process. On average, ill health increases with advancing age, and we may expect that social organizational involvement will decline with age simply because of increased restrictions on mobility or frailty. However, there may be some compensation through involvement in different types of organizations with advancing age, for example, increasing involvement in organizations that do not require physical fitness for participation. Second, aging is associated with various other social and economic changes. Some may accompany widowhood, especially for women, in terms of loss of a car (driver). Others reflect declines in the value of private pensions with advancing age. Changes in social activities with advancing age thus may primarily reflect other social and economic changes rather than declines in health or aging per se.

Finally, chronological age defines membership in a particular birth cohort or generation. The group of people aged 60 and over today represent a span of over 30 years and encompass enormous diversity. Some writers have considered how attitudes and behavior vary among birth cohorts or whole generations. Karl Mannheim (1952) linked the process of the formation of generations to social change, arguing that not only do generations relate to being born in the same era, but that those who live through a period of rapid social change share a "historical-social conscience" or collective identity that influences their attitudes and behavior and distinguishes them from preceding and succeeding generations. The present social activities of older people can only be understood by reference to their prior life course. For example, older women's and men's current financial circumstances are intimately tied to their previous role in the labor market and thus their pension acquisition. There is likely to be substantial continuity of social activities and interests from adult years through to later life.

Cross-cutting these various meanings of aging are gender and class. In terms of physiological aging, older women have greater reported levels of disability than older men (Arber & Cooper, 1999) and therefore may experience more constraints on their social activities because of mobility difficulties. Class inequalities in health mean that older people previously in working-class occupations are more likely to suffer ill health and disability in their sixties and seventies than are professionals or managers (Arber & Cooper, 1999). Social and economic changes with advancing chronological age are more pronounced for women than for men. In terms of cohort changes, the lives of women have changed enormously this century with the growth of women's employment, the availability of contraception, and the liberalization of abortion. These profound changes have had less effect on the oldest generation of older women but more effect on the young elderly and midlife women. The current generation of older women have had a very different life course from that of older men. Many of the oldest generation of women left the labor market when they married or had children and either did not return to paid employment or returned to part-time rather than full-time work as their children became less dependent (Dex, 1984). Thus, when we compare age groups of older people in their sixties through their eighties, we are comparing men and women from distinct age cohorts with different labor market experience and life history.

CLASS, EDUCATION, AND MATERIAL RESOURCES

There is a growing diversity among older people relating to inequalities in income in the form of pensions. In the United Kingdom, private pension provision has grown over the last 30 years, leading to increases in inequality linked to class and gender (Ginn & Arber, 1999). Those in professional and managerial occupations usually retire with substantial occupational pensions, whereas manual workers often have no occupational pension or only a very modest pension, barely sufficient to bring the older person above poverty level. For two-thirds of British women over age 65, their only pension income is from the state, whereas this is the case for only one-third of older men (Ginn & Arber, 1999).

Class forms a fundamental division across British society (Arber & Cooper 2000). For older people, their class position can be best signified by their main occupation during working life. Conventionally, women's class has been measured by her husband's occupation if she is married and by her own occupation if she is not (Goldthorpe, 1983). However, among older women it is not feasible to measure class using the conventional approach, because of the high proportion who are widowed with no data available about their late husband's occupation. Therefore, the only alternative is to measure occupational class based on their last occupation, which for the current generation of older women may have been before marriage, many years earlier.

An individual's educational level is likely to influence his or her tastes and interests and thus the type of social organizations joined. Educational qualifications can be applied to all adults and are generally stable throughout the life course. However, there are cohort differences in the level and significance of educational qualifications with younger age cohorts more likely than older cohorts to have degree-level qualifications and with lower educational attainment among the current cohort of older women than among men.

Within British society, income and material resources of the household, as reflected in car and home ownership, are closely tied to class and earlier position in the labor market. For older women, lack of a car may be a critical issue. Fewer women in their eighties were car drivers because of the restricted nature of women's roles in the mid-twentieth century. Thus, widowhood often represents a double blow for these women, losing their husband and at the same time their mobility to visit places, friends, and social organizations in the "family car." Older women's social worlds may be more limited to the extent that they do not have a household car at their disposal.

It is expected that class, educational qualifications, and material resources will all have independent effects on older people's membership in social organizations. A key concern is to what extent the general decline in health and socioeconomic resources with advancing age is also associated with a decline in membership of social organizations, while also bearing in mind that the more disadvantaged material resources of older women and working-class older people may provide added constraints on their membership in social organizations.

MARITAL STATUS IN LATER LIFE

Widowhood is a fundamental experience of later life and is normal for older women. Three-quarters of men over 60 in Britain are married or cohabiting and therefore have a partner to rely on and to accompany them to social organizations should they wish to do so, whereas among women over 60, fewer than half are married (British Household Panel Study, 1999). Half of women in their seventies are widowed; among those over 80, three-quarters of women are widows. Thus, widowhood is normative for older women, whereas only 14 percent of men over 60 are widowers, increasing to two-fifths among men over 80.

Many research studies fail to consider older people who have never married (6 to 7 percent of older men and women) and the increasing proportions who are divorced. Solomou and associates (1998) found that divorced and never-married older men reported less practical and emotional support from family and friends than those who were married. Therefore, social organizational membership may be particularly important for older divorced and never-married men as sources of sociability and self-identity. The expectation may be that widowed older people will seek to replace their lost partner by involvement in social organizations as a compensation. We examine to what extent widowhood leads to a growth in social organizational membership as an alternative source of companionship and identity and whether this is more likely for widowers than widows. We might expect the never-married and divorced to be more involved in social organizations, since they do not have a marital partner to fall back on as a source of sociability and companionship.

BENEFITS OF SOCIAL ORGANIZATION MEMBERSHIP

Membership in social organizations is characterized as volitional, representing a willingness of the individual to engage in an organized or sociable pursuit. The focus in this chapter is not on organizations that have been set up "for older people," such as day care centers, but on organizations that the older person chooses to join (Davidson, et al., 2002). Social organization membership may be more important in later life when other opportunities for social interaction have been closed, such as those relating to formal roles in employment, childrearing, and marriage (Atchley, 1994). Role theory suggests that the retired will seek to replace their lost roles with community-based activity.

Membership in social organizations may have a range of beneficial features, particularly for older people:

1. Involvement in organizations provides a source of *sociability*, which is likely to lead to better *social integration*. Organizational involvement may reduce social isolation and the potential for loneliness, enhancing broader feelings of psychological *well-being*.
2. Involvement in sports organizations is likely to directly promote *physical fitness* and *health*.
3. Organizations may provide both a source of and confirmation of *self-identity*. This is likely to be particularly salient in later life, when other sources of identity, relating to paid employment and roles as a parent or partner, are no longer available.
4. Organization membership may bring feelings of *self-worth* and *self-esteem*, for example, involvement in organizations associated with doing something for others. Involvement in community organizations often involves undertaking *altruistic activities* for others or making a contribution to the community.

There may be differences among older people in their preferences for involvement in different types of organizations, particularly relating to class and educational background. For example, Mein and associates (1998) found that higher-grade civil servants felt guilty that they were no longer socially productive, whereas those from the lower grades felt they had earned their retirement. Thus, middle-class older people may be more inclined to engage in informal organizational activities that provide a source of self-esteem, whereas working-class older people may be primarily concerned about maintaining sociability.

TYPES OF SOCIAL ORGANIZATIONS

Different types of social organizations vary in the extent to which they provide each of the potential benefits just enumerated. We categorize social organizations into five types, as follows:

Social organizations include social clubs for older people, workingmen's clubs, and those that provide entertainment such as bingo. These are likely to provide sociability and social integration, but not the other three benefits.
Sports organizations are varied, including bowling, golf, tennis, and exercise clubs. They are likely to fulfil the first two benefits, plus potentially providing a source of self-identity, for example, as a good bowler or a golfer with a low handicap. Playing sports and games may also bring a sense of self-esteem from successfully maintaining activity when this is seen as unusual at a certain age, for example, playing tennis at 75 or swimming in competitions at 70.

The following three types of organizations are more outward-looking, being guided either by a spirit of altruism or by shared interests or principles:

Interest groups include membership and involvement in political organizations and environmental pressure groups, as well as groups associated with paid work or professional roles. Among older women, the Women's Institute forms an important interest group. Involvement in such organizations may bring sociability, self-identity, and self-esteem.
Community groups include residents and tenants associations, scouts, guides, parents organizations, and various other voluntary activities. Involvement in such organizations is likely to yield feelings of self-worth and self-esteem, as well as self-identity and sociability.

Membership in *religious groups* may solely comprise taking part in religious services as an individual, but it is often a source of sociability, communalism, and friendship. Religious membership may also be a source of self-identity, as well as providing the opportunity to do things for others, resulting in greater feelings of self-worth and self-esteem through altruistic activities.

Thus, all types of organizational membership are likely to result in sociability and reduce social isolation. Social and sports organizations have in common that they are leisure oriented and consumption oriented. Social organizations are predicated on sociability, and especially for men are often associated with the consumption of alcoholic drinks. Membership in sports organizations will usually provide benefits in terms of physical fitness, but it may also increase self-esteem because of being seen as a good sportsperson. Being involved in interest and community groups and religious organizations is likely to bring benefits in terms of a source of self-identity and feelings of self-worth, as well as sociability.

AIMS

This chapter examines the involvement of older men and women in different types of social organizations that are likely to vary in their impact on an older person's sociability, self-identity, and self-esteem. The specific questions to be addressed are:

1. Does organization membership decline with increasing age? If so, can this be explained solely by a decline in health and other material resources that facilitate participation?
2. Is there evidence of substitution of different types of organization membership with advancing age?
3. Do widows and widowers have higher levels of social participation than married older people, which could be seen as compensating for the loss of their partner? In other words, does social organization membership substitute for marriage?
4. How do class and differential material resources relate to membership in different types of social organizations that vary in their provision of sociability, self-identity, and self-esteem?
5. Does social organization membership in later life represent a perpetuation of bases of inequality associated with class, education, and material resources?

DATA AND METHODS

The chapter is based on analysis of the 1999 wave of the British Household Panel Survey (BHPS) (1999). The BHPS began in 1991 when a representative sample of approximately 10,000 adults living in some 5,500 households was interviewed about a range of topics including family structure, health, finances, and material circumstances (Taylor, 1992). In 1999, additional Scottish and Welsh households were added, resulting in over 15,000 individuals completing an interview. The use of weights ensures that this larger sample remains representative of Britain at the end of the twentieth century. The analysis focuses on the over 3,500 women and men age 60 and over interviewed in 1999.

Questions relating to informal organizations ask respondents to which (if any) of a specified set of groups they belong. We examine all those who say they are members of groups. In addition, for religious organizations, we include those who say they attend religious services at least once per week (even if they say that they are not members of a religious organization). For trade unions and professional associations, we only include those who say they are *active* in these organizations. The BHPS data provides no information on the frequency of attendance or nature of activity in these organizations.

Class is based on the individual's current occupation or on their last occupation if they are not in paid employment and is coded into the Registrar General's social classes (Office of Population Censuses and Surveys, 1990). As preliminary analysis showed little difference between skilled manual and semiskilled/unskilled workers in their social organization membership, these groups were combined into a single manual class.

Educational level is based on the individual's highest qualification achieved. Income is measured using total household income after housing costs are met and following adjustment for household composition using the McClements scale. The two measures of health are reporting that health problems affect moderate physical activity "a lot" and a subjective assessment of health as "excellent, good, fair, or poor."

AGE AND GENDER DIFFERENCES IN SOCIAL ORGANIZATION MEMBERSHIP

There is surprisingly little overall difference in the proportions of older men and women who are members of social organizations. Three-fifths of men and women over 60 belong to one or more organizations (see Table 6.1). The lack of gender difference in overall levels of membership hides major gender differences in the types of organizations attended. Older men are over twice as likely as women to be members of social groups or sports clubs: 21 percent of men compared to 8 percent of women belong to social groups, while 16 percent of men and 7 percent of women belong to sports clubs. These two types of organizations are focused on sociability, although sports clubs may also provide opportunities for self-esteem and self-identity. In contrast, women are more likely to belong to religious organizations—nearly one-third of older women and 19 percent of men.

One-fifth of older women and men are members of community groups, such as tenants or residents associations, or voluntary organizations. These organizations generally serve others in the community and provide sources of self-identity and self-worth, as well as sociabil-

TABLE 6.1. Percentage of Men and Women Who Are Members of Different Types of Organizations, Age 60 and Over

	Men	Women	All
Social group	20.8	7.9	13.5
Sports club	15.6	6.7	10.6
Religious organisation (plus	13.7	23.6	19.3
weekly church attendance)	18.7	30.5	25.4
Community group	21.5	22.0	21.8
Tenants/residents	13.8	13.5	13.7
Voluntary service	6.5	7.6	7.1
Parents/school	1.0	1.0	1.0
Scouts/guides	1.0	0.9	1.0
Other community	4.7	3.5	4.0
Interest group	17.9	23.6	21.2
Political party	7.0	5.1	5.9
Environmental group	3.7	2.8	3.2
Trade union (active)	1.3	0.2	0.7
Professional (active)	2.9	0.7	1.7
Pensioner group	5.9	9.3	7.8
Women's Institute	-	8.3	4.7
Other women's group	-	2.4	1.4
Other organisation	10.8	11.5	11.2
Any organisation	61.6	59.4	60.4
3 or more organisations	12.9	14.0	13.6
N=	1,553	2,004	3,556

Source: British Household Panel Survey, Wave 9: 1999 Computer files (authors' analysis)

ity. Similarly, there is little gender difference in membership of interest groups, although men are more likely to be involved in political parties, environmental groups, and trade union or professional associations. Women are more likely to be involved in groups that support their members as well as others in the community, such as the Women's Institute and pensioner groups.

A modest decline in overall membership in social organizations is found with increasing age (figures not shown). In their sixties, around two-thirds of men and women belong to one or more organizations, while above age 80, just over half do. Advancing age leads to an equivalent decline in membership for older men and women, but this decline is not so dramatic as some commentators might have expected. Although there is a remarkable similarity in the extent of organization membership between men and women in different age groups in later life and a surprisingly modest decline between the sixties and the eighties, this stability reflects a changing composition of types of organization membership by gender and with advancing age.

When the proportion of older men who are members of the five main types of organizations is considered across age groups, there is a parallel decline in membership of social groups and sports clubs, falling from over one-quarter belonging to social groups in their sixties to 15 percent over age 80, while membership of sports clubs falls from one-fifth to under 10 percent. Alongside the declines for sports and social group membership, there is stability with age for men's membership in other types of groups, although some suggestion of a slight increase in community and religious group membership for men in their seventies.

Fewer women than men are members of social groups and sports clubs in their sixties (12 percent of women), and the fall is very dramatic to only 3 to 4 percent of women over age 80. Older women's involvement in religious organizations is higher than men's involvement across the age range and increases with advancing age, reaching over one-third among women over 80. This contrasts with a decline in women's involvement in community groups and little change in interest group membership.

Our data suggest that organization membership that provides primarily sociability declines with age, but that there is substantial continuity or increase in membership of organizations that also provide sources of self-identity and self-esteem. For women there is a clear decline with age in membership in social groups, sports clubs, and community groups, whereas for men the decline is only clear-cut for social and sports clubs.

AGE AND GENDER DIFFERENCES IN SOCIAL AND HEALTH RESOURCES

A key concern is to what extent gender and age differences in membership in various types of organizations can be explained by increased disability and lower levels of income and other material resources that may be needed to facilitate organization membership. A range of different indicators shows that material and health resources deteriorate with advancing age, and older women are generally more likely to be disadvantaged than older men.

Reports of health problems that limit activities "a lot" increase from 10 percent of men aged 60 to 74 to one-third aged 85+. For women, the increase starts at an earlier age and is steeper, reaching half of women over 85. Variations in home ownership with age largely reflect cohort differences, with younger cohorts being more likely to be home owners.

Car ownership follows a similar pattern, but shows a much steeper gradient with age and is more distinctly gendered. Not having a household car increases from 21 percent of women in their early sixties to 88 percent over age 85, whereas the parallel increases for men are from 11 percent to 67 percent. Changes in levels of car ownership with advancing age reflect several factors: declining health, which curtails driving; the effects of disadvantaged material circumstances, reducing the possibility of owning and running a car; and older cohorts of women, who were less likely to be car drivers.

There are cohort and gender differences in the acquisition of educational qualifications. The proportion of older people with no qualifications rises from half of men in their early sixties to 78 percent at 85+, and for women the respective proportions move from 64 percent to 85 percent. Being in the lowest quartile of household (equivalized) income increases with age, reaching over one-third of men and women in their eighties. Given the accumulation of socioeconomic and health disadvantages with advancing age, we now examine to what extent class, income, educational qualifications, car ownership, and housing tenure might explain the declines in membership in different types of social organizations in later life.

AGE, GENDER, AND MEMBERSHIP IN ANY ORGANIZATION

As discussed earlier, the proportion of older men and women who are members of any organization declines from two-thirds in their sixties to just over one-half above age 80. This decline in membership in any social organization with increasing age can be entirely explained by poor health, lower income, and fewer resources of older people with increasing age. We use logistic regression to predict membership in any social organization, comparing two separate models. Model A includes age in five-year age groups and a variable that combines gender and marital status. This shows that the odds of membership fall from 1.00 for those aged 60 to 64 (the reference category) to about half this value among people over 85. Model B also includes highest educational attainment, occupational class, household equivalized income, housing tenure, car ownership, and two measures of health. Once these variables are included in the model, there is no longer a statistically significant effect of advancing age on organization membership.

Older men who are never married or divorced have a 50 percent lower odds ratio of being a member of a social organization than married men. This lower level of membership only changes slightly when the various material resources and health are included in Model B. Thus, older never-married or divorced men are the group most likely to be isolated from organizational contacts, and this is not explained by their poorer socioeconomic circumstances.

Membership in organizations is most likely among materially and culturally advantaged older people; those with a degree have an over four times higher odds ratio of membership than older people with no qualifications. Similarly, older people with higher levels of household income and those who own their home are more likely to be organization members. Thus, older people with greater levels of material and cultural capital (in the form of education) are most likely also to benefit from social organizational capital.

MEMBERSHIP IN DIFFERENT TYPES OF ORGANIZATIONS

Various types of social organizations are likely to provide different benefits in terms of sociability, self-identity, and self-worth. Organizations with a purely social orientation enhance sociability but are less likely to provide sources of self-identity and self-worth, whereas membership in interest and community groups are likely to also yield sources of self-identity and self-esteem. This section examines the factors associated with being a member of the five different types of organizations identified in Table 6.1: social, sports, interest, community, and religious groups. For each type of organization, a logistic regression model is analyzed that includes age (in five-year age groups), a combined gender and marital status variable, educational attainment, class, household equivalized income, housing tenure, car ownership, and two measures of health.

Membership in social and sports clubs declines very markedly with increasing age even after controlling for socioeconomic and health variables. Men are more likely to be members than women. Widowers have a high level of membership (odds ratio of 2.4 for sports clubs and 1.57 for social organizations compared to 1.00 for married men). This suggests substitution of social and sports organization membership among widowers providing alternative sources of social support when men no longer have a marital partner. This contrasts with divorced and never-married men, who have lower membership in social and sports clubs than married men.

Married women are somewhat more likely to be members of social clubs than widows, possibly accompanying their husband to such organizations. There is a slightly higher membership in sports clubs among widows than married women. Limitations of health are strongly associated with lower levels of membership in both sports and social clubs.

Social club membership has a divergent class pattern of membership compared to the other four types of organization. Older people previously in manual occupations, with no or low educational qualifications and who rent rather than own their home, are more likely to be members. Thus, more disadvantaged older people are members of social clubs, which are likely to provide important sources of sociability. Sports club membership among older people is not divided by class, income, or education, although car owners and those who own their home are more likely to be members of sports clubs.

The pattern of membership in interest groups, such as political and environmental groups, and in community groups, such as residents associations and voluntary organizations, is broadly similar. Membership in these organizations increases rather than decreases with advancing age, once socioeconomic and health resources are included in the models. The greatest likelihood of membership in community organizations occurs for people in their early seventies, and for interest groups, the greatest likelihood of membership is at over age 80. Thus, there may be some evidence that older people reduce membership in sports or social groups and replace this with interest-group and community-group membership as age increases. The effect of health limitations on membership is less than for sports and social groups.

Interest and community groups are primarily the province of older women, whereas sports and social groups are primarily the province of men. There is no evidence that widowhood for either men or women leads to an increase in membership in interest or community groups. In fact, widowed men have a very low likelihood of membership in interest groups (.55), compared to married men (1.00), whereas divorced and never-married women are particularly likely to be members.

Interest and community group membership is heavily skewed toward older people with more education, those who previously worked in professional, managerial, or white-collar occupations, those with a higher household income, and those who own their home. Car ownership is less essential showing a nonsignificant relationship with interest-group membership and a modest association with community-organization membership. These types of organizations are likely to provide sources of self-identity and self-esteem as well as sociability and are primarily the province of better educated and materially-advantaged older people.

Membership in religious organizations has substantial similarities with interest and community group membership, but also distinct differences. Religious membership is highest among people in their late seventies and early eighties, after socioeconomic status and health are controlled. Women are much more likely to belong to religious groups than men, with never-married older women having a particularly high odds of membership. Widowed women are somewhat more likely to be church members than married older women, suggesting possibly increased attendance following widowhood. This contrasts with older men, where there is no difference in religious membership according to marital status.

Class and educational qualifications are positively associated with religious membership but not income or car ownership, suggesting that cultural capital in the form of education and previous class position are important, but not current material resources. Health limitations are not statistically significantly related to membership in religious organizations, unlike the other four types of organizations. However, subjective (or self-reported) health is better among those who attend religious organizations.

DISCUSSION AND CONCLUSIONS

Three-fifths of men and women over 60 in Britain are members of one or more social, leisure, community, or religious group. There is a modest decline in organization membership with increasing age among older people, but this can be entirely explained by increased disability and declines in material resources, which hinder participation. Thus, the overall levels of organizational membership do not vary with age, after controlling for health and other material and cultural resources. However, there is evidence of substitution of different types of organization membership with advancing age. For both men and women, there is a decline in membership in social and sports clubs and an increase in membership in religious organizations and interest groups, while the level of membership in community groups peaks in the early seventies.

British widowers are more likely to attend social and sports clubs than married older men, after controlling for age and resources. These higher levels of social and sports club participation of widowers than married men suggest some compensation through organization membership following the loss of their wives. There is no parallel evidence for widows that they are substituting for the loss of their husbands through increased membership in social and sports clubs. However, widows are slightly more likely to be involved in religious organizations than married women. Older men who are divorced or never married have significantly lower membership in any organizations than married or widowed older men, indicating that they may be a socially isolated group in later life. However, older divorced and never-married women are more socially involved in interest, community, and religious organizations.

A key finding is the strong class and education inequality in social organization membership in later life. Working-class older men and women are more likely to attend social clubs than the middle class, but there is a much higher membership in the other four types of organizations among older people who are middle class, more educated, with a higher household income, home owners, and have a household car. Social clubs are therefore the province of working-class older people, providing them with sociability and reducing social isolation, but they are less likely to provide sources of self-esteem and self-identity. This contrasts with membership in community and interest groups, which provide a source not only of sociability, but also self-esteem and self-identity; they are to a much greater extent the province of middle-class and more advantaged older men and women. Thus, social organization membership in later life represents a perpetuation of bases of social inequality associated with class, education, and financial and material resources.

NOTES

We are grateful to the Data Archive at the University of Essex for permission to use the British Household Panel Survey data. This research is supported by the Economic and Social Research Council (ESRC) as part of the Growing Older Programme, grant number L480 25 4033.

Tables and figures on which the analysis in this chapter has been based are available on request from S.Arber@surrey.ac.uk.

REFERENCES

Arber, S., & Cooper, H. (1999). Gender differences in health in later life: A new paradox? *Social Science and Medicine, 48*(1), 63–78.
Arber, S., & Cooper, H. (2000) Gender and inequalities in health across the life course. In Ellen Annandale & Kate Hunt (Eds.), *Gender inequalities in health.* Buckingham, U.K.: Open University Press.
Arber, S., & Ginn, J. (1995). *Connecting gender and ageing: A sociological approach.* Buckingham, U.K.: Open University Press.
Askham, J. (1994). Marriage relationships of older people. *Reviews in Clinical Gerontology, 4,* 261–268.
Atchley, R. C. (1994). *Social forces and ageing.* Belmont, CA: Wadsworth Publishing.
British Household Panel Study. (1999). *Wave 9: 1999 Computer Files.* Colchester, U.K.: University of Essex, Institute of Social and Economic Research.
Carnegie Inquiry into the Third Age. (1993). *Life, work and livelihood in the third age: Final report.* Dunfermline, U.K.: Carnegie UK Trust.
Davidson, K. (1999). Marital perceptions in retrospect. In R. Miller & S. Brownings (Eds.), *With this ring: Divorce, intimacy and cohabitation from a multicultural perspective.* Stamford, CT: Jai Press.
Davidson, K., Daly, T., Arber, S., & Perren, K. (2002). La masculinitê dans un monde feminisie: le genre, l'age et les organisations sociales. In C. Athias-

Donfut & P. Tripier (Eds.), Vieillir jeunes, actifs et disponibles? Special issue of *Cahiers der Genre, 31*, 39–58.

Dex, S. (1984). *Women's work histories: An analysis of the women and employment survey* (Number 46). London: Department of Employment Research Paper.

Ferraro, K. (1984). Widowhood and social participation in later life: Isolation or compensation? *Research on Aging, 6*(4), 451–468.

Ghee, C. (2001). Population review of 2000: England and Wales. *Popular Trends, 106*, 7–14.

Gilleard, C., & Higgs, P. (2000). *Cultures of ageing: Self, citizen and the body.* Essex, U.K.: Pearson Education.

Ginn, J., and Arber, S. (1999). Changing patterns of pension inequality: The shift from state to private pensions. *Ageing and Society, 19*, 319–342.

Goldthorpe, J. (1983). Women and class analysis: In defence of the conventional view. *Sociology, 17*(4), 465–487.

Kohli, M., Rein, M., Guillemard, A-M., & van Gunsteren, H. (Eds.). (1991). *Time for retirement: Comparative studies of early exit from the labour force.* Cambridge, U.K.: Cambridge University Press.

Laslett, P. (1989). *A fresh map of life.* London: Weidenfield and Nicolson.

Mannheim, K. (1952). The problem of generations. In Karl Mannheim, *Essays on the sociology of knowledge.* London: Routledge and Kegan Paul.

Mein, G., Higgs, P., et al. (1998). Paradigms of retirement: The importance of health and ageing in the Whitehall II study. *Social science and medicine, 47*(4), 535–545.

Office of Population Censuses and Surveys. (1990). *Standard occupational classification,* vol. 3. London: HMSO.

Solomou, W., Richards, M., et al. (1998). Divorce, current marital status and well-being in an elderly population. *International Journal of Law, Policy and the Family, 12*, 323–344.

Taylor, M. (1992). *British Household Panel Study user manual: Introduction, technical report and appendices,* vol. A. Colchester, U.K.: University of Essex.

Wenger, C., Davies, R., et al. (1996). Social isolation and loneliness in old age: Review and model refinement. *Ageing and Society, 16*, 333–358.

7

The Secret World of Subcultural Aging: What Unites and What Divides?

Andrew Blaikie

INTRODUCTION

Half a century ago, the *American Journal of Sociology* ran a special issue on aging. Contributors included Clark Tibbitts, Robert Havighurst, E. W. Burgess, and David Riesman. Alongside the predictable range of topics covered—labor force participation, retirement problems, and role flexibility—there was considerable interest in retirement migration, the social life of retirement communities, and, inspired perhaps by the early work of Donald Cowgill, a focus on the leisure activities of groups of older people whose lifestyles appeared at odds with received notions of disengagement (Cowgill, 1941; Hoyt, 1954; Michelon, 1954). While cultural shifts were broadly implied, only Riesman considered these explicitly. As a social psychologist, he was concerned with the responses of individuals to their own aging: some ("the autonomous") "[bore] within themselves psychological sources of self-renewal... independent of the strictures and penalties imposed on the aged by the culture"; others ("the adjusted") had "no such resources within them but [were] the beneficiaries of a cultural preservative (derived from work, power, position, and so on) which sustains them, although only so long as the cultural conditions remain stable and protective"; finally, "the anomic," "protected neither from within nor from without, simply decays" (Riesman, 1954, p. 379).

Subsequently, Arnold Rose (1965) recognized that cultural predispositions were not simply a matter of personal reactions or adjustments to the values of society at large and that some kind of status system, based on the distinctive values of a subculture, might also exist among older people.[1] The conditions of existence for such a phenomenon were historically unprecedented and included demographic and medical advances (more older people staying healthy until greater ages), migration patterns (both the outmigration of younger people from rural and inner-city areas and older people's self-segregation into retirement communities), and shifts in social organization (rising compulsory and voluntary retirement).

Assuming that because of such processes "the elderly tend to interact with each other increasingly as they grow older, and with younger persons decreasingly," he postulated the emergence of an age-graded counterculture in which all older people, though some more than others, were potential members of a group that opposed the rest of society (Rose, 1965, p. 4). All that would be required for "the elderly" to transform themselves from an observable social category to an active cultural group was self-conscious identification with their peers.

In the decades since, the limitations of such thinking have been manifest in the failure of this cultural model to materialize. For example, Rose predicted that "the elderly seem to be on their way to becoming a voting bloc with a leadership that acts as a political pressure group" (Rose, 1965, p. 14). However, without needing either to enumerate the observed factors responsible or to invoke the postmodern doxy of diversity and difference, it is abundantly clear that older people no more form a monolithic category than do members of any other age group. Thus, although there might be a logical case for pensioners uniting to campaign for better pensions by supporting a particular party, their failure to do this either effectively or consistently has been due to both synchronic and diachronic variations in alignment. Older people's voting behavior indicates that most think now as they did when they first entered work: their present, shared circumstances are less important in determining preference than lifelong convictions drawn from a broad range of differing ideologies and predicaments. Moreover, the term *pensioner* embraces several age cohorts, each with its own generational awareness of social change. Older people are further segregated among themselves according to income, health status, gender, and ethnicity. Meanwhile, retirement itself acts to disperse and disconnect individuals who were once collectively focused around workplace matters (Blaikie & Macnicol, 1989, pp. 77–78).

Against such fissiparous tendencies among the old, there are many countervailing arguments for solidarity between generations, not least those involving the continuing importance of family ties. Nevertheless, a subculture is taken to be a self-conscious minority group, and the minority with which we are concerned, unlike other minorities comprising members who live in them for all or most of their lives, is defined by age. It may, therefore, be most instructive to compare the experiences of older people with those inhabiting other age-based subcultures, such as youth, not least because the latter have already been much analyzed.

CULTURES OF YOUTH AND AGE

It has been argued that the rise of youth cultures in the second half of the twentieth century was due primarily to increases in disposable incomes and a lengthening of the gap between childhood and adulthood (Frith, 1984). If one regards the transitions from work through retirement to deep old age as a mirror image of those from infancy through childhood and adolescence to adulthood, then undoubted parallels may be found. A case can certainly be made for the enhanced spending potential of some Third Agers (though by no means most), while the period likely to be spent in retirement prior to the onset of deep old age has expanded considerably. Similarly, as economic recession has led to a questioning of some imputed causes of the emergence of youth culture—unemployed or impoverished youth are more likely to remain dependent either by residing longer with their parents or staying in education or both—so the real value of the state pension has fallen, thereby limiting options for most dependent elders.

Young people construct subcultures that reflect their subordinate status in relation to home and education. However, the orientation of older people is significantly different: Childhood and youth represent stages in which the young are socialized via parental control and compulsory schooling, whereas retirement has a wholly voluntaristic relation to further learning for those who have been socialized long ago. Nevertheless, the retired do share a potentially antagonistic relationship with those belonging to other generations, particularly middle-aged adults in high-status positions, from the micro level of family dynamics to the macro level of political decision-making. Whether for positive or negative reasons, both youth and Third Age cultures emphasize leisure rather than work. Both also have the potential for dividing into subcultures that may be either oppositional to the mainstream or accommodated within it. To this extent, while most subcultures are by definition subordinate, some may emphasize difference while remaining comfortable with the overlying popular culture. These include subgroups whose shared identifications vary from inhabiting "lifestyle enclaves," based upon expressions of shared patterns of appearance, consumption, and leisure activities, to the fluid "neo-tribes" whose elective affinities go no further than enjoying "the being together of everyday life" (Bellah, et al., 1988; Maffesoli, 1996).

Finally, youth subcultures differentiate themselves by expressions of style, ideology, and behavior, most visibly through dress and musical tastes. Similar distinctions are discernible among older people, although cultural responses have tended to differ. Since the baby boom generation is now entering its Third Age, however, confusions arise as a consequence of the aging of youth cultures. Do the rock icons of the 1960s now constitute rebels of the older generation, or are they simply aging shadows of their former selves, worthy of nostalgia but no more (Strausbaugh, 2001)?

THE OPACITY OF AGING

In 1965, Rose suggested that older people had been neglected by sociologists because "the aging have been a low prestige segment of the population, and only those interested in social reform have been willing to study them." Nevertheless, he continued, "the objective trends seem to point to a higher status for the aging in the future, so we can anticipate that even the sociologists will find it respectable to conduct research in this field" (Rose, 1965, p. 15). With hindsight, his forecast appears overly optimistic to say the least. Why, when the relative proportions of national populations surviving into their Third Age throughout the West and across much of the developing world have grown so dramatically (Laslett, 1987), have youth subcultures continued to be analyzed so fully, yet elder subcultures so little?

In addressing this paradox, one might begin by asking: Why has aging proven unattractive to study? Subcultural aging is often hidden—hence a "secret world"—in ways that parallel the formal secrecy surrounding sexual behavior in the not-so-distant past. Although the conduct of older people in groups may well be perfectly obvious to those people themselves, its shape and meaning are rather less clear to the rest of us. One reason why social scientists knew little about everyday sexual activity until intrepid investigators like Kinsey reported in the late 1940s was because many behaviors, though commonplace, were officially taboo, thus not openly discussed (Weeks, 1990, pp. 76–77).

Many have pointed to a similar prohibition surrounding aspects of bodily and mental decline, such as incontinence, dementia, and, of course, death. Yet the oversight is not simply a problem that may be remedied by better social bookkeeping. Behind the taboo lies apprehension, a fear of the negative aspects of our own aging; hence it could be argued that a culture that vaunts youth is, in fact, a culture in denial. Some even contend that "gerontophobia" is a particular affliction of those who study aging (Green, 1993). Because many experiences of aging have been subjected to stigma through processes of social marginalization, they have become embarrassing to talk about, particularly where intimate bodily care is involved (Lawler, 1991). (See also Julia Twigg's chapter in this book.) By association and metaphor, all later life has been distanced from the mainstream of personhood (Hockey & James, 1993, pp. 45–72).

This willful failure to see into the social dynamics of later life—what I would call the opacity of aging—is exacerbated by ageism within the academy, especially within cultural studies. A subculture may be defined as "a system of values, attitudes, modes of behaviour and lifestyles . . . which is distinct from, but related to the dominant culture of a society" (Abercrombie, et al., 1994, p. 416). Not only must it be distinct, but also the very fact that it is a subculture assumes that power lies elsewhere, within the dominant culture. For this reason, sociologists have been attracted to subcultures of gender, "race," class, and particularly youth, but not age.

In the rebellious years of the middle and late 1960s, the self-image of student dissatisfaction was that of a generation at war against the old political and ideological certainties (Inglis, 1993, pp. 14–15). Such resistance found intellectual coherence in the subsequent development of cultural studies focused on how people constructed their own cultures "from below." Stimulated by the Centre for Contemporary Cultural Studies in Birmingham, a whole school of theory grew from ethnographic studies of youth subcultures. Meanwhile, older people were entirely ignored. Arguably this reflected the antipathies of 1968 toward all that was regarded as outdated. Moreover, youth rebellion was seen as significant because those who "matured too early" (teenage mothers, child prostitutes, criminals, even murderers) or alternatively refused to mature (being unemployed and not "settling down") clearly posed threats to the potential smooth running of society. Both youth and pensioners hold a dependent status in the social system, but the relationship to power differs. Young people are perceived as the parents and workers of the future in ways that retired people by definition cannot be (Blaikie, 1999a, p. 131). Thus although resistant subcultures may have existed among the old, they were overlooked. Instead, as the "burden of dependency" became a pretext to set workers versus pensioners in the late 1970s, so the playing field for generational battles became one of social policy (Johnson, et al., 1989). The calculus here was one of accounting for welfare, and in fueling the energies of the political economy theorists, it deflected studies of aging—including those of social exclusion—away from culture and toward the social structure. It has indeed been argued that "social gerontology remains tied to concerns over lack and need, and still defines much of its subject matter around these themes. Attempts to move it away from this emphasis upon disability and the impoverishments of age are still met with considerable resistance" (Gilleard & Higgs, 2000, Preface).

Thus, before we can even begin to consider aging subcultures, we are hampered by a profound double disregard: Our popular perception is one of unwillingness to contemplate the presumed negative aspects of later life, while academic discourses mirror the marginalization of later life as a phase in which cultural concerns have little apparent impact upon social or economic issues. These two agents of division themselves provoke the first apparent unity among the aged, that which reifies retirement as something that somehow exists of itself as an independent entity, a social space into which all must fall on the point of leaving work and inhabit thereafter for the rest of their lives. Gerontologists are less happy with this, of course, precisely because it represents a constructed homogeneity that does violence to the diversity of later life. They are disposed to react by noting that several age groups coexist as pensioners, each cohort exhibiting a different age-consciousness, and that older people are segregated among themselves, according to income, health status, gender, geography, and ethnicity (cf. Sara Arber's chapter in this book). The retired population is also fractured according to sociologically-imposed classifications—Third and Fourth Ages, midlife and later life, young old and old old (cf. Hans-Joachim von Kondratowitz's chapter in this book). A third set of divisions thus concerns the fragmentation of later life itself (Blaikie, 1999b, pp. 77–83).

Yet, as Figure 7.1 indicates, the axes along which our culture might fracture are equally lines through which solidarities may be drawn. In two areas, there exists potential for either unity or division. These are, first, the relationship between the aged and the nonaged, and, second, relationships between the older age groups themselves. The concept of the Third Age is critical here. Insofar as it represents a blurring of the boundaries between midlife and later life, a "severing of the chronological bonds," it proposes unity across the lifespan (Featherstone & Hepworth, 1989). However, its very definition as "an era of personal fulfilment" presupposes degrees of wealth and health that conspire to divide the retired into happy Third Agers and the less fortunate Fourth Agers (Laslett, 1989, p. 4). All the notion of the Third Age does is to marginalize the very old still further. For the newcomer stepping out

UNITY	DIVISION
Reification of retirement	Opacity of aging
	Deep old age as taboo
	Generational bias of cultural studies
	Social policy emphasis
	Gerontologists favor diversity
	Modernist impulse to classify
Aged and nonaged (Third Age)	Aged versus nonaged (Fourth Age)

Cultures of resistance	
UNITY	DIVISION
Liminality: middlescence parallels adolescence	Double deviance
Subcultural identification	Institutional marginalization, concealment, and depersonalization

Cultures of incorporation	
UNITY	DIVISION
Consumer culture	Individualism or lifestyle enclaves
Purchasing youthfulness	
Political solidarity?	Declining citizenship?

Cultures of consolation	
UNITY	DIVISION
Coherent self-narratives: continuity with earlier sense of self	Postmodern fragmentation
Generational identifications	Generational identifications
Imagined community	Paramount reality

Figure 7.1. Potential Factors Uniting or Dividing the Culture of Aging

onto the brink of later life the choice is paradoxical: Either one opts for retirement as a catchall that unites all pensioners but sets them apart from the rest of society, or one joins the Third Age movement, thus condemning the very old to the greater stigma of the Fourth Age and ultimately, of course, worsening the prospects for one's own deep old age.

Analytically, such thinking is concerned with age categories rather than with social groups. Thus, although conceptual cleavages may be mapped onto empirical realities, as implied, group membership on the ground must fulfill three sociological criteria: first, people must interact with one another in accord with enduring and morally established patterns; second, these interacting persons must define themselves as members of the group; and third, these people must be defined by others as belonging to the group (Merton, 1968; pp. 339–340). Given these provisos, we might discern three routes by which older people strive to maintain identity and esteem: cultures of resistance, cultures of incorporation, and cultures of consolation.

CULTURES OF RESISTANCE

Late midlife is not unlike adolescence in that both represent transitional life stages that create personal problems—teenage trauma or midlife crisis—as well as providing a degree of social freedom to experiment with norms, values, and conduct. Since we know a good deal about youth subcultures from ethnographic studies, we might suggest parallel avenues for gerontological research. For example, unemployed school dropouts become delinquents because committing crime is a means of both obtaining goods that they cannot otherwise afford and temporarily relieving the boredom of enforced leisure. Late midlife brings similar problems for those making the shift from work to retirement. Thus it should come as no surprise to learn that so-called Bus Pass Bandits do exist. A recent British television documentary with this title investigated people in their seventies and older who were involved in fraud, embezzlement, bank robberies, and bootlegging (Channel Four Television, 2001). Although the interviewees had turned to crime partly to alleviate poverty—as one said, "I can't see how any pensioner . . . can live an adequate life"—most had other motives, be they rectifying perceived injustice, "doing something to keep me going," or a need for sociability, challenge, and "being somebody." (John was one of seventeen "decent old boys, who took up tobacco smuggling for fun and a better pension." He remarked, "I'd never been in court. I'd never been in prison. I'd never been nothing.")

The incompatibilities of age and crime were nonetheless made apparent, as for instance in the case of an older bank robber.

> Eighty-three-year-old "Bang Bang" Charlie has 579 convictions. It seems a shame he couldn't make it round figures but, as he said, "When you go in a bank with a gun your heart goes 'Boom. Boom. Boom.' My heart couldn't take that. I've had five heart attacks. I've one eye, cirrhosis in my liver and this leg here." What's worse, the cashiers started to laugh. Bank robbery is a young man's game. (Banks-Smith, 2001, p. 22)

This account, like several similar reports in British newspapers, attracted public attention less because of the existence of such criminals than because of the way in which they contradicted the stereotyped image of older people as essentially passive and law abiding (Blaikie, 1999b, p. 187). A marked cognitive dissonance exists between popular attitudes about older people and their actual behavior. Indeed, several of the interviewees remarked that they had exploited the stereotype of passive conformity to fool their victims. Meanwhile, most press reports make fun of old people behaving like teenagers. A near riot at a community hall was presented in farcical terms as " 'Oldies' barney at the bingo!" (Notarangelo, 1996, p. 1). Unlike their youthful counterparts, older people have not indulged in ritualized gang warfare or Bacchanalian pop festivals. Since such phenomena are not expected of them because of their age, those who do defy the norm become doubly deviant.

In similar ways, those who deliberately grow old disgracefully by flaunting their sexuality, making faces at carers, or simply, in the words of the poem *Warning*, wearing purple may be said to be indulging a politics of self by fashioning particular repertoires of resistance from the meagre resources available to them (Joseph, 1974). Morinis' conclusion regarding alcoholic Skid Row Indians—that "their lives are their manifestos"—is equally applicable to the urban bag lady or the aged slum dwellers of many inner cities (Morinis, 1990, p. 362; Stephens, 1976). Somewhat rhetorically, Ascherson refers to

> the 47 percent of people over 75 who live alone, and who frequently revert to their existence as teenagers. Their room is a tip of familiar possessions; they eat any old biscuits or cold sausages lying around; they delight in doing things their way. They are usually deaf, but specially deaf to the scoldings of the authoritarian young. (Ascherson, 1998, p. 2)

The point about isolation is significant; for unlike with youth culture, rebellion remains individualistic and is thus quickly nullified as eccentricity.

Maintaining a sense of self is an interactive process, but as one enters the Fourth Age and more particularly its medicalized, institutional settings, the ability to engage in collective dialogue is reduced. Moreover, resisting depersonalization requires self-consciousness and self-control, both of which become increasingly difficult to maintain with the onset of cognitive and physical impairments such as dementia and incontinence. As revelations of elder abuse attest, under the spatial control of the total institution or within the confines of the family home, power relations often remain hidden. Subversive inclinations, often perpetuated through "tiny gestures of defiance and small acts of personal insurrection" clearly exist, but neither setting provides a context for their emergence into the public gaze (Hockey & James, 1993, p. 131).

CULTURES OF INCORPORATION

At the opposite extreme are those elders who trumpet the virtues of Third Age living. Rather than oppose mainstream trends, many older people have embraced consumer culture. The concept of subcultures presumes that minority groups can be identified by their patterns of resistance. However, in a consumer society, popular culture is better characterized as conservative and commercialized. Rather than being alternative or politically radical, many youth are now simply hedonistic, while their ethics have slipped toward "hedonistic individualism" (Redhead, 1997).

The roots of teenage consumerism lie in the 1950s, when marketing opportunities were found in unlocking the reserves of disposable income held by the first mass generation who left school and found jobs but who did not yet have to settle down and grow up (Abrams, 1959). Equally, the growth of the contemporary grey market, and particularly the recognition of a potential bonanza from the baby boomers, encourages Third Agers to think about holidays, health, and leisure, thus exploiting a desire not to grow old by purchasing products and services that "combat the signs of aging" while pursuing the pleasures of youth. A cursory look at any of the glossy magazines aimed at older people over the past 20 years reveals this (Featherstone & Hepworth, 1995).

Collectively, these desires are expressed through what Bellah calls "lifestyle enclaves," social networks "formed by people who share some feature of private life [and who] express their identity through shared patterns of appearance, consumption, and leisure activities, which often serve to differentiate them sharply from those with other lifestyles" (Bellah, et al., 1988, p. 335). The truth of this observation is evident in the analyses of consultants whose "psychographic segmentation" defines evermore specific niches within the post-50 population—Woopies, Jollies, Glams, Primelifers, GoGos, NoGos, Retire Aware, Wind-Down, Lifestyle Adjustment, Leisure Years, and so on (Ostroff, 1989). Against the strictly individualistic interpretation of consumerism, the lifestyle enclave suggests a degree of collective support through shared endeavor. Nevertheless, Bellah and associates go on to note that "whereas a community attempts to be an inclusive whole, celebrating the interdependence of public and private life and of the different callings of all, lifestyle is fundamentally segmental and celebrates the narcissism of similarity" (Bellah, et al., 1988, p. 72). Thus, for example, the Saga holidaymakers[2] who flock to the Costas and now further afield and the snowbirds who winter in Florida, the more permanent residents of American sun cities or British migrants to seaside resorts are essentially segregationist (King, et al., 2000). Although one might expect the apparent blurring of chronological boundaries to encourage age-integrated living or continuing-care communities, migration trends, holiday preferences, and housing markets are all niche-driven and reflect a desire among many older people to separate themselves from younger generations.

In a worst-case scenario, the growing incorporation of elders into consumerism through lifestyle enclaves heralds the decline of a cohesive moral agency or shared values. However, not all collective behavior is hedonistic, and pockets of ethical communitarianism also prevail. Expressions of committed generational solidarity still exist among those engaged in the "old" politics of the struggle for better pensions. Nevertheless, despite the reciprocal relationship between state policy and interest group activity, the last half century has not seen older people gaining great influence within the political process (Pratt, 1993). In part, of course, this has been because the cohorts from which pensioners emerge have always been politically, economically, and socially divided and, if anything, have become more polarized at higher ages. Instead, the quest for participative citizenship appears to be aligned to a politics of lifestyle. Whether one belongs to the street people or the leisure fanatics or the educated, bourgeois vanguard that is the University of the Third Age, a shift is occurring where, as with the new social movements, change can be brought about less by chipping away bureaucratically at the policy agenda and rather more by raising consciousness within the civic environment (Melucci, 1989). However, there are indications of generationally-based cultural conservatism here in that older people have more readily retained the styles of citizenship to which they have been used than younger people: for example, a massively higher proportion of people aged 65 and over (79 percent) bothered to vote compared with those aged 18 to 24 (38 percent) in the most recent United Kingdom general election.

CULTURES OF CONSOLATION

Gilleard and Higgs (2000) aver that "the ageing of populations has coincided with the working through of the modernist project." Arguably, the fixed categories of "retirement" and "old age pensioner" belong, like structured dependency theory, to the era of the strong welfare state, while much that may be said about contemporary aging finds echoes in postmodern theories of self and identity, where the old certainties of belonging have given way to fragmentation and risk. Lifestyling certainly suits this supposition. But what about those whose resources and health status are so constrained that the very notion of lifestyle appears luxurious and unattainable? Do such older people simply accept the logic of postmodernity and slowly fall apart, or do they seek ways to defy disintegration by maintaining stability and self-esteem? Indeed, since by definition subcultures are social groups, can isolated Fourth Agers, for all they fulfill the criteria of alienation and anomie, be considered members of such entities if they cannot be observed interacting?

Evidence from the research—Kaufmann's aptly titled *The Ageless Self* being a good example—suggests that because we regard identity as central to understanding ourselves, we will go to considerable lengths to sustain a coherent sense of self (Kaufmann, 1986). The connection between such a project and the role of subcultures or other social groups is not immediately apparent, since psychological and emotional elements of aging have not been so frequently examined as externally observable behavior, particularly because the links between the two are still less explored (Ruth & Kenyon, 1996). However, several researchers have analyzed personal narratives as routes to comprehending aging cultures. These may be linked to what Mills (1940) first called vocabularies of motive, the particular ways in which people justify their views and behavior. For instance, Rory Williams (1990) has considered the importance of the Protestant work ethic in directing the perceptions of older Aberdonians about death and illness, his argument being that a generational worldview may act as a categorical imperative by which all questions of morality are being tested. Illness suggests sloth and sin; health reflects the right attitude and sound moral fibre.

While this strikes a chord with the "time signatures" devised by marketers to classify sets of values belonging to specific cohorts, recent research by Conway (2000) extends the possibilities by focusing on how vulnerable older people bolster their ontological security. He argues that when they feel socially marginalized they try to make sense of the world using notions of "imagined community" to justify a moral sense of self grounded in reciprocity. With increased individualization and the loss of significant others, an identification with the past-situated mores of dead relatives provides the basis for navigating reality, a rationale for action. His interviewees talk of a better past when their families and neighbors were "a little world on our own," then project this idealized image onto their values in the present. This reconnection with the past provides the key resource for sustaining biographical continuity while becoming a strategy for coping with the fractured present. However, precisely because the community is imagined, it can only act as a palliative bolstering self-esteem; it is not a concrete resource. For all the resistance to change it may provoke, ultimately it becomes a consoling anachronism (Conway, 2000, p. 231).

CONCLUSION

Aged 66, William Shaw's mother sold her house in Leeds, bought a motor home, and joined the Saga louts (Shaw, 2001, p. 28).

> I was expecting throngs of happy revellers dancing in the moonlight and crashing out on idyllic beaches at dawn. I got silver-haired sunseekers. (Coyle, 2001, p. 14)

These throwaway lines from journalists give the impression of aging in the twenty-first century as a Gadarene pleasure rush to sunny climes. Recently, too, both the embrace of cyborg possibilities and the critique of aging as a "socially constructed disease" have questioned the decline narratives of biological essentialism (Featherstone, 1995; Gilleard & Higgs, 1998; Gullette, 1997). Yet, notwithstanding religious beliefs, in the final instance the corporeal inevitability of aging is a paramount reality for all of us, against which we can but construct temporary escape attempts (Cohen & Taylor, 1991). These may be fulfilling, even liberating, but they are by definition fragile and temporary alternatives to the obduracy of being old: it will not go away (Berger & Luckmann, 1991). Depending on their circumstances, older people may turn to crime, to lifestyle enclaves, to imagined communities, or to a range of other collective resources. Some survival mechanisms are more visible than others, some outer-directed, others involuntary. Yet whether they opt for resistance, consumerism, or contemplative coming to terms, each mode will provide identity symbols defining its members as distinct from others. Indeed, subcultures of aging lend evidence to the claim that "identities are constructed through, not outside, difference" (Hall, 1996, p. 4). Thus they can only have meaning in relation to what they are not. The motives and experiences that unite older people into groups are also what divide them from one another and from the rest of us.

Cultures of aging have a symbiotic relationship with the aging of cultures. Under the classificatory paradigm of modernity, Western societies have been remarkable for their age-gradedness, most notably in the articulation of retirement as a means of separating working and nonworking populations (Kohli, 1986, 1988).[3] Given the apparent fragmentation of those categories under postmodern conditions, where the identification of a single dominant culture is in itself problematic, generational schisms are not always easy to pinpoint, still less to reconcile with straightforward intentions of resistance, incorporation, or consolation. Yet, in the same way that "normal" aging has emerged to counterbalance the professional obsession with pathology, so too older people have developed subcultures in defiance of dysfunction. For them the world as it is does not work. Accordingly, rather than being simply compensatory, in the sense that membership confers moral recompense for failure in society, subcultures of aging help us to see what may be wrong with society itself. They serve as reminders that neither fatalistic dread nor the expectation of fulfillment is a wholly appropriate way to apprehend later life.

NOTES

1. I am indebted to Haim Hazan for the reference to Rose's work.
2. Saga is a British travel and amenities company catering specifically to older people.
3. Clearly, this discussion has concerned only Western societies. For an overview of the position of elders in other contemporary cultures, see Sokolovsky 1997.

REFERENCES

Abercrombie, N., Hill, S., & Turner, B. S. (1994). *The Penguin dictionary of sociology*. Harmondsworth, U.K.: Penguin.
Abrams, M. (1959). *The teenage consumer*. London: Routledge and Kegan Paul.
Ascherson, N. (1998, November 15). Keep on running . . . . *The Observer Review*, pp. 1–2).
Banks-Smith, N. (2001, May 2). Take the money and run (TV review). *The Independent* , p. 22.
Bellah, R., Madsen, R., Sullivan, W. M., Swidler, A., & Tipton, S. M. (1988). *Habits of the heart: Middle America observed*. London: Hutchinson Education.
Berger, P., & Luckmann, T. (1991). *The social construction of reality*. Harmondsworth, U.K.: Penguin.
Blaikie, A. (1999a). Can there be a cultural sociology of ageing? *Education and Ageing*, 14(2), 127–139.
Blaikie, A. (1999b). *Ageing and popular culture*. Cambridge, U.K.: Cambridge University Press.
Blaikie, A., & Macnicol, J. (1989). Ageing and social policy: A twentieth century dilemma. In A. M. Warnes (Ed.), *Human ageing and later life* (pp. 69–82). London: Edward Arnold.
Channel Four Television. (2001, May 1). Bus Pass Bandits. *Cutting Edge* documentary.
Cohen, S., & Taylor, L. (1992). *Escape attempts*. London: Routledge.
Conway, S. (2000). "I'd be unhealthy if nobody wanted me any more": A sociological analysis of the relationship between ageing and health beliefs. Unpublished Ph.D. thesis, University of Hull, U.K.
Cowgill, D. (1941). Mobile homes: A study of trailer life. Unpublished Ph.D. thesis, University of Pennsylvania.
Coyle, J. (2001, March 11). Go, go, GOA-away, I yelled . . . . *The Observer* , p. 14.
Featherstone, M. (1995). Virtual reality, cyberspace and the ageing body. In C. Hummel, & C. J. Lalive D'Epinay (Eds.), *Images of aging in Western societies* (pp. 246–286). Geneva, Switzerland: Centre for Interdisciplinary Gerontology.
Featherstone, M., & Hepworth, M. (1989). Ageing and old age: Reflections on the postmodern life course. In B. Bytheway, T. Keil, P. Allatt, & A. Bryman

(Eds.), *Becoming and being old: Sociological approaches to later life* (pp. 143–157). London: Sage.

Featherstone, M., & Hepworth, M. (1995). Images of positive aging: A case study of *Retirement Choice* magazine. In M. Featherstone & A. Wernick (Eds.), *Images of aging: Cultural representations of later life* (pp. 29–48). London: Routledge.

Frith, S. (1984). *The sociology of youth*. Ormskirk, U.K.: Causeway Books.

Gilleard, C., & Higgs, P. (1998). Ageing and the limiting conditions of the body. *Sociological Research Online 3*, 1–16.

Gilleard, C., & Higgs, P. (2000). *Cultures of ageing: Self, citizen and the body*. Englewood Cliffs, NJ: Prentice-Hall.

Green, B. S. (1993). *Gerontology and the construction of old age: A study in discourse analysis*. New York: Aldine de Gruyter.

Gullette, M. M. (1997). *Declining to decline: Cultural combat and the politics of midlife*. Charlottesville: University Press of Virginia.

Hall, S. (1996). Introduction: Who needs "identity"? In S. Hall & P. du Gay (Eds.), *Questions of cultural identity* (pp. 1–17). London: Sage.

Hockey, J., & James, A. (1993). *Growing up and growing old: ageing and dependency in the life course*. London: Sage.

Hoyt, G. C. (1954). The life of the retired in a trailer park. *American Journal of Sociology, 59*(4), 361–370.

Inglis, F. (1993). *Cultural studies*. Oxford: Blackwell.

Johnson, P., Conrad, C., & Thomson, D. (Eds.) (1989). *Workers versus pensioners: Intergenerational justice in an ageing world*. Manchester: CEPR/Manchester University Press.

Joseph, J. (1974). *Rose in the afternoon*. London: Dent.

Kaufmann, S. (1986). *The ageless self: Sources of meaning in later life*. Madison: University of Wisconsin Press.

King, R., Warnes, T., & Williams, A. (2000). *Sunset lives: British retirement migration to the Mediterranean*. Oxford: Berg Publishers.

Kohli, M. (1986). The world we forgot: A historical review of the life course. In V. W. Marshall (Ed.), *Later life: The social psychology of aging* (pp. 271–303). London: Sage.

Kohli, M. (1988). Ageing as a challenge for sociological theory. *Ageing and Society 8*, 367–394.

Laslett, P. (1987). The emergence of the Third Age. *Ageing and Society 7*, 113–160.

Laslett, P. (1989). *A fresh map of life: The emergence of the Third Age*. London: Weidenfeld & Nicolson.

Lawler, J. (1991). *Behind the screens: Nursing, somology and the problem of the body*. Melbourne: Churchill Livingstone.

Maffesoli, M. (1996). *The time of the tribes: The decline of individualism in mass society*. London: Sage.

Melucci, A. (1989). *Nomads of the present: Social movements and individual needs in contemporary society*. London: Radius.

Merton, R. K. (1968). *Social theory and social structure*. New York: Free Press.

Michelon, L. C. (1954). The new leisure class. *American Journal of Sociology, 59*(4), 371–378.

Mills, C. W. (1940). Situated actions and vocabularies of motive. *American Sociological Review, 5*, 904–913.

Morinis, A. (1990). Skid Row Indians and the politics of self. In F. R. Manning & J-M. Philibert (Eds.), *Customs in conflict: The anthropology of a changing world* (pp. 361–368). Peterborough, Ontario: Broadview Press.

Notarangelo, R. (1996, December 18). "Oldies" Barney at the Bingo! *Scottish Daily Mirror*, p. 1.
Ostroff, J. (1989). *Successful marketing to the 50+ consumer: How to capture one of the biggest and fastest growing markets in America.* Englewood Cliffs, NJ: Prentice-Hall.
Pratt, H. J. (1993). *Gray agendas: Interest groups and public pensions in Canada, Britain, and the United States.* Ann Arbor: University of Michigan Press.
Redhead, S. (1997). *Subculture to clubcultures.* Oxford: Blackwell.
Riesman, D. (1954). Some clinical and cultural aspects of aging. *American Journal of Sociology, 59*(4), 379–383.
Rose, A. (1965). The subculture of the aging: A framework for research in social gerontology. In A. M. Rose & W. A. Peterson (Eds.), *Older people and their social world: The sub-culture of the aging* (pp. 3–16). Philadelphia: Davis.
Ruth, J-E., & Kenyon, G. (1996). Introduction: Special issue on ageing, biography and practice. *Ageing and Society, 16*, 653–657.
Shaw, W. (2001, March 11). Happy campers. *The Observer Magazine*, pp. 28–31.
Sokolovsky, J. (Ed.). (1997).*The cultural context of aging: Worldwide perspectives.* Westport, CT: Bergin & Garvey.
Stephens, J. (1976). *Loners, loser and lovers: Elderly tenants in a slum hotel.* London: University of Washington Press.
Strausbaugh, J. (2001, August 12). Unplug the oldies—for good. *The Observer Review*, pp. 5–6.
Weeks, J. (1990). *Sexuality.* London: Routledge.
Williams, R. (1990). *A Protestant legacy: Attitudes to illness and death among older Aberdonians.* Oxford: Clarendon Press.

8

Political Mobilization and Political Identity among Swedish Pensioners 1938–1945

David Gaunt

In Gothenburg in January 1938, irate groups of older people stood outside the poor law authority. They had just been inside to collect their combined pension plus poor law assistance. Their hopes had been high. A new pension reform came into effect on this very day. The new pension would be ten crowns greater each month than before. The dismay was great as each of them was forced to sign a receipt giving them exactly the same amount as the month before. What had happened to the extra ten?

Patiently the poor law administrators explained: Well, yes, you have received ten crowns more in pension—and pointed to that figure. But, they also said, poor law supplementary support was means-tested, so those extra ten crowns had to be deducted, otherwise they would be breaking the law. The outrage among the elderly was enormous—the authorities have "confiscated" our pension raise! This outrage was worsened by the knowledge of the pensioners' powerlessness. The authorities could fall back on the national law, which did indeed give them the right to reduce assistance if a client had other income.

The poor pensioners of Gothenburg were mostly of working-class background and were loyal to the Social Democrats or other left-wing political parties. Gothenburg, with over 250,000 inhabitants, was the second largest city in the country and the major port, shipbuilding, and industrial center. The national government was social democratic and had been reelected with a thumping great victory in 1936 after a campaign focused on the issue of raising pensions. The new pensions were termed "Per Albin pensions" after party leader Per Albin Hansson. The Social Democrats won a clear majority and with ease voted through a pension reform. The new pensions were to begin being paid in January 1938. The city government of Gothenburg was also in Social Democrat hands. The governing board of the poor law authority was also dominated by Social Democrats. How was it possible that this massive political mobilization had resulted in the paradox that the poorest of pensioners did not get a raise?

One of the angriest in the crowd outside the poor-law authority was disability-pensioner John Björnheden, age 64. He was to become the leading figure of the radical pensioner movement. In a letter written later, he gave his version of the situation.

> What would you say if, when the Riksdag agrees to give an extra hundred crowns to the elderly and, if they receive even the smallest amount of assistance, the municipality takes it? They have the law on their side, so in this case we are powerless. Minister of Social Affairs [Gustav Möller] expressed hope that the municipalities would not do so, and most are humane enough to let the elderly keep the extra amount without drawing in the previous support. But when Gothenburg's poor law authority withdrew the extra ten crowns, it gave the impulse to form a pensioner organization. And in the old fashion go out and fight. They had one weapon left, the right to vote.[1]

Bad feelings among the poor pensioners did not improve once the government washed its hands, saying that the local authorities were in the right to reduce support. The government appealed to local authorities to abstain from such a reduction, but it could not hinder them. No broad public opinion in media demanded a rectification. The poor elderly felt themselves abandoned. In 1938, about 39 percent of old age pensioners in the larger towns and cities were dependent on poor law support. This made up a very great proportion of the aged workers.[2]

LEFT-WING POLITICS AND PENSIONS

Labor politics was complicated, and there were several articulate parties to the left of the Swedish Social Democrats. The Social

Democrats split at the end of World War I, and two communist parties eventually evolved out of this break. One communist party kept loyal to Moscow, while the alternative party attempted to develop a type of domestic communist ideology. In the elections of 1936, the two communist parties won 16 percent of the vote. In addition, there was a strong syndicalist movement. The Left Socialist party evolved in the 1930s through persons who broke with communism and attempted, unsuccessfully, to rejoin the Social Democrats. The Social Democrats under the pragmatic leadership of Per Albin Hansson modified many of the extreme ideological positions in its earlier party programs. This especially irritated the elderly, who had grown up on radical socialism. The radical left-wing was quick to recognize the potential of their disillusion.

Left-wing politics in Gothenburg were more radical than elsewhere in Sweden. One of the left-wing parties, the Left Socialists had its headquarters there. This party was led by Albin Ström, who also had a seat in the Riksdag (Parliament) and published the weekly newspaper *Arbetar-Posten*. He seized the opportunity to fish for votes among the pensioners. The *Arbetar-Posten* accused the Social Democrats of having "tricked" the elderly to vote for them. The newspaper also announced that an open public meeting for pensioners would be arranged in February 1938. The theme was set: "Demand that the pension goes to the elderly, not to the ... poor law authority."[3]

A letter was sent to Prime Minister Hansson. But there was no reaction. Open protest meetings continued and during the summer of 1938, the idea of building a pensioner association took form. A founding meeting was held toward the end of August with over 800 persons attending. By September 6, 1938, the by-laws were established and members began to enroll. In the newspapers, the group was described as a *kamporganisation*, that is, an "organization for struggle."

It is difficult to be certain of the background of the membership since lists have not been preserved. But one of the leaders, John Björnheden, wrote an autobiographical sketch that indicates the social standing of part of the membership. He was born outside wedlock in a rural parish in 1874. He never knew his father, and his mother died when he was very young. The local authority auctioned him off to the lowest bidder, and he thereby became the foster child of a farm family. His schooling was the minimum. He joined the navy and then the merchant fleet. When he could no longer serve on ships, he tried his hand at farming and at selling real estate.[4] He is thus a low-status worker with little education, no relatives, no savings, and a low pension and dependent on poor law assistance.

Björnheden emerged as a spokesman of a radical faction, and he was elected treasurer of the first Gothenburg pensioner association. He talked of fighting a political struggle to force through general increases in pensions, when other elderly would have been satisfied with added income from lotteries, jumble sales, and philanthropy. At a very early stage, Björnheden argued that pensioners needed to vote for parties that supported their interests. In his view, the pension was a question of citizenship rights.[5] In the final analysis, Björnheden had few followers, and he was just too extreme for the majority of the association.[6]

Seeing the need for an alternative, Björnheden and a handful of others began to plan for a national league of pensioners. The first meetings were held early in 1939, and the group began placing articles in newspapers.[7] This group became known to the public at the May Day Parade that year. Prime Minister Hansson had come to Gothenburg to hold the traditional political speech. As the parade was being assembled, representatives of the local pensioner organizations turned up and managed to buttonhole Hansson. Björnheden gave him a prepared manifesto in which he termed the older workers to be "Branting's old soldiers." During 50 years, they fought and marched under the "banners of the Social Democrats," they had formed the first unions, they had suffered under the General Strike, and they had built up society. Now, he said, "we live in misery and distress." He used the term "rationalized out" to describe their social position. It was particularly important to separate pensions from poor law administration. Toward the end of the manifesto, he used a rhetorical turn that was later to become classic in pensioner politics.

> We people's pensioners, when we were active and healthy, built up this country. We feel as if we are citizens in a democratic state and we want our problems to be solved in a respectful and democratic way. Therefore, we protest that our pension or part of our pension shall be paid in a disgraceful form and that we therefore are seen in the eyes of public opinion and are treated by authorities as living on social assistance. . . . At the moment we people's pensioners are living in conditions that are unworthy of a free and democratic land.[8]

There was some factual base to his claim. Persons who were close to 70 years of age were born in the 1870s. The industrial breakthrough in Sweden is often dated to the 1880s, dating that is particularly true for large cities. This meant that as this generation began working life many of them were attracted from the countryside to industrial and service sector jobs in towns and cities. Björnheden is typical of this movement.

The Swedish Social Democratic Workers Party provisionally organized in 1882 and was formally constituted in 1889. Thus, the effort to build and to consolidate a social democratic party was a major part of their youth, and one can assume that they deeply absorbed the ideological positions taken during this formative period. From the start, the leader of the party was Hjalmar Branting, who died in 1925. In the beginning, both he and the party were open for radical Marxist thinking; this influence declined later as Branting assumed a revisionist stance. Ideological division resulted in hard running battles with the party left-wing opposition, which was only partially defused when the left-wing split away in 1917.

Thus, the Social Democratic party this generation had experienced in their youth was a party fired with hard ideological language and constant attempts to organize competing radical groups. The pensioners constantly called forth the memory of Branting. Björnheden wrote in 1942, "If they had continued to follow Branting's party program, no remarks would be needed. Instead songs of praises would be sung, at least from the elderly."[9] On the letterhead of the journal *Pensionären* appeared a quotation taken from Branting promising care for the elderly and disabled.

The elderly participated in the major battles for association in trade unions. Most trade unions were closely allied to the Social Democratic Party, but there was also a successful rival revolutionary syndicalist movement founded in 1910 called Sweden's Workers' Central Organization (SAC).

It was also true that the poorest pensioners were dependent on the local poor law administrations. This was part-and-parcel of the very first Pension Act of 1913. There were many complications to this act. The act was formulated during a conservative government and was voted through during a liberal government. One of the chief worries was that if individuals knew that they would receive old age pensions, they would cease to work. Thus, the pension sums had to be very small. Local poor law administrations could give means-tested "communal pension supplements." But this presented a second complication because the existing Poor Law Act had been adopted as far back as 1871. The poor law authorities traditionally felt the need to bully, penalize, and otherwise humiliate recipients. Some left-wing Social Democrats considered voting against the People's Pension Act because of the clearly inadequate sums involved, particularly for older workers in towns and cities where the cost of living was very high.[10]

The People's Pension Act stated that if older persons with small pensions applied to the poor law administration for support, the sum up to a specified amount could be given, and this amount would not be considered poor relief. But it also meant that applications from the aged had to be first dealt with in the normal poor law authority manner. The only difference was that part of the sum that the elderly received would be "free" from stipulations of repayment out of future income. However, any other assistance received from the poor law sources would still be subject to those regulations.[11] Borrowing a Danish expression, this procedure was termed "poor law administration without the poor administration effect." The meaning of this was that the poor law administrators themselves were considered to be "humane" and that the experience of receiving "poor relief" was hereby removed. This step proved to be a mirage; most municipalities did not use this two-step procedure, but only applied the single poor law relief. During the years of deep depression in 1932 and 1933, about 14,000 individuals received these "communal pension supplements"; of these, 11,000 lived in the two cities of Gothenburg and Stockholm. This was a small number compared to those dependent on poor law assistance. The number of old age pensioners (over 67 years of age) who received the straight old-fashioned poor relief was 92,000 in 1935. The proportion of the aged receiving poor relief grew steadily from 16 percent in 1923 up to 20 percent in 1935 and decreased slightly to 18 percent in 1941.[12]

THE NATIONAL LEAGUE FORMS

By turning directly to Prime Minister Per Albin Hansson, the aged poor showed that they expected a positive reaction. There was no response.

In September 1939, the Swedish People's Pensioners National League formed in Gothenburg, with a provisional leadership whose task was to organize agitation and to build up a national movement. At that time, there were only five local associations, mostly in western Sweden. The provisional leadership was a small group.[13] John Björnheden was secretary and main agitator and also became editor of the membership quaterly *Pensionären.* On the provisional board, there were two other pensioners, but surprisingly there were also two younger librarians with left-wing political orientations. The vice secretary was Edvin Trettondal-Eriksson, who was chief librarian in the suburb of Mölndal and a well-known radical. He belonged to the communist party and was chairman of the "Friends of the Soviet Union." The vice chairman was Gunnar Lundstedt, who was librarian at the Workers' Further Education Association (ABF). Even Lundstedt was a known radical figure, even though he actually never broke with the Social Democrats. Trettondal-Eriksson was 43 years old, and Lundstedt was 52 years old.

The presence of these younger intellectuals within an organization for pensioners deserves some comment. It is conceivable that they represent opportunistic political forces that attempted to use the pension issue in order to embarrass the Social Democratic mainstream. It is also conceivable that they also tried to break the ingrained party loyalty of the elderly voters. There are several indications in Björnheden's writings that one aim was to build a political party for pensioners. He often alludes to the potential resource of the votes of the elderly. Lundstedt mentions later that he had seen Björnheden as the logical Riksdag candidate for a pensioner's political party.[14]

From its small beginnings in 1939 and 1940, the Swedish People's Pensioner National League had a double agenda. One goal was open, to work for the improvement of the material conditions of the pensioners. The other goal, however, was hidden and consisted of trying to jockey into position to form a pensioner political party on the labor movement's left wing. It took a while before this double goal became apparent. Whether Björnheden was wittingly or unwittingly being used is hard to say. His politics were formed in Branting's time, and he was thus used to a party in opposition filled with critical ideological debates about differing lines of action. He was not used to an established party in government willing to sacrifice ideological purity for the sake of a workable compromise. Perhaps he had not noticed that the Social Democratic Party no longer tolerated the chaotic ideological dissension of its formative period. At any rate, Björnheden's editorial writings and agitation were consistently antigovernment, and he refused to moderate his language, even when fellow pensioners disapproved the dirt throwing and personal attacks.[15] The bad language and personal attacks were clearly counterproductive if the main aim was to induce the government to engage in a dialogue with the pensioner association. Of course, such language might have served a purpose if the point was to undermine the credibility of the government.

By 1940, the Swedish People's Pensioner National League had decided its by-laws, been registered as a legal association, and could collect dues. Agitation began. The provisional board decided to send Björnheden to Stockholm in order to build up an organization there. The two trips turned out a major fiasco, mainly because of Björnheden's scathing pen and tongue. Hereafter, the Social Democratic Party took clear position against the National League. Both trips were coordinated by the leftist Social Democrat member of Riksdag Fredrik Ström, a novelist who had briefly joined the communists. In July, Björnheden actually met with Gustav Möller.[16] He also talked at workers' meetings and was interviewed in the major daily newspapers *Dagens Nyheter* (independent liberal) and *Social-Demokraten* (considered to be the government's voice).[17] In November, Björnheden returned to Stockholm to meet with leading officials and politicians at a lunch arranged by Fredrik Ström. At the lunch was the head of the National Board of Social Affairs, the social mayor, a major philanthropist, and the director of Stockholm poor law administration. Björnheden made a short speech that did not go down well. It is hard to reveal the exact words that he used, but he probably used arguments based on articles he had just written.

In June, he had published an article referring to the pensioners as the "pariah of the people's home."[18] The "people's home" was a slogan adopted by Per Albin Hansson in 1928 as the symbol for a future society based on a family-like equality of treatment; there were to be no "stepchildren." Björnheden wrote: "How long shall [the politicians] ignore the cries of the pensioners. . . . There are hundreds of thousands of undernourished [pensioners] in this country. They do not call it famine, because they are ashamed of it." Although pensioners ate only potatoes, salted herring, and porridge, they still had too little at the end of the month. In another article from that time, he attacked the government for granting extra wages to municipal workers (because of high prices), but not to the elderly. In autumn, Björnheden published a new article, "The People's Pensioners—A Dark Chapter."[19] The association had been collecting monthly statements of income and outlay from the membership. He used some of them in this article. For instance, there was the case of a retired fisherman who received 26:50 crowns per month in pension. (Today, it would equal US$2.60, but was, of course, worth more back in 1940). His expenditure, however, was 74 crowns. The fisherman's economy would have been even worse, if he did not live in his own cottage. With sarcasm Björnheden thundered: "People's home—the model state—the triumphant paradise of democracy—this is Sweden." He heckled the people's pension as a "poor shrunken castaway social reform." If Björnheden said anything like this when he met the Minister of Social Affairs or lunched with leading social administrators, then it is clear that they would hardly have been inclined to help him or his league. As Björnheden wrote many years later,

> I wrote to Fredrik Ström and asked him directly if he would lead the way for us. . . . He invited me to Stockholm and I went, received over 20 names to begin going about to the social democratic leaders. It was a sad wandering. Surprised faces and negative response—there was no need for any pensioners associations. Those matters should be left in the hands of our elected representatives. . . . A compact no everywhere. . . . Then I was invited to speak in City Hall for twenty [persons] Ström had invited. The idea was that they would give us help, but after my talk, I was defeated. Just to think, what a perfect opportunity I let go down the drain. After my talk silence fell, no one said a single word.[20]

Probably Björnheden was not being false in his surprise that no help was forthcoming. His combative slogans and extreme statements were, probably, not meant to be taken at face value, but rather were thought to function as a shrill alarm clock. This might function on public opinion but was the wrong way to enter a dialogue with persons who were already engaged in the management of elder care or in the formulation of policy. Björnheden indirectly accused these persons of inadequacy, and he questioned their intentions and sincerity. It was a predictably bad beginning, and it is odd that Björnheden did not foresee the consequences.

Terms like "pariah" and "famine" and "undernourished" connect to the famine and casteless groups in India. Surely this was intended as a torpedo against the facade of the "people's home," in which no one was supposed to be treated unfairly. But it was a bit too much. Government and officials could see that this person was no incremental reformist with whom it was possible to cooperate, but instead he was a flaming orator. The headache for the government was that Björnheden could probably swing public opinion since the pensions were undeniably inadequate and consumer prices were rising. The thought that he might lead the pensioner movement was frightening. There was a risk that he could mobilize the pensioner voters, and an election would soon have to be held. Even if leading politicians insisted that pensioner associations were unnecessary, some like Gustav Möller became interested in building a pro-government organization in order to defuse Björnheden.

THE GOVERNMENT BACKS DOWN

The political situation came to an acute culmination at the end of 1940. At this time, it became apparent that the government had lost control over the pension issue. The government had, since Björnheden's visit to Stockholm, been preparing extraordinary legislation to give all pensioners an additional 16 percent. A special bill had been slowly progressing through the committees and departments. News of the preparations were known and somewhat dampened irritation among the elderly. Pressure was building up.[21] It would also be a good tactic as part of the coming election campaign. However, on December 2, 1940, Per Albin Hansson and Gustav Möller met and decided to place the extra pension bill on ice and not present it before the Riksdag when it reopened for sessions after the New Year break. Möller then discussed the postponement with the representative council and with the Riksdag group; both groups agreed to the change.[22] Fredrik Ström was a member of the Riksdag group, and he immediately informed Björnheden. He asked for hundreds of the monthly budgets that members had sent in. The Swedish People's Pensioner National League laid up a strategy to bombard the press with the need for the reform.[23] By the time the Riksdag reopened, the government bill with the raised pension was back on the agenda and sailed through the legislature. Newspapers were quick to attribute this success to the pensioner association. *Ny Tid*, the Social Democrat daily, wrote that the pressure of the association had resulted in "that the powers of state more quickly dealt with [the pension issue] that otherwise would have been the case." The syndicalist weekly *Arbetar-Kuriren* wrote that the main reason that extra pensions "even came up to discussion is proof that the action of the pensioners is a factor to be counted on. Had they been silent they would have got nothing."[24] For Hansson and Möller, this turn of events must surely have been a nightmare. That a group of pensioners could force the government to change its agenda through a rapid mobilization of extra-parliamentary opinion must have been hard to swallow.

Increasingly, the National League was accused of being communist or of being a communist tool. This campaign culminated just as the provisional National League board was calling a formal foundation congress in the autumn of 1941. *Social-Demokraten* in a lead article accused Björnheden, Lundstedt, and Trettondal-Eriksson of running a cover organization for communists. Ny Tid repeated the accusation in a lead article stating that the league could only please "communists and other persons and groups working on the fringe of the labor movement."[25]

THE GOVERNMENT STRIKES BACK

In early 1941, a new aggressive line could be noticed among Social Democrats. On an agitation trip to the industrial center of Norrköping, Björnheden found that the local pensioners were being threatened by the local trade union association. If the purpose was to form a pensioner association, they would have to pay rent for the use of the Union Hall, which they of course could not afford. A local Social Democrat member of the Riksdag appeared and held a short speech to the effect that there was no need for a pensioner association since it would not "have any task to fulfill." Björnheden got the impression that this was part of a policy originating higher up. He wrote a letter of complaint to the steering committee of the Social Democratic Party expressing his feeling that a clampdown was being put into effect. He emphasized that the elderly in general were Social Democrats and expected greater understanding for their plight. The Party Committee wrote back and denied that it had made any decision against building pensioner associations.[26]

In secret, however, plans were being made to build up a parallel organization among the pensioners. This was not discussed in higher official circles, and thus adequate written evidence is lacking. One must infer intention from the course of events.

The Björnheden provisional group had its mind set on constituting the formal Swedish Pensioners National League in the autumn of 1941 on the occasion of its first national congress. As there were a number of local associations with sizeable membership, the time was right. It was a disappointment that the league had not been established in the largest cities, but it had spread outside of the west coast area into the central and northern mining and timber communities and some medium-sized manufacturing towns. The only associations that were known to be hostile to the idea of joining the National League was that of some local Gothenburg pensioners associations that had personal grudges against Björnheden or other members of the provisional board.[27] Because of the opposition of the Social Democratic Party, support was being sought from left-wing parties, and leading Left Socialist and syndicalist personalities would participate. The date of the National Conference was announced to be November 23, and the place was Gothenburg.[28]

A RIVAL ORGANIZATION EMERGES

On the Social Democratic side, there was considerable activity. A large pensioner association began to organize in Malmö in February 1941. Its chairman was Karl Pettersson, a retired master carpenter. Malmö was the hometown of both Prime Minister Hansson and Minister of Social Affairs Möller. This local association received considerable support from the local trade union association.[29]

Two anti-Björnheden pensioner associations in the Gothenburg area agreed, together with the newly formed Malmö association, to build a rival Swedish Peoples Pensioner National Organization. They set up an interim board and announced a call for a congress on November 16. It was also to be held in Gothenburg. The names of the two associations were nearly identical, the place for the two congresses was the same, and the dates of the two meetings were only one week apart. The membership bulletins would also be very close in name: *Pensionären* and *Folkpensionären*. In early November, Gustav Möller traveled to Gothenburg and spoke with the anti-Björnheden groups.[30] Developments went very quickly. If one only uses existing documents, it appears that the decision to hold the congress on November 16 was first taken at the meeting in which Möller spoke, that is November 9. Thus, the congress had less than one week to prepare. It is very unlikely that this haste was accidental.

At the Social Democratic loyal pensioner association congress on November 16, the Swedish Peoples Pensioner National Organization elected as chairman Karl Pettersson, the leader of the Malmö association. Upon his election, he made a speech in which he insisted that the very word "struggle" should be "stricken from the agenda of the people's pensioners." He stressed the need for associations to support its membership and to give them activities and entertainment. These words were clearly addressed against the National League, which emphasized the need for political struggle.[31]

The opposing Swedish Peoples Pensioner National League held its congress the next week. Almost as a comment on Pettersson's remarks, this congress passed a resolution that it was to be dedicated to "struggle." In an opening speech, the librarian Gunnar Lundstedt remarked on the unfortunate split within the pensioner movement and stated that the Social-Democratic press had attacked the National League as a communist cover. There were undeniably many members who belonged to the syndicalist movement, but they were definitely not communists. The National League elected chairman stressed the need for "struggle" to avoid being reduced to a simple "beggar's organization."

The two rival organizations were very close in name, but far apart in the matter of means and goals. The National League had an established polemical stance. It had proved capable of manipulating opinion and could create problems for the government. However, it did not have many members. When it adopted a constitution, it had no more than 500 paying members.[32] It was saved by its intellectual and radical tone, which appealed to opinion-makers with strong ideological commitments. The rival National Organization was closely linked to the Social Democratic Party and grew very quickly. By 1944, it had 41,000 members.[33] Often the trade unions would encourage their older members to establish local associations linked to it. In the very beginning, the National Organization sought and received economic support from the Social Democratic party and from the Trade Union Organization.[34]

ACUTE NEED FOR PENSION REFORM

The rivalry of the two groups led them to a state of isomorphism. It proved impossible to hold a loyal party line, as the problems of survival on pensions was increasingly acute. The National Organization was forced to put pressure on the government to raise the pensions. The accusation that the National League was a communist front was not always effective, as toward the end of the war—particularly after 1943—the political star of communism was on the rise.

In 1944, the situation came to a new head. A complete reform of the pension system was needed; without it, the party risked losing its grip on the elderly. The Social Democratic Party Steering Board discussed whether it should make a statement of support for the loyal People's Pensioners National Organization. Per Albin Hansson and some others expressed the view that pensioner associations were unnecessary since the interests of the elderly were the concern of the Riksdag. But a different board member presented the case: There were two associations. "One of these is communist. I think that it would be clearly politically useful if we made a statement." For Gustav Möller, solution of the pension problem became an "incredibly important point... particularly since the people's pensioners in the larger communities have organized themselves."[35]

The rivalry between the organizations was a tedious mud-slinging affair, in which neither organization showed its best side. Through most of the 1940s however, the National League had the advantage over the National Organization since it several times renewed its opposition platform. A rhetorical feat was the quick adoption of some of the ideas in the British Beveridge Plan. That plan was published at the end of 1942, and by January 1943, Björnheden began to promote what he called the "pensioners' own Beveridge Plan." He made a speech under this title in the summer of 1943. In this pension, payments would be totally free from means-testing; payments were to be 160 crowns per month for single pensioners and 260 crowns per month for married couples, with free hospital and sick care, extra money for clothes and furniture, and the building of special housing for pensioners—a total of just over 2,000 crowns per year plus free medical care.[36] From 1944 on, there was a breakthrough in political opinion about the need to improve the situation of the pensioners. Some of the "pensioners' own Beveridge Plan" ideas were eventually accepted.

The Social Democrats began to plan a strategy to win pensioner votes in the elections of 1944. There was great disappointment over the slow working of the Committee for Social Care in preparing a pension reform. The Steering Board was particularly irritated that the Social Democratic committee members were in agreement with the nonsocialist members, which made it impossible to state a distinctive party line. Gustav Möller explained, "Previously it was [easier] to make a concrete program and as you remember we resigned from the [coalition with the Agrarian Party] in 1936 over the pension issue. Then our party program demanded a minimum pension. That people ought to be able to live on it. But how shall we now manage to make our demands concrete? What sums shall pensioners get so as to get out of [poverty]?" He obviously wanted a single figure, but the Committee on Social Care entangled itself in complicated calculations of sums varying from place to place because of varying costs of living.[37] The Steering Board was not pleased, and in the end the party lost many votes over the pension issue.

In the May Day parades in 1944, the radical pensioners were on the march. Much press and newsreel coverage was given to the Stockholm United Pensioner Association, who formed their own section under their own banner. Among the slogans on the banners were "Raise the People's Pensions," "Away with the Poor Law," and "Freedom to All the People." Afterward, a retired Stockholm mayor, the aged humanitarian internationalist Carl Lindhagen, spoke. The assembly adopted a statement expressing disappointment that government had done so little to improve pensions. To close the meeting, they sang the Swedish national anthem "Du gamla, du fria" (You Old, You Free), which in this situation attained a connotation it normally did not have.[38] Even the official Social Democratic May Day Parade speeches—like those of Möller, state secretary Tage Erlander, and the Trades Union chairman—noted the need for pension increase. It was obvious that pension reform was to become a major issue in the elections in the autumn of 1944. Even the nonsocialist parties—particularly the liberal Peoples Party, but even the conservative Party of the Right—were interested in the pensioner vote.[39]

As it turned out, the Social Democrats lost over 110,000 votes in the 1944 elections, compared with the previous election. The Communist Party increased to just over 18 percent of the vote, which was a great embarrassment. Even the liberals appeared to have won votes on the pension issue. In analyzing the loss, the party concentrated on social policy, particularly on pensions. Gustav Möller was in trouble, and the rising star Tage Erlander demanded a complete renewal of social policy. The party members of the Committee for Social Care were vilified for not being sufficiently radical, for being overly interested in thrift, and for always being in agreement with the nonsocialist members of the committee. In a letter to the chairman of the Committee for Social Care, Bernhard Eriksson, Olivia Nordgren described Erlander's diatribe. He had said that weak social policy had caused the poor election results. He called on the need for renewal. "It is not certain that our social policy solution should follow the old line. . . . [We need] truly energetic preparation for proposals on social care issues for the 1946 Riksdag. We must be radical, radical!"[40] Here was perhaps the first indication that it would be the relatively unknown Erlander who would be chosen the new party chairman after Hansson (who died in 1946), and not Möller, the favorite of the old guard.

Great expectations were placed on the coming pension reform bill, which could be proposed in 1946. Pressure from both pensioner associations was in effect all through the preparation of the bill. One of the first battles was to force the Committee for Social Care to actually come up with a clear proposal. This committee as a rule took a very long time on every issue and was extremely attached to complicated schemes for regional equality. Sometimes it was paralyzed by the need for individual local adjustments. In the end, the members could not agree on a single proposal. The major issue was that the members wished to retain income testing and the control functions of the poor-law authorities. Many of the members had a background in professional social work and saw it as an integral part of a welfare society; public pensioner opinion demanded freedom from any such means testing. In the proposal of November 1945, there were three alternatives, of which two were politically interesting. Alternative II would give each pensioner 1,000 crowns per year after means-testing (this would give smaller amounts to persons with any other source of income). Alternative III would give 1,000 crowns per year to each pensioner without any means testing at all. Naturally this meant that Alternative II would be inexpensive for state finances while Alternative III would be very expensive. In high-level party discussions, Prime Minister Hansson spoke in favor of the cheaper Alternative II, since it also would not give money to persons with large incomes. The Minister of Finance favored the cheaper alternative. Möller himself said that he could accept Alternative II even though he preferred the expensive alternative of 1,000 crowns to every pensioner.[41] To some it appeared as if Möller and the party majority were being forced by outside circumstances to accept the expensive reform.

What decided the issue was that the Party of the Right declared itself in favor of 1,000 crowns for all. This forced the government to abandon the idea of the means-tested alternative. It simply could not afford to lose the pensioner vote. The exact background of the position of the Party of the Right is not known. However, increasingly during the war the nonsocialist parties had become engaged in issues of social welfare. The initial dislike of social welfare that expressed itself in opposition to any form of state pensions had disappeared. Even their voters had benefited from the state pensions and would receive the higher pensions. Even they were interested in economic security and medical care at low cost.

The story of the Swedish pensioners' political mobilization indicates that a small but radical group could control opinion and could force government to increase the tempo of pension reform. In this way, the Swedish case is somewhat similar to what happened in England. There, the Old Age Pensions Association started in 1938 and formed itself after some struggle into a National Federation of Old Age Pensioners Associations. This organization was free from trade union affiliation. Its rhetoric was in its most extreme version similar to that used in Sweden. It put pressure on politicians through petitions with thousands of signatures. A first petition in July 1939 collected about five million signatures. This created considerable raising of consciousness and did lead to some increases in pensions. But it did not lead to permanent influence over policy.[42]

The Swedish case differs, since the two rival pensioner organizations there after a few years began taking the same stance. The organization shaped to defuse the old age question turned on its creator. By the end of World War II, opinion about the conditions of old age pensioners was a very crucial electoral issue and would continue to be central to political debate throughout the 1950s.

NOTES

1. John Björnheden to Josef Kjellgren, March 21, 1945, Kjellgren Collection, Royal Library, Stockholm.
2. David Gaunt, Från Brantings soldater till folkhemmets paria, in Lennart Levin (Ed.), *Sveriges pensionärsförbund. Kommunistiskt, borgerligt, opolitiskt?* 1939–1999 (12) (Stockholm: SPF förlag, 1999).
3. *Arbetar-Posten* issues of February 11, February 18, and February 25, 1938.
4. Björnheden's autobiographical scetch is in the Ivar Lo-Johansson Collection, Uppsala University Library, volume 545 k:2.
5. John Björnheden, Vad vill pensionärsföreningen?, *Arbetar-Tidningen*, November 25, 1938.
6. Schism i folkpensionärs förening, *Ny Tid*, December 21, 1938.
7. Folkpensionärernas förening, *Arbetar-Tidningen*, April 21, 1939; and Gunnar Lundstedt, Arbetarklassen och folkpensionen, *Göteborgs Posten*, March 23, 1939.
8. Folkpensionärerna till statsministern, *Morgon-Tidningen*, May 2, 1939; Ers Excelens, vi lider nöd, *Arbetar-Tidningen*, May 5, 1939; *Arbetar-Posten*, May 5, 1939.
9. John Björnheden, Brev, *Pensionären*, Christmas issue 1942, 17.
10. Åke Elmér, *Folkpensioneringen i Sverige* (Lund: Gleerups, 1960), 31–33.
11. Ibid., 208–209.
12. Ibid., 306.
13. Minute books for the Swedish Pensioner National League are at the League's national headquarters in Stockholm.
14. Gaunt, Brantings soldater, 17–18.
15. Ibid., 50–51.
16. National League Minutes for April 4, 1940; Björnheden's annotation in his pocket calendar for March 15 and July 7, 1940. His yearly pocket calendars are deposited in Gothenburg City Archives.
17. Folkpensionärer bilda sin egen riksorganisation, *Social-Demokraten*, July 5, 1940.
18. John Björnheden, Folkhemmets paria, *Arbetaren*, June 12, 1940.
19. John Björnheden, Folkpensionärer—ett mörkt kapitel, *Arbetaren*, October 23, 1940.
20. John Björnheden to Ivar Lo-Johansson, January 2, 1949, in Lo-Johansson Collection, Uppsala University Library; the meeting is referred to in *Göteborgs Handels-och Sjöfartstidning*, November 26, 1940.
21. Folkpensionärers riksförbund gå till kungs, October 31, 1940; Folkpensionärer kräva full kompensation, *Göteborgs Posten*, November 6, 1940.
22. Se volume Miscellaneous annotations 1929–1940, in Per Albin Hansson Collection; Social Democratic Riksdag Group Minutes for December 4, 1940; Social Democratic Representative Council, December 3, 1940, point 4. All of this is in the Swedish Labour Movement Archive and Library, Stockholm.
23. 500 pensionärer visa sin budget för riksdagen, *Göteborgs Tidningen*, December 15, 1940; John Björnheden, Fattighjälp, *Arbetaren*, December 19, 1949; Editorial article, De folkhemska pensionärerna, *Arbetaren*, December 28, 1940; John Björnheden, Folkpensioner och fattigvård, *Arbetaren*, December 28, 1940; John Björnheden, Nu går det inte längre, *Arbetaren*, January 4, 1941.

24. Editorial article, Folkpensionärsföreningar, *Ny Tid,* October 7, 1941; *Arbetar-Kuriren,* December 7, 1940.

25. Editorial article, Kommunister fiska bland de gamla, *Social-Demokraten,* October 14, 1941; rebuttal from John Björnheden, Ett genmäle till Social-Demokraten, *Arbetaren,* November 4, 1941; Editorial article, *Ny Tid,* October 7, 1941; Editorial article, *Svenska Dagbladet,* October 28, 1941.

26. John Björnheden to Swedish Social Democratic Workers Party Steering Board, March 9, 1941; Minutes of Social Democratic Workers Party Steering Board, point 33, for April 9, 1941 and appendix, point 35, for the same date. All material in Swedish Labor Movement Archives and Library, Stockholm.

27. Folkpensionärer bilda ny Göteborgsförening, *Göteborgs Handels och Sjöfartstidning,* September 30, 1941; Folkpensionärs strid, *Göteborgs Tidningen,* October 3, 1941; Storm kring pensionärer i Göteborg, *Göteborgs Posten,* October 3, 1941.

28. Gaunt, Brantings soldater, 31–33.

29. Elmér, Folkpensioneringen, 160–168; Håkan Jönsson, *Det moderna åldrandet: Pensionärsorganisationernas bilder av äldre 1941–1995* (Lund: Lund Dissertations in Social Work 2. 2001), 66–74.

30. Elmér, Folkpensioneringen, 163.

31. Landets gamla ha bildat ny sammanslutning, *Göteborgs Posten,* November 14, 1941.

32. Gaunt, Brantings soldater, 32.

33. Elmér, Folkpensioneringen, 167.

34. Swedish Social Democratic Workers Party Steering Board, Working Committee Minutes, March 26, 1942, point 34, Swedish Labor Movement Archives and Library, Stockholm.

35. Swedish Social Democratic Workers Party Steering Board, January 16, 1944, point 8; April 23, 1944, point 21.

36. Pensionärer ha sin Beveridge-plan klar, *Arbetaren,* July 31, 1943.

37. Swedish Social Democratic Workers Party Steering Board Minutes, April 23, 1944, 17–18, Swedish Labor Movement Archives and Library, Stockholm.

38. Otium, 1944:1 and 1945:1.

39. Peter Baldwin, *The politics of social solidarity: Class bases of the European welfare state 1875–1975* (Cambridge, U.K.: Cambridge University Press, 1990), 136–144.

40. Olivia Nordgren to Bernhard Eriksson, November 5, 1944, Eriksson Collection, volume 2, Swedish Labor Movement Archives and Library, Stockholm.

41. Swedish Social Democratic Workers Party Steering Board, December 9, 1945; Riksdag's Group Minutes, January 29, 1946, and March 5, 1946, Swedish Labor Movement Archives and Library, Stockholm.

42. John Macnicol & Andrew Blaikie, The politics of retirement, in Margot Jeffreys (Ed.), *Growing old in the twentieth century* (London: Routledge, 1989), 21–42.

REFERENCES

Baldwin, P. (1990). *The politics of solidarity: Class bases of the European welfare state 1875–1975.* Cambridge: Cambridge University Press.

Elmér, Å. (1960). *Folkpensioneringen i Sverige.* Lund, Sweden: Gleerups.

Gaunt, D. (1999). Från Brantings soldater till folkhemmets paria. In Lennart Levin (Ed.), *Sveriges pensionärsförbund: Kommunistiskt, borgerligt, opolitiskt? 1939–1999* (pp. 6–79). Stockholm: SPF förlag.

Jönson, H. (2001). *Det moderna åldrandet. Pensionärsorganisationernas bilder av äldre 1941–1995*. Lund, Sweden: Lund Dissertations in Social Work.

Macnicol, J., & Blaikie, A. (1989). The politics of retirement. In Margot Jeffreys (Ed.), *Growing old in the twentieth century* (pp. 21–42). London: Routledge.

9

The Making of Older Immigrants in Sweden: Identification, Categorization, and Discrimination

Owe Ronström

INTRODUCTION

The story presented here is a Swedish one, but only partly so. A specific Swedish set of problems stems from a common understanding of a general economic decline in the public sphere, which in combination with a decreasing will to pay taxes to solve other people's problems has resulted in restrictions and cutbacks in welfare expenditures. The making of older immigrants is from the outset inscribed in this often-told story: "Money's not enough anymore!" A result is a growing tendency to use public resources to solve acute problems, rather than to provide general and regular services. I will also address a more general, not only Swedish, set of problems: discriminating practices that develop from making public resources available to certain marginalized "problematic" categories or groups, but only if they accept being stamped as problematic, thus marginal. The effect of the acceptance of this labeling is an affirmation and strengthening of that marginal position.

It is often said that Sweden most likely is the country that has invested most in projects to integrate immigrants. The results, however, are meagre indeed. Integration of the immigrated population is not more successful in Sweden than elsewhere. One plausible reason is unforeseen countereffects: The money spent on fighting discrimination on individual and group levels has produced discriminating practices on a structural level.

THE RESEARCH PROGRAM "CULTURE OF AGING"

The empirical base of this paper is the research program "The Culture of Ageing." This six-year program, led by the historian David Gaunt and me, employed more than one dozen researchers from a number of disciplines. Together we set off to study as many aspects of aging as a cultural phenomenon of which we could think. We studied dancing, music-making, narratives, food, clothes, old age in religious texts, the pensioners' movements, representations and images of aging, the struggle for the old person's right to work, and much more.[1]

A number of studies were designed to deal specifically with the making of older immigrants in Sweden. We started by surveying the growing Swedish literature on the topic and went on to investigate how and why a number of old age care institutions in the Stockholm area were established—institutions intended for immigrant Finns, Jews, Syrians, Italians, and Greeks (Ponzio, 1996; Ronström, 1996a). It is results from these studies, conducted between 1993 and 1996, that I will draw upon in this chapter.[2]

THE STUDY OF OLDER IMMIGRANTS IN SWEDEN: THE BEGINNINGS

In the late 1970s, a public discussion about older immigrants started. The first research reports were published in the early 1980s. In the 1990s, older immigrants had become firmly established in the public discourse as a specific social category, with its own set of problems that should and could be solved.

A significant part of the interest in older immigrants was raised by officials, by authorities at different levels, from local to national. This is again a part of the Swedishness of this field. As noted by leading scholars on immigration, a large part of Swedish official immigration policies has been induced from above, with little or no influence from the immigrants themselves (Hammar, 1988, p. 19, 1994, p. 16). The power over the definition of both the problems and the solutions has been in the hands of Swedish authorities. One reason is that the whole field of "invandrare," the Swedish word for immigrant, from the outset has been created, shaped, and developed by officials and researchers, in close cooperation. Much research has been initiated and paid for by social authorities. A substantial part has been produced by professionals commuting between research, social work, and social administration. As in some cases the researchers and the officials have even been the same persons, it is not by chance that the researchers and the officials have had common interests and common ways of thinking and talking to fall back upon.

Much of the research about older immigrants in Sweden has been dominated by a social technological perspective and by ideas about increasing social problems and possible, but not yet found, solutions. For this reason, research about older immigrants to a large extent has focused on social problems, loss, deprivation, and the like. Also evident among the producers of this research are social pathos, empathy, an eagerness to induce rapid social improvement, and a strong will to make the world better for everybody. This important feature of the discourse about problematic social categories such as older immigrants follows directly from the social technological perspective.

It is no big surprise, then, that the picture of older immigrants that has been built up during the last 20 years is dark. Older immigrants constitute a growing problem, not least because of their rapidly growing numbers. In 1996, there were about 110,000 older immigrants in Sweden, about 7 percent of all people over 65. In 2010, it is estimated that the numbers will have doubled. Most of the older immigrants come from neighboring countries in Europe, but the number of immigrants from farther afield is growing fast. Generally, older immigrants are depicted as having bad health, low income, poor living standards, and low life expectancy. One of the greatest problems, maybe even the greatest, according to a widespread picture, is that older immigrants speak little or no Swedish and thus, as the standard Swedish expression has it, "live outside society." This has to do with the common tendency in Sweden to translate the widely used concept *culture* into *language*. Bad Swedish is seen as a mark of non-Swedishness. It is because immigrants speak bad Swedish that they are not fully integrated, and it is because they are not fully integrated that they continue to speak bad Swedish. The Swedish language—often called only "the language"—is understood as the main entrance to Swedish society and Swedish culture.[3] Thus, a person proficient in speaking Swedish will be considered Swedish, well integrated into Swedish culture. This is an important reason for investing in language courses for immigrants and for treating low proficiency in the Swedish language as a major social and cultural problem.

THE MAKING OF NEW SOCIAL CATEGORIES

Producing new social categories is a complicated process with its own inherent logic. This is how it is often done in Sweden: First, the fact that there is a certain group or category with a specific set of problems is established. Then, it is stated that the number of people belonging to this group or category is increasing. The next step is to declare that too little is known, that nothing yet has been done, and, of course, that something should, could, and must be done. The point of departure is a growing social problem; the goal is to find the right means to solve the problem. There seems to be little space for questions and reflection between these positions.

Looking back on this problem-driven production of social categories, it is not hard to see that the struggle for social reforms and improvements, for making life better for deprived people, in combination with often very strong social engagement and feelings of solidarity among the active social workers and officials, has often led to a simple patronizing of the clients. It is paradoxical how easily a strongly stressed cultural relativism and antiethnocentrism could be integrated into a "von oben" perspective, from which the identified marginalized groups could be patted on their heads.

What we stand in front of here is the Janus-face of altruism: the two sides of "What you want people to do to you, you should also do to them." Fundamentally, to help, to take care of somebody, starts with establishing a social construct according to which one part is seen as dependent on the other. It proceeds by identifying what the helper, if in the same situation, would like to be helped with and finally goes on to secure that the person in need, the dependent, will get precisely that. The helper controls the identification of the person in need as well as the identification of what he or she needs. When combining two marginalized social categories, such as "old people" and "immigrants," into a doubly marginalized new category, "older immigrants," it is all too easy for the necessary reflections to give way to the ready answers that start with "we have to do something immediately, or it soon will be too late!"

NEW PERSPECTIVES

What answers are there then to the question of why "older immigrants" was invented as a social category in the late 1970s and early 1980s? First, the numbers of old immigrants increased radically during this period. When they were few, the problem was small. Then their numbers grew—and so did the problem of how to deal with them. Second, not only have they become more numerous, but their problems have also increased and become more severe. Most studies of older immigrants have departed from these two standpoints.

These answers, however, are far too simple. Growing numbers and problems may be necessary conditions, but there is more to it. People from many places have lived in Sweden for centuries. A reason that the number of old immigrants in Sweden seems to have grown during the last decades may well be the simple fact that we had not previously bothered to count them! All these immigrants have grown old in Sweden, and all have had their problems. Still, it was not until the late 1970s that they had become identified as a problematic social category. In fact, several ethnic groups, among them Finns, Estonians, and Jews, have striven for years to organize care systems for "their" elderly (Karupää, 1994; Ronström, 1996a,b). Up to the 1970s, only the Jews had succeeded. Why?

Another approach is to look for answers in other directions. One possible answer has to do with the way officials in social security institutions work. A central part of their work is to identify problematic groups, investigate their problems, and then solve them. For all kinds of professionals, developing their work as professionals is of fundamental importance. For social workers, one way to develop their profession is to identify new groups of people hitherto unknown to officials as in need of their services (Arnstberg, 1989). When such a new group has been identified and categorized, the social and cultural "contents" of that group will develop as a result of a complex interplay between the categorizers and the categorized. The process is often characterized by "alter casting" (Weinstein & Deutschberger, 1963; Lange & Westin, 1981), whereby the dependant part is molded in a form created for it by the categorizers.

Yet another viable explanation is compatibility: As there are older immigrants in other countries, (which in the Swedish context most often should be read United States), there must be older immigrants also in Sweden, although we might not yet be aware of it. A variation on the same theme is when seemingly successful institutional solutions to specific social problems in other countries are imported as models also for solving problems in Sweden. An example is the introduction of the Greek KAPI[4] in Sweden during the 1990s.

A fourth and more general type of explanation is that a change in the patterns of social categorization in Sweden as a whole now is taking place (and, as it seems, not only in Sweden, but also in many other countries in the Western world). There seems to be a overall tendency to move from class-based to ethnically-based social categorizations (cf. Lundberg, Malm, & Ronström, 2000).

A fruitful approach to the question of why "older immigrants" was invented as a new social category is to follow Ivan Illich (1975) and many others, who have pointed to the simple fact that all systems in a sense produce their users. When there is a system for distributing resources to older immigrants, there will be older immigrants asking for these, and precisely these, resources. If we from this perspective look back to the question of why for 20 and more years there exists a social category called "older immigrants" in Sweden, the possible answers must be found by not looking too much in the direction of the fingers that point at older immigrants. Instead, it is necessary to turn around and look at those to whom the pointing hands belong. What 40 years of gerontological research has taught us, writes anthropologist Christine Fry (1990), is that the elderly belong to the most heterogeneous parts of the populations in industrialized societies. People are born different; no two people live the same lives. Therefore, people accumulate differences through their lives and will become increasingly unique the older they get: "The longer they are here the more time they have to experience life and to become increasingly unique physically, psychologically, and culturally" (Fry, 1990, p. 129). Once this is accepted, it will be obvious that the answer to the necessary question of why people, when growing old, despite their inherent differences, become treated as more and more similar cannot be found among the aged.

Instead, as Fry urges us, we should investigate the social and cultural factors that shape the way people make a living (Fry, 1990, p. 129). To these factors belong a structure where certain people, as professionals, with the best of intentions and the best of reasons, make a living from identifying, categorizing, and also potentially discriminating against marginalized groups. A closer look at the material generated by our studies reveals that a small number of key actors are constantly recurring. They are often middle-aged, with university education, often in sociology, social work, and the like. They are trained to lead, to take initiatives, and have often worked with social questions, care, and social policies for many years. They take great personal interest in immigrant and old age issues, and, not least important, they are in position to assemble large public resources for that purpose.

OLDER IMMIGRANTS?

Here it is necessary to dwell also upon the question of what kind of category "older immigrant" is. From the perspective of the studies we have been conducting, age and ethnicity can be described as two differently constructed "frames" for categorization. Not only are they different, but they also have a tendency to compete with each other. Both are widespread, widely used, and therefore pregnant with meaning. What happens when they are combined? Theoretically, there are some different possibilities. One is that the old age aspect becomes dominant, while the immigrant/ethnic aspect becomes subordinate. The other is, of course, the other way around: Age becomes a part of the overriding ethnic aspect. A third possibility is that a new "older immigrant" category with traits from both is established, as in the American concept "eth-elders" (Driedger & Chapell, 1987). A fourth is that the old immigrant does not fit into any existing category, based either on age or on ethnicity. Old immigrated individuals thus end up in a conceptual vacuum and become socially and culturally invisible.

As far as we have been able to see, in Sweden today there is substantial empirical support for all four possibilities. An example of the first is the older immigrants' contact with the health and care systems. A founding principle in Swedish welfare policies is to treat all citizens equally, which in Sweden as a rule has been translated to "in the same way." As a result, there is a well-established practice with strong ideological support to treat old people as fundamentally the same, irrespective of origin and need. The immigrant/ethnic aspect becomes subordinated under the age aspect. The second possibility, where the age aspect is subordinated and the ethnic aspect is accentuated, can be exemplified with Poles, Hungarians, and other immigrant groups in Sweden that have no specific activities geared toward "their" old people. Instead, they have tended to treat the aged as an integral part of the ethnic communities.

An example of the third, the amalgamation of age and ethnicity into a new category, can be exemplified by some ethnically-based pensioners' organizations and some homes and institutions for non-Swedish elderly. In Rinkeby, a suburb in north Stockholm, there is a home for the aged, where people of mostly Hispanic origins have spontaneously moved in. Here, according to a recent dissertation based on fieldwork at this institution, it seems that new meanings of "old immigrant" are being lived out (Olsson, 1995).

Examples of the fourth possibility may at first be harder to find, because of the resulting invisibility. But it is a fact that many immigrated old people are estranged from Swedish pensioners' associations, do not want to live in Swedish institutions for the aged, and at the same time for different reasons choose to stay out of the social networks and institutions formed by their compatriots. Studies point to such problems among for example Kurds, Iranians, Finns, and Swedes from Finland (Songur, 1992; Hajighasemi, 1994; Heikkilä, 1994, 1996). Many of these immigrants have come individually to Sweden and lived their whole lives without much contact with the Swedish welfare system or the organizations of their fellow countrymen. For people estranged from the Swedish society in which they have spent most of their lives and who do not find the imagined community with fellow "ethnics" strong enough, the consequences in later life may be frightening.

SUMMARY AND CONCLUSION

It seems that in Sweden today old age is becoming increasingly ethnicized or, if you wish, that ethnicity has achieved an increasingly strong age aspect. Many ethnic groups are now on their way to identify "their elders" as a special category. Swedish authorities have set up special solutions to meet the special needs and problems of older immigrants. A growing number of researchers have done their best to explore this new social category. But at the same time, Swedish pensioners, through their organizations, have started to display themselves publicly as a group "with their own culture," by using the same expressive and rhetorical means and models that since long have been used for the same purposes by ethnic groups. Thereby Swedish pensioners in a sense also have become increasingly "ethnicized" (Ronström, 1994, 1997, 1998).

What are the possible reasons behind this ethnification of old age? Perhaps this simply is what everybody has wanted all the time, but have not until now been able to carry out. Another is that it is what some have wanted and successfully achieved, and therefore what others have begun to take after—a version of the "domino theory," as presented by Ernest Gellners in his famous work about nations and nationalisms: If one starts, others have to follow or simply disappear (Gellner, 1987). A third is that although there have always been older immigrants, it is not until recently that we have discovered them, which of course is a prerequisite for taking any steps at all to improve their situation. A fourth is that it is not until recently that we have invented or constructed older immigrants as a socially and culturally relevant category.

Support for all these explanations can be found in our research: the first two mostly among representatives of the immigrants' organizations and Swedish social officials, the latter two more commonly among researchers. But, as a conclusion, it seems that old immigrants themselves have played only a very small part in the production and dissemination of the concept of "older immigrants." Instead, it seems as though the concept as well as the ongoing ethnification of old age/aging of ethnicity in Sweden as whole primarily result from the efforts of Swedish officials and researchers. From this perspective, you could view a large part of the resulting "multicultural Sweden" and "the ethnics" in Sweden, not only as an answer to a growing diversity due to immigration of new foreigners, but also as an arrangement of the ruling elite, to make it possible to uphold its ruling functions in society.

NOTES

1. A list of reports from the research program "The Culture of Ageing" is published in Hyltén-Cavallius, 1999.
2. See Ronström, 1996 a, b.
3. See, for example, the discussion in Sjögren, Runfors, & Ramberg (Eds.), 1996.
4. Greek abbreviation for Kèndra Anìktìs Prostasìas Ilikiomènon ("Center for Open Care of the Elderly").

REFERENCES

Arnstberg, K-O. (1989). *Socialarbetare*. Lund, Sweden: Studentlitteratur.
Driedger, L., & Chappell, N. (1987). *Aging and ethnicity: Towards an interface*. Toronto: Butterworths.
Fry, C. L. (1990). Cross-cultural comparisons of aging. In K. F. Ferraro (Ed.), *Salient perspectives in gerontology*. New York: Springer.
Gellner, E. (1987). *Culture, identity and politics*. Cambridge, U.K.: Cambridge University Press.
Hajighasemi, F. (1994). *Invandring på gamla da'r—sextio äldre iranier berättar*. Socialtjänsten, FoU byrån, rapport 1994:6.
Hammar, T. (1988). Kunskapens makt eller vem är det som styr? *Invandrare och Minoriteter*, 4–5, 19–23.
Hammar, T. (1994). *Om IMER under 30 år. En översikt av svensk forskning om internationell migration och etniska relationer*. Stockholm: Socialvetenskapliga forskningsrådet.
Heikkilä, K. (1994). *Mer än halva livet—en studie om äldre finländska invandrare i Stockholm*. Socialtjänstens FoU-byrå rapport nr 1994:2. Stockholm.
Heikkilä, K. (1996). På väg mot en mer nyanserad bild av äldre finländska invandrarnas situation. *Socialmedicinsk tidskrift*, 7–8, 385–391.
Hyltén-Cavallius, C. (1999). *Näring för minnet. Pensionärsmat, smak och historia*. Rapport från forskningsprogramt Åldrandets kultur no 11. FoU rapport nr 1999:18. Stockholm: Socialtjänstförvaltningen.
Illich, I. (1975). *Den farliga sjukvården*. Stockholm: Aldus.
Karupää, M-A. (1994). *En koffert i Tallinn: Estniska pensionärer i Stockholm*. Socialtjänsten, FoU byrån, rapport 1994:4.
Lange, A., & Westin, C. (1981). *Etnisk diskriminering och social identitet*. Stockholm: Liber Förlag.
Lundberg, D., Malm K., & Ronström, O. (2000). *Musik, medier, mångkultur. Förändringar i svenska musiklandskap*. Gidlunds, Sweden: Hedemora.
Olsson, E. (1995). *Delad gemenskap. Identitet och institutionellt tänkande i ett mulitetniskt servicehus*. Linköping Studies in Arts and Science 134. Linköpings Universitet.
Ponzio, S. (1996). *Äldre, invandrare och äldre invandrare*. FoU byrån rapport nr 1996:18. Stockholm: Socialtjänsten.
Ronström, O. (1994). "I'm old an' I'm proud." Dance, music and the formation of cultural identity among pensioners in Sweden. *The World of Music*, no. 3, 5–30. Berlin: International Institute for Traditional Music.
Ronström, O. (Ed.). (1996a). *Vem ska ta hand om de gamla invandrarna?* Rapport från forskningsprogrammet Åldrandets kultur nr 2. FoU rapport nr 1996:3. Stockholm: Socialtjänsten.

Ronström, O. (1996b). Äldre invandrare: från teori till praktik. *Socialmedicinsk tidskrift 7–8*.

Ronström, O. (1997). *Russindisco och seniordans. Pensionärers nöjen och modernitet.* Rapport från forskningsprogrammet Åldrandets kultur no 7. FoU rapport nr 1997:14. Resursförvaltningen.

Ronström, O. (Ed.). (1998). *Pigga pensionärer och populärkultur.* Stockholm: Carlssons.

Sjögren, A., Runfors, A., & Ramberg, I. (Eds.). (1996). *En bra svenska? Om språk, kultur och makt.* Mångkulturellt Centrum, Botkyrka.

Songur, W. (1992). *Att åldras i främmande land.* Socialtjänsten, FoU-rapport nr 1992:15. Stockholm.

Weinstein, E. A., & Deutschberger, P. (1963). Some dimensions of altercasting. *Sociometry, 26*, 454–466.

10

Women Aging and Body Talk

Chris Gilleard

INTRODUCTION

In this chapter, I propose a general framework to interpret the conflicting and contrasting discourses about the aging body in contemporary society. I will focus on the aging of women's bodies, the various practices through which women understand and interpret their changing bodies and the structures that shape those practices.

The experience of bodily aging is a topic curiously ignored by mainstream gerontology. In her book entitled *Women and Aging*, published as recently as 1999, Linda Gannon has nothing to say about the subjective experience of aging. Throughout her book she makes no mention of the aging of skin and hair, of changes in fat and muscle distribution, no reference to aging and appearance, or the use of the body as a source of personal and social identity—indeed, nothing about the psychological and social reality of women confronting their own aging. Instead, her chapters address cancer, cardiovascular disease, menopause, and osteoporosis (Gannon, 1999).

Although they avoid such a narrow biological focus, social gerontologists who write about gender pay equally scant attention to women's subjective understandings of aging. Rather, they focus on the contrasting demographic profiles of men and women in later life, stressing differences in their economic and physical health status (cf. Arber & Ginn, 1991). Their central task remains "the nature of the relationship between gender and age-based systems of inequality and capitalism" (McMullin, 1995). In either case, the subject of the aging body remains tucked out of sight, submerged beneath overdetermining biological and socioeconomic structures.

The humanities have been more ready to acknowledge the subjective experience of aging. Women's experience of their aging bodies has been a central focus for a number of writers such as Anne Basting, Frida Furman, Margaret Gullette, and Kathleen Woodward.[1] Adopting a more or less post-structuralist perspective, these authors have begun to examine the complex and varied meanings that aging has for women and how those meanings are represented in books, films, and the media (cf. Basting, 1998; Gullette, 1997; Woodward, 1999[2]). They also share an explicitly normative goal of altering and improving the status of older women.

While such subjective accounts provide a valuable contrast to more structural approaches, they risk leaving unanalyzed the broad social relationships within which age is experienced and from which meanings are drawn. Such blindness to social structure is evident in Kathleen Woodward's comment that: "Along with race, gender and age are the most salient markers of social difference" (Woodward, 1999, p. x). No room here, it seems, for social class!

Finding a path between these two lines of approach, the structuralist and the subjective, might appear a reasonable option. However, I do not wish to address this topic simply to find a middle ground. My intention, rather, is to draw upon this subjectivist tradition while trying to develop a more critical, historically-situated understanding of women's accounts of bodily aging. To that end, I shall concentrate first upon the social and cultural practices that fashion women's accounts of growing old, before going on to considering how these accounts reflect and relate to broader social and cultural processes that are implied in the "postmodernization" thesis of society.[3]

TECHNOLOGIES OF UNDERSTANDING

Toward the end of his life, Foucault had begun to reframe the focus of his work. He saw as the central concern of his writing the technologies that "humans had employed to develop knowledge about themselves." These technologies developed to address a question that, according to Foucault, was first raised at the end of the eighteenth century, namely, "What are we in our actuality—what are we today?" In addressing this question, he wrote

> there are four major types of . . . "technologies," each a matrix of practical reason: (1) technologies of production which permit us to produce, transform or manipulate things; (2) technologies of sign systems, which permit us to use signs, meanings, symbols or signification; (3) technologies of power, which determine the conduct of individuals and submit them to certain ends or domination, an objectivising of the subject; (4) technologies of the self, which permit individuals to effect by their own means or with the help of others a certain number of operations on their own bodies and souls, thoughts, conduct and way of being. (Foucault, 1988, p. 18)

To understand how accounts of bodily aging can be used to address the question "What is aging in its actuality?", I shall draw heavily on Foucault's ideas, especially his ideas on the "technologies of individual domination, the history of how an individual acts upon himself [sic], . . . the technology of the self" (Foucault, 1988, p. 19). Later I will consider how the discourses and practices constituting these technologies of the self link into Foucault's other three "technologies" of production, signification, and power.

Body-oriented technologies of self-care have been pursued through three interrelated practices, each reflecting differing material representations of the body. The cultural evolution of these practices has contributed, serially and cumulatively, directly and indirectly, to women's understanding of their aging bodies.[4] These technologies represent a focus upon the body as a subjectively understood surface of identity that needs to be worked upon (for example, through the use of cosmetics and hair dyes), the body as an instrument of the self that needs to be developed, strengthened, and cultivated (for example, through jogging and workouts at the gym), and the body as an agency-enabling structure, ever subject to risk, that needs to be "tended" (for example, through dieting and the use of dietary supplements). To my mind, these represent the central practices of self-care through which women in the twentieth century have addressed the aging of their bodies; even when eschewed or abandoned, they continue to provide an interpretive framework for the subjective experience of aging.

The development, practice, abandonment, and rejection of these technologies have had a major influence on how women think, talk, and write about aging. By saying this, I do not mean to imply that other forms of discourse about aging are not still employed, predating these consumerist technologies of the self. The idea that there are distinct "seasons of life," for example, continues to be used as a regulatory framework when speaking about and interpreting aging, even though it dates back to antiquity.[5] But by tracing the impact of these "new" practices on women's discourse, we can distinguish their relative influence and contrast them with previous ways of talking and writing about age and the aging body. Such analyses can help illuminate the changing actuality of aging in the twenty-first century.

THE TOP AND BOTTOM OF AGING

Keith Dutton has argued that photography and later the cinema first fully revealed the actual human body to public display. Before that, he states, most Europeans "would hardly have ever seen a completely unclothed body save in the most intimate of domestic circumstances" (Dutton, 1995, p. 97). Equally important was the introduction of private bathrooms as a standard feature of twentieth-century housing, for without that newly introduced "private space" within the household, most women would rarely have found themselves in a position to regard their own unclothed bodies. In 1900, the typical household in England and America had no separate bathroom; by 1950, bathrooms were the norm in most households.[6] Before the twentieth century, public and personal gaze were directed toward the face and head. The traditional attention given to the face and hair still dominates technologies of self-care, but the exclusivity of that vision has passed.

The modern shift from the face and the head to the whole body is reflected and reproduced in the history of the cinema. After the introduction of cinematic narrative, the first "physical" focus was upon the face—witness the close-up traditionally associated with the film pioneer D. W. Griffith.[7] The close-up helped foster the Hollywood "star system"—and the star system, by acting as the principal reference for "the look," stimulated the mass marketing of cosmetics and the expansion into working-class lives of beauty and hairstyling salons.[8]

Developments in the 1940s and 1950s shifted the focus toward the torso and the mass fashioning of a whole-body aesthetic that soon after led to the rise of such body culture and body hygiene practices as slimming, tanning, and toning. The development of these body technologies were historically ordered by technological and economic processes, many linked to developments within film and the media. They gradually eroded the salience of more class-based cultural practices that had been transmitted through the personal dressers and the more exclusive fashion and beauty salons frequented by upper-class "society" women. The emergence of a mass, all-embracing, and highly visual culture, articulated by Marshall McLuhan in the 1960s, revolutionized the social text of the body.

The representation of aging still focuses upon the traditionally public aspects of the body, the face, and the head. Key features include facial lines and wrinkling, sagging jowls, and greying hair. Developments in the hairdressing salon, the cosmetic industry, and the allied personal-care retailing industry have fostered new discourses of choice and agency around these "age" signifiers. While premodern/early modern attempts to hide the signs of aging were the subject of ridicule, these new body-surfacing technologies have proved more popular and more resilient. Materially, this resilience has come about because the products used have been tested against the harsh light of the camera.[9] Culturally, they have gained legitimacy as the supremacy accorded to "foundationalist" views of nature has been eroded (in part by technological developments within the cosmetic industry itself). As hair dyes skin-lifting, antiwrinkling, and age spot–removing creams fill the counters of drugstores and supermarkets, individual attempts to mask or minimize signs of aging are more likely to be criticized for their complicity with patriarchal capitalism than for their presumption in tricking "nature."

The more private changes in the whole body's surface—changes in the shape and structure of the body, its skin, muscles, and sinews—have received rather less public airing. Despite the fact that the unclothed torso serves as one of the principal social texts for identity, few cosmetic products have been marketed that directly address the greying of pubic hair or that seek to cover, conceal, or combat the lines and wrinkles on the belly and buttocks. The signs of aging that spread over the hidden surfaces of the body represent the last frontier within the postmodern life course—and are still awaiting cultural reconstruction.

Nevertheless, much has happened over the last century to render the body a more complex (plastic) site from which to read social identities. The development of the photographic and cinematographic close-up, the arrival of cosmetics on the counters of Woolworth's, the mass marketing of women's magazines, and the increasing availability of private bathrooms have contributed to the emergence of this new culture. Practices such as putting on one's face, carrying mirrors in handbags, and getting a hairdo were incorporated into the experiences of young women in the interwar years. The cinema, the hair salon, and the cosmetic counter of the department store were the sites of the new mass market in self-care that explicitly incorporated the aspirations and means of the working classes. The new technology they displayed required a greater degree of personal reflexivity across all classes and eventually across all generations. The modern manipulation of one's appearance is a cultural practice that was transmitted across a particular generational cohort rather than a practice that was passed down through the generations. It took place within and indeed formed the foundations of a new, intragenerational system of mass cultural reproduction. Class-based, intergenerational modes of cultural transmission were outflanked and—at least as far as body-based cultural practices are concerned—they have now become of marginal social significance.

The transformation of the hair salon from individual cubicles to an open salon is a good example of how this system of cultural reproduction spread. When the salon was first introduced toward the end of the nineteenth century, it sought to mimic the experience of upper-class women employing a private dresser in their own bedroom to cut and style their hair. Each chair was set in its own cubicle, and the hairstylist ministered to the customer's needs as a "private practice." After the popular impact that film stars such as Clara Bow and Jean Harlow had on hair styles, the individualized cubicles were removed, and the salon opened out as a new cultural space where women could meet and watch each others' hair being styled "in public."[10]

As a direct consequence, women reaching retirement age in the 1970s and 1980s had spent much of their adult lives not going out in public without their face on. Visits to the hairdressing salon had been part of their generation's lifestyle. Both practices had as their theme identity and change (delivering "a new you"). How and under what circumstances women decide to retire from this kind of identity work remains an underresearched and poorly understood process. Clearly, many women do stop using makeup and do stop dyeing their hair. Some stop visiting the hairdresser, and for some women, the decision to give up these cultural practices may be sudden and irreversible. Once the decision to sport a head of white hair is taken, it is rarely reversed. As Frida Furman has written of the beauty salon, "Who says this is a morally trivial space?" (Furman, 2000, p. 20).

The issue of deciding when to stop may also surround antiaging cosmetic surgery, a practice whose origins lie in the events of World War I. The decision to have repeated face-lifts, skin tucks, and so on may change as abruptly and finally as the decision to stop dyeing one's hair. Whether a common "body drop" is evident in both cosmetic use and cosmetic surgery is not established. There may well be different temporal trajectories in the rate at which different cosmetic practices begin and end. How women explain their decisions to stop or continue these body-surfacing practices has not been researched. Public discourse about cosmetic surgery is just beginning.[11]

Such discourse will grow. Cosmetic surgery is fast becoming a common, if not yet a mass experience, both in the United States and in parts of Western Europe. Much of it addresses the same cultural issues, resisting the body drop of aging. While the most popular procedures concentrate largely upon the face, figures from the various U.S. cosmetic surgery organizations suggest that other areas of the body have increasingly become targets for intervention. We are beginning to experience the "bottoming out" of aging, as the whole aging body gets ready to go onstage.[12]

AGING AND PHYSICAL CULTURE

Unlike body-surfacing technologies, the focus of physical culture technologies is clearly aimed at the bottom of aging. The workout is concerned with shape, size, and fitness; and the bottom (the backside) is a key signifier of the postmodern virtue of fitness. For women, the development of the workout and related fitness regimes followed the cosmetic/cinematic revolution. These practices became more culturally salient in the latter decades of the last century, from the 1960s onward. The history of physical culture had previously been dominated largely by male-oriented practices.

For most of Western history, there were no female athletes.[13] Women's sports emerged as public events in the late nineteenth century, and even today, women's athletics are frowned upon and even banned in many countries. The introduction of public education for girls provided the strongest impetus for the development of physical exercise. The emergence of what came to be called (in Britain) "gymslip culture" spread as women were drafted into the various protomilitary organizations formed at the time of World War II, and matters of physical fitness and stamina took on greater significance.

Previous physical culture practices that targeted girls or women had focused upon their posture. Women's fitness and later their fatness were twentieth century concerns. The introduction of physical culture clubs into working-class areas in the interwar years was largely a male preserve. Only after World War II did a leisure industry emerge that interwove the themes of strength, shape, and stamina as part of a gendered identity. Spurred on by the cultural endorsement of thinness in the 1960s, Weight Watchers and other physical culture organizations introduced more and more working-class women to the regime of the gym and subsequently the leisure center.

Figures suggest that women now outnumber men in the use made of such centers and clubs. The periodization of these practices is important. Adult women began attending physical exercise classes in significant numbers only in the 1960s and 1970s. Before that, women's experience of physical exercise had been confined to school or protomilitary organizations catering to young women. Not until the 1980s did the focus shift from shape and size to the maintenance of lifelong fitness and exercising specifically to resist the processes of bodily aging.

Even these themes are interwoven, for there is as much concern to maintain health as there is to resist an aging appearance.

One consequence of the timing of these practices is that it is the cohort of women approaching retirement in this century who have developed a tradition of going to the gym and working out. Swimming makes an interesting contrast, since it reflects a tradition reaching back to an earlier period of municipal public baths, elementary school swimming lessons, and seaside holidays where swimming became associated with having fun. As a result, it is one form of body culture that is already widely incorporated in later lifestyles.

One unexplored aspect of the growth of exercise programs, workouts, and other forms of physical culture for women is the extent to which they afford the opportunity for an emerging locker-room culture. Just as the opening out of the hair salon allowed women to share a discursive practice around this new self-care technology, so the increasing use of the gym can be seen as expanding the social space where aging and bodily practices can be reflected upon by women as a group. Discovering a social space where women can be at ease with their actually aging bodies may provide an opportunity for younger generations to revise their own expectations of age and aging. Alternatively, the changing room may become a site where an unexpressed fear and loathing is fostered by the sight of "uncultivated bodies," reinforcing a sense that "I will not let myself go like that."[14]

LONG LIVES AND LEAN DIETS

The experience of aging derived from looking at oneself and others forms an important part of both personal and social identities as "older people." The interior experience of aging—the way that one's body feels and how those feelings change—is less easily incorporated into one's social identity. Developing a discourse about the inner experiences of aging relies heavily, in consequence, upon already-existing discourses of health and illness.

From childhood onward we learn to talk about symptoms—our aches and pains and the general malaise of our insides. It would be tedious to rehearse all the themes that medical sociology has applied to develop an understanding of these processes. Discussing one's experience of aging in terms of physical symptoms is common and can be found in subjective accounts of aging going back to antiquity.[15] Indeed, this kind of discourse still permeates gerontology, providing a comfortable medium for researchers, governments, and health care workers. "Lay" and "professional" discourse about health and illness, however, have become less distinct as health and disease occupy an increasingly salient position within contemporary culture.

The rise of what David Armstrong has called "surveillance medicine" has intensified the process of self-scrutiny. On many counts, including the rising sales of vitamins, minerals, and dietary supplements, we have become a more health-conscious society. Looking after our health is a major concern for all classes and for all adult age groups.[16] By implication, we are more vigilant for signs of ill health. Health checks are ubiquitous. Even when well, we are encouraged not to drop our guard, to remain vigilant, keeping our hearts healthy and our bodies fit through self-imposed regimens of the body. In a sense, the signs of aging have become elided with the signs of ill health, and the former have come to serve as an index of the latter.

Despite this common concern for health and fitness, there are differences in the traditional patterns of symptomatology that characterise the different stages of life. Transient symptoms, arising from external circumstances such as falls, sports accidents, fights, exposure to adverse elements, or contact with other people who are ill typify the experiences of young adults. In contrast, symptoms that arise exogenously in youth appear endogenously in later life. These symptoms, which signify the faults and flaws of the body and its organs, persist and accumulate, gradually forming a backdrop against which life is lived. Epidemiological research indicates that only a minority of those aged over 60 report being free from any form of illness.

Despite age-associated variations in symptomatology, there is little evidence that men and women evaluate their health more negatively as their age increases. It seems as if health has been incorporated into a more general sense of well-being, while symptoms have begun to lose their defining significance as determinants of health. Health talk itself has become a social discourse of floating signifiers, whose referents range from skin color, muscle tone, and the ingestion of vitamins to repetitive activities performed as leisure. Perceptions of health become disconnected from specific symptoms. As health risk overrides symptomatology, it extends beyond the frame of the body to cover a widening variety of environments and activities with which individual bodies are engaged. The distinctiveness of aging as a site for learning a body talk based upon symptoms begins to wane, faced with the all-pervasiveness of risk. Though older people seem to experience more symptoms and talk more often with each other about them, these kinds of conversations do not actively frame an aging identity. Rather, they are confined to the personal sphere of "intimate conversations" and "private consultations." The public space of health, however, extends to and incorporates all generations.

Two separate questions arise concerning the focus of such alternative body talk. Does the consumption of "antiaging" products map sufficiently closely on to the consumption of "health-promoting" products that both can be thought of as serving a similar function of developing and sustaining identity in later life? By continuing to consume health-promoting products, does one resist ill health and aging? Second, does the experience of aging depend more or less upon how one talks about one's health rather than about one's illnesses? By choosing to carry on an existing "health-promoting" lifestyle, despite pain or weakness, does one see oneself resisting old age? By abandoning "health-promoting talk," choosing instead to define one's body by accounts of its symptoms, does one accede to "old age"? We have little understanding of the relationship between women's views of their health, the practices that they employ to maintain their health, and the reflexive use of "illness" versus "health" discourses in self-ascribed aging.

We know little of the temporal trajectories of taking up and abandoning the consumption of the various nutraceuticals, dietary aids, and other health-focused products, how such patterns of use change over time, and how this might relate to self-ascribed aging. Cross-sectional surveys suggest that the self-conscious pursuit of healthy lifestyles becomes less common with increasing age, but this may well mask a cohort effect in the practices of self-care. The recent history of diet in Western society gives us clues how such cohort effects might operate.

The concerns of poor old people had been whether or not to eat. Choosing what to eat was determined by cost not calories. Patterns of consumption in Britain indicate that even now food still constitutes the major item of expenditure for those over the age of 75. Men and women in their 50s and 60s, in contrast, spend more on leisure goods and services. For today's middle-aged cohorts, food comes lower down the rank order of consumption. It seems clear that food and the selection of food also provide an emerging space in which the discourse of bodily maintenance is expressed.

The emergence of a more health-conscious culture, the changing emphasis of medicine from diagnosis and treatment to public surveillance and the identification of premorbid risk, and the increasing significance of food choice as the expression both of identity and "agency" provide some of the contexts for talking and thinking about aging as a process that is subject to personal control. These new contexts are creating new, shifting cultures of aging expressed and reflected in the shifting discourses and practices through which women address their bodily aging.

These processes were first expressed in body-surfacing technologies and later in the pursuit of physical (body) culture. This third form of self-technology—the dietary and health care regime—reflected in the rise of nutraceuticals, health-conscious diets, and the assumption that one can eat one's way out of aging—is the latest to arrive.[17] What these discourses share, of course, is their emphasis upon subjectivity and agency. Their origins are to be found in the emergence of mass consumer culture, and their development is fostered by the widening role played by the market in commodifying more and more aspects of personal and civic life. Choosing whether and how to age is a central element of the differing and contradictory discourses of aging that are becoming evident in the various generations of women who have reached the age of 60 over the last half century. It is a process that is historically situated and closely connected with the selective emergence of women into those public places where mass culture is formed. Whether it is also a site of resistance, a countercultural site for women to define new forms of subjectivity remains to be seen.

WOMEN AGING AND RESISTANCE

Having spent some time outlining bodily-focused technologies of the self that constitute the contemporary practices defining (and defying) later lifestyles, I would like to examine the relationship of these practices to Foucault's other three systems of technology (of production, signification, and power). In doing so, I wish to draw out the particular significance of gender in developing a more culturally informed approach to aging studies.

First, I address the link between the technologies of the self and technologies of power and governmentality. Are technologies of the self subordinate to processes of individual and social control? Should we view technologies of the self as simply the cultural superstructure of a patriarchal capitalist state that is intent on fashioning among women a mystified consciousness concerning the actuality of aging and womanhood, in order primarily to expand production within its established framework?

Next, I examine the link between the technologies of the self and technologies of signification. Is aging—especially bodily aging—such a gendered site because aging is framed as a process of nature and nature is constituted within the modern vision as essentially "female"? If so, is it therefore more productive, more emancipatory to see nature as constituted out of discourse and the technologies of self, vehicles through which we construct representations of both aging and womanhood? Maintaining such post-structural indeterminacy may help guarantee that both age and gender remain fluid and open. Alternatively, should we seek a closer understanding of the material realities of aging abstracted from consideration of the gendered body? Would such a more resolutely modern approach allow us to better define, determine, and redesign our aging bodies, resisting the post-structural temptation to let the aging body's gendered images flower beneath the desires of the market?

Finally, I turn to the relationship between technologies of the self and technologies of production? Can discourses about aging and gender be interpreted without linking them explicitly to the position men and women occupy within the systems of production? Is an emancipatory technology of the self merely one that privileges the position of well-off retired men while further marginalizing and excluding poor aging women? If women's aging is defined by their unequal status in both the public and the private spheres, will it be men, primarily, who age, while women grow old?

POWER AND SELF-CONSCIOUSNESS

To what extent are technologies of the self mediated through relationships of social power? Is not only the technology but also the very "self" that is being developed and cared for a function of gendered power relationships? Sandra Bartky has written:

> The woman who checks her makeup half a dozen times a day ... who worries that the wind or rain may spoil her hairdo, or who feeling fat monitors everything she eats has become just as surely as the inmate a self-policing subject, a self committed to a relentless self-surveillance. This self surveillance is a form of obedience to patriarchy. (Bartky, 1990, p. 80)

Naomi Wolf, too, has written of the terror of aging that drives women into their subjection before the cosmetic counter, the diet books, and the surgeons' scalpels. She argues:

> Since middle class Western women can best be weakened psychologically now that we are stronger materially, the beauty myth ... draws on more technological sophistication and reactionary fervor than ever before ... [and] ... the unconscious hallucination grows ever more influential and pervasive because of what is now conscious market manipulation: powerful industries—the $33bn a year diet industry, the $20bn cosmetics industry, the $300m cosmetic surgery industry and the $7bn pornography industry—have arisen from the capital made out of unconscious anxieties and are in turn able to use, stimulate and reinforce the hallucination in a rising economic spiral. (Wolf, 1990, pp. 16–17)

Other women writers have pointed out the relentless and inescapable pursuit of "age-denial" that women can be caught up in, with the only route out a kind of capitulation to "exclusion" from contemporary society. Diana Meyers writes:

> If aging women do not hide the signs of age, conventional beauty ideals and the facial legibility postulate authorise us to read their faces as a mark

of inner corruption ... labouring to stay young-looking is a way of shunning devolution and defilement. (Meyers, 2000, p. 39)

The assumption that women are "disciplined" by their antiaging labors is a central theme in Wolf's *The Beauty Myth* and forms a constant motif for other feminist writers such as Germaine Greer and Margaret Gullette. As a reactance, it calls up an ideology, a type of discourse that is perfectly captured by Gulette's theme of "declining to decline"—a resistance that itself adds yet further layers of contradiction. This discourse itself can be further challenged since what constitutes resistance and what constitutes capitulation is rarely clear, as both Furman and Meyers have pointed out.[18]

It would be naïve to believe that the cosmetics industry is wedded to a particular ideology of femininity. The industry is quite capable of rebranding its products and will happily redefine age as beauty if that will help sell them. For example, L'Oreal now markets a hair color product called "Gray Chic"—"so you can play with grey in the most natural way with shades from crystal clear and silvery to tones with subtle hints of colour" (cited from an advertisement in the January 2001 issue of *Modern Maturity*).

These paradoxes of resistance are evident in many post-structuralist writers and in many "postmodern" cultural practices. One particular example can be seen in the work of photographer Jacqueline Hayden in her "Figure Model Series." Here, the photographer exhibits pictures of nude men and women in "new versions of classical poses," offering their aging bodies to the public gaze "denuded of social context" (Cristofovici, 1999). Simply challenging one aesthetic with another, the argument remains contained within the sphere of imagery, competing photographic fictions of a life. In the end, all that such soft-focused images reveal is the omnivorous capacity of the camera to "create the beautiful and ... use it up" (Sontag, 1979, p. 85). A slightly more engaged approach can be seen in the recent use of photographs of aging women modeling fashion in glossy British weekend magazine supplements. Although including "age and aging" as intrinsic parts of the contemporary culture of consumer society, along with disability and deformity, such mediated forms of resistance do little more than expand the portfolio of images floating freely before the market.

Resistance to the overdetermined image of bodily aging calls forth more complex discourses and practices. But the underbelly of this resistance is an equally encultured sense of fear and shame about the body that cuts across all adult age categories. To speak of a youth culture does not mean that youth has it easy. Escaping into old age, embracing the body drop itself, may offer some kind of relief for many for whom the struggle to embrace or resist an image and identity as a modern woman has proved too burdensome. The invisibility of older women so widely descried may, for some women, be sought as a personal good, a final resolution to an otherwise endless treadmill of effort and labor. As Baudrillard has pointed out, the most powerful form of resistance is indifference to the social. Yet, even that discourse which advocates "letting it go" invariably requires that this choice is communicated, that it too constitutes a kind of voice. Frida Furman quotes one of her beauty salon customers as saying: "at this point in my life I'm relaxing and it's fine, no big deal . . . I wear a size 14 instead of a 10. . . .I don't really care anymore." For Furman, however, this constitutes a voice of resistance, a representation of a potential "counterculture" (Furman, 2000, p. 19).

Such paradoxes abound. Cosmetic surgery is used by an increasing number of women in their late 50s and early 60s (10 percent of women aged 55–64 reported having surgery in the latest AARP *Modern Maturity* commissioned survey). There is a greater tolerance for cosmetic surgery and a greater tendency for those who have had surgery to want to repeat it. Women are nine times more likely to have surgery than men. At the same time, the survey reports that most U.S. women do not see appearance as an extremely important part of their lives. Over 90 percent of men and women in a *Modern Maturity* survey reported being satisfied with their appearance (*Modern Maturity*, April 2001).

To relate these evident contradictions in the practices of "managing aging" to the emerging cultural understanding of aging, it is important to recognize that just as advertisers shift and reverse their focus, so do consumers. Such shifts increase as the arenas for body talk and body practices expand. The notion that an internalized agism is driving women to consume endless amounts of cosmetics is too simplistic, just as it is simplistic to believe that a deliberate stimulation of age terror is being fostered as a backlash to women's increasing economic resourcefulness. The search for a new aesthetics of aging can always be incorporated into the texts of the market. The reframing of aging as "fashion" as much reflects as it resists the cultivation of cultures that global capitalism thrives upon.

ALL SMOKE AND MIRRORS: SIGNIFYING AGE

Mother nature made old age and death sisters. With such an understanding, the medical men of the nineteenth century outlawed old women from their modern new hospitals (Smith, 1990, p. 254). Medicine feared and still fears both. Rather than treating old age, geriatric medicine emerged in postwar health care systems charged with the task of removing "the aged" from medical and surgical wards, albeit professing sympathy for their aged state while so doing. Maintaining an essentialist dichotomy between normal and abnormal aging, modern medicine has traditionally refused to treat, halt, or reverse old age. That which cannot be cured must be endured. Throughout the nineteenth and twentieth centuries, technological medicine had no truck with age and aging, and consequently old age became a "natural" criterion for withholding investigation and treatment.[19]

Post-structuralism has scant regard for this "essentialist" discourse. "Women," like "aging," represent no more than a regulatory frame whose discourse "congeal[s] over time to produce the appearance of substance, of a natural sort of being" (Butler, 1990, p. 33). As the state limits its role to providing a safety net for old age, so the space by which later life can be understood and practiced widens; for increasing numbers of people, this widening cultural space offers both opportunity and uncertainty. Nature becomes ungendered, and becomes plastic.

Within this new post-structural arena, women writers are beginning to address and, by addressing, to reconstitute the subjective experience of aging. In a challenging collection of essays, extracts, and reports from exhibitions, Kathleen Woodward sought to establish "an arena of visibility... for the virtually invisible subject of older women" (Woodward, 1999, p. x). The aging of a generation of feminist writers and activists has no doubt played a part in these new developments. But I also believe that aging has become such a cultural issue because it is now beginning to escape from the limits previously set by modern social policy and modern biomedical discourse.

Throughout modernity, writing about the aged tended to be writing about a social category of need or an account of the disease and dysfunction that were seen as naturally associated with old age. Within such discourse, the aging body was merely a repository of need, a signifier of disability—what aging bodies can or cannot do, what assistance should be given them. But with the development of personal toiletries, hair dyes, dietary and exercise regimes, and a new focus upon positive health and fitness as core postmodern virtues, an alternative discourse is emerging that uses age as a contrasting context for lifestyle choices. Some of the underlying postulates of this discourse have been identified by Diana Meyers—"that people's inner nature can be deciphered from their outward appearance—the facial legibility postulate that an attractive inner nature is embodied in an attractive face" (Meyers, 2000, p. 30). Fit, healthy, and attractive bodies are seen as desirable to all classes and across all generations. They are, if not a universal right, at least a universal aspiration.

Not looking good reflects badly upon the kind of person one is and the extent to which one is or is not a participant citizen in contemporary society. As more of life is lived within public spaces (viz., the rise of urban lifestyles, less time spent at home and more time spent shopping, eating out, visiting leisure and entertainment centers), so the body becomes an increasingly important site for the social texts of identity and difference. The constancies Meyers noted become more salient as the assumptions that are required if one is to negotiate life in public become more widely shared.

With the increased use made of the body as a means of establishing personal and social identities, the evident work that is put into creating and maintaining an identity has taken on a greater sense of worthiness. The aim is respect, to be well regarded. Old-looking people risk being disregarded and disrespected. Such disrespect/disregard is a product of the social gaze. Older people are becoming a visible minority, subject to the dominant gaze of a non-old majority. Since public spaces exist for the purposes of immediate use, the historical situatedness of aging is overshadowed by its visible distinctness. Age then becomes a matter of "street credibility." As social relationships are increasingly shaped by consumerist considerations, so individualized bodies become more salient as the site of social text. As time and nature cease to be significant reference points for living life, masking age becomes less an act of violation than an act of self-expression.

Traditionally women rather than men have been considered the object of others' gaze (others being both men and women). The reflexivity of the twentieth century has accentuated that self-as-other gaze, which both demands identity work and exposes all worked identities to the risk of invalidation by the leakage of an alternative "spoiled" identity. Older women often comment about being surprised to discover that a publicly reflected image of some "older other" is in fact oneself.[20] Women have become used to preparing their public identities in front of personal mirrors—in the bathroom, the hallway, or the bedroom. These are intimate personal spaces typically shielded from the public gaze. Public mirrors have no sense of this history; they are the unprepared surfaces that reflect and by their reflection support modern lifestyles. Necessary elements, they are a source of both fear and reassurance. Within their reflected gaze, they contain the power to legitimate our public existence. Mirrors and cameras have replaced nature as the source of personal as well as social identities.

To retreat from this site of both affirmation and rejection, to escape from the discourse and practices of reflexive modernity, is to retreat not into nature (as it was for nineteenth-century romantics) but to retreat from all social and cultural meaning. As personal discourse ceases to be embedded in the broader cultural discourse of society and as self-care practices cease to connect with the practices of anonymous yet significant others, the consequence is cultural suicide. If no one looks and no one listens, personal narratives become irrelevant; nature takes her course.

GENDER AND THE GINI COEFFICIENT: DIVERSITY AND DIFFERENCE

Money talks. Spending one million pounds advertising a particular brand name increases the likelihood that identity, that brand name, will dominate public discourse. Yet money alone will not secure the success of that marketing strategy. So it can be argued that the successful use of technologies of self-representation will not be confined to those with money. Still, money helps. Opinions about how much it helps vary. For some writers pursuing structural accounts of age and gender, the status of the aging body depends crucially upon access to income and wealth in later life. The ability to maintain a fit, youthful, attractive, healthy body—to be the embodiment of the third age—has been ascribed to the interactive impact of gender and class. Women as they age accumulate more ill health at the same time as they accumulate poverty. The inequalities that ensure that working-class women end up with the poorest health and upper-class men end up with the best health have been explored at considerable length—and with mixed empirical support.[21]

Does this mean that the impact of "ageism," of unfavorable interenerational comparisons of worth and status by the "young" of the "old" can only be ameliorated by providing more opportunities for greater intragenerational comparisons? It seems possible to argue that greater disparities, greater evident differences among older people, actually ensure more opportunities for a wider range of self-care practices and identity-forming discourses than would arise if later life were made more socially and economically equal—for example, by the hegemony of the old age pension.

A frequent theme in past accounts of aging has been the elimination of difference (of class, gender, ethnicity, sexuality, able-bodiedness). Aging has been viewed primarily as a process of desexualization, disablement, and impoverishment. Already evident in premodern writings, such ideas formed part of the modern scientific discourse of the nineteenth century. Von Kondratowitz gives one particular example from a nineteenth century German medical textbook:

> In [old] age the sexual function gradually ceases, sexual difference turns into indifference again and . . . the sexes come to resemble each other once again in respect of appearance and the condition of the whole body, as they did in childhood. (*Enzyklopädisches Wörterbuch*, cited in von Kondratowitz, 1991, p. 148)

Class has formed a strong vertical division within modern society that ensures the segmented transmission of culture from one generation to the next. If most people were poor, the cultures of aging that were transmitted were those of lack, poverty, and hardship. Rising incomes across the twentieth century have meant that most older people have experienced an improving quality of life for themselves and their children. As successive cohorts have become better off, participation in consumer culture has become horizontally segmented. Cultural transmission has become an increasingly horizontal process. Class-based cultures are aging into the distance of history.

The consequence is a growing heterogeneity within generations. If the vertical cultures of class tended to be monolithic, the horizontal spread of culture fosters difference and diversity. That diversity appears to be growing, as fashion cycles speed up and as identities and the voices and bodies that represent them expand into the cultural spaces of postmodern society. Much contemporary writing about aging originates from an aging but not an old-aged cohort of women. They are voices from the baby boom generation located in a cohort whose expenditure on leisure goods and services now exceeds that on material necessities of food and shelter. Talking about, rehearsing, and reflecting upon their own and others' aging are possible now in a way not available a couple of generations ago. The rise of "difference" in a context of increasing affluence across the whole of the adult life course will see more complex discourse around aging than has previously been expressed. Issues concerning resistance to and acceptance, denial, and transcendence of bodily aging will not be resolved as a result, but they do contribute to the gradual dissolution of modernity's monolithic ageist culture. Recognizing the relevance of gender is part of that process, acknowledging the increasing diversity and increasing differentiation that constitute the actuality of aging in the twenty-first century. Premature demands for an equalization in the experience of aging risk foreclosing on the possibilities inherent in our increasingly longer lives. The new trend evident in women's writing, talking, and thinking about bodily aging can be seen as representative of this new culture.

SUMMARY

My aim in this chapter has been to outline an approach toward viewing "body talk"—the discourses and practices concerning the body—as a means of expanding our understanding of the actuality of aging. Drawing upon Foucault's ideas of the technology of self, I have suggested that there are three main body practices through which women can talk about the subjective experiences of aging. These technologies are concerned with body surfacing, body shaping, and body well-being. The cultural practices associated with these technologies—insofar as they have emerged as practices within women's lives—are historically situated within the changing structures of status and power, of signification and meaning, and of economic wealth and resourcefulness of late modernity.

I have emphasized in particular the power of retail capital to commodify an ever-widening arena of personal and social life, the undermining (through science, technology, and progressive urbanization) of nature as a gendered, foundational ethic through which women traditionally have made sense and understood the limits of their lives, and the growing intragenerational heterogeneity in material, social, and cultural wealth and expenditure that has followed the collapse of modern class society.

Only within this historical, material, and political context can we properly examine and contextualize women's accounts of aging, drawing out from such subjective accounts both the heterogeneity of individual lives and the underlying structures through which postmodern culture extends its tributaries. Such an approach may provide a useful theoretical framework from which both quantitative and qualitative empirical studies can be undertaken within this emerging field of cultural gerontology.

NOTES

1. A point that has already been alluded to by Featherstone and Wernick when they wrote, "It is from the humanities then that we find attempts to grapple with the meaning of the aging process" (Featherstone & Wernick, 1995, p. 2).

2. Though not without considerable ambivalence, as Anne Basting has noted, writers such as Woodward are at pains to point out that "there can be no postmodern poetics of the aging body" (Basting, 1998, p. 144).

3. As outlined in Crook, Pakulski, & Waters (1992), especially pp. 133–134.

4. I do not mean that body technologies have created the discourse; rather, they serve as a focus for new and counter discourses concerning the actuality of aging.

5. See Daniel Levinson's two books, *The Seasons of a Man's Life* and *The Seasons of a Woman's Life*, or Gail Sheehy's *Passages* and *New Passages* (Levinson, 1978, 1997; Sheehy, 1986, 1996).

6. For a description of housing at the turn of the last century for England, see Rowntree (1902) and, for America, see R. S. Lynd and H. M. Lynd, *Middletown: A study in American culture* (New York: Harcourt, Brace, 1929). For a twentieth century overview, see A. Holmans, Housing, in A. H. Halsey (with J. Webb) (Ed.), *Twentieth Century British Social Trends* (London: Macmillan, 2000), especially p. 479; and T. Caplow, L. Hicks, and B. J. Wattenberg, *The First Measured Century* (Washington: AEI Press, 2000), especially p. 98.

7. Of course, many early narrative films had action scenes involving "whole bodies." These bodies were costumed characters, however, with the scene focusing upon the agency of the characters rather than the physical appearance of the actors' bodies as a property of the actors themselves.

8. See Caroline Cox's discussion of the role of 1920s and 1930s Hollywood stars in shaping hairstyles (Cox 1999).

9. Examples of the mockery of antiaging practices can be found in George Minois's accounts of sixteenth century attitudes toward old age. He cites Erasmus, who seems to have been particularly scathing of both men and women, the latter "forever smearing their face with make up and taking tweezers to their pubic hairs" while the former are "so eager to be young that one dyes his white hair, another covers up his baldness with a wig [and] another wears borrowed teeth taken from a pig perhaps" (Minois, 1989, pp. 256, 260).

10. See Cox, 1999, p. 97.

11. For example, it has recently been a front-page issue for the AARP's monthly magazine, *Modern Maturity* (March/April 2001).

12. For examples of photographic exhibitions, stage shows, and other modes of displaying the aging body, see Kathleen Woodward's book, *Figuring Age* (1999).

13. It is said that the Greeks introduced nudity into athletics in order to make sure no women were "surreptitiously" taking part.

14. A quotation by one of Laura Hurd's seniors in her article on older women's negotiation of aging illustrates this. "You wouldn't believe some of them in the changing room. Walking around naked with their ugly bodies. There's nothing I hate more than an ugly woman. Their big fat asses hanging out and their big fat stomachs hanging over. Egad. It's awful!" (Hurd, 1999, p. 432).

15. See, for example, descriptions given in Minois (1989).

16. Over 90 percent of every adult age group over 24 felt having good health was the most important thing in life. (Table 8.21 in Hansbro & Bridgwood, 1997).

17. Almost every self-help book promoting an anti aging lifestyle will incorporate at least one chapter on food and diet, making the obligatory reference to "antioxidants" and the life-elongating power of calorie restriction.

18. Furman, 2000, p. 15; Meyers, 2000, pp. 29–30.

19. See the editorial on ageism in the *Journal of the American Medical Association* (Wetle, 1987).

20. "Passing my reflection in a shop window I am taken by surprise at the sight of a striding woman with white hair: she is still wearing the bangs of her late youth, but there are shocking pockets and trenches in her face: she has a preposterous dewlap: she is no-one I can recognize" Cynthia Ozick, cited by Nancy Miller in her chapter "Marking Time" in Kathleen Woodward's book, *Figuring Age* (1999, p. 4).

21. The literature on social class and health in old age has been reviewed in our book, *Cultures of Ageing* (Gilleard & Higgs, 2000, pp. 155–160).

REFERENCES

Arber, S., & Ginn, J. (1991). *Gender and later life*. London: Sage Publications.

Armstrong, D. (1995). The rise of surveillance medicine. *Sociology of Health and Illness, 17*, 393–440.

Bartky, S. L. (1990). *Feminity and domination: Studies in the phenomenology of oppression*. New York: Routledge.

Basting, A. D. (1998). *The stages of age: Performing age in contemporary American culture*. Ann Arbor: University of Michigan Press.

Butler, J. (1990). *Gender trouble: Gender and the subversion of identity*. London: Routledge.

Caplow, T., Hicks, L., & Wattenberg, B. J. (2000). *The first measured century.* Washington: AEI Press.
Cox, C. (1999). *Good hair days.* London: Quartet Books.
Cristofovici, A. (1999) Touching surfaces: Photography, aging and an aesthetic of change. In K. Woodward (Ed.), *Figuring age: Women, bodies, generations* (pp. 268–296). Bloomington: University of Indiana Press.
Crook, S., Pakulski, J., & Waters, M. (1992). *Postmodernization: Changes in advanced society.* London: Sage Publications.
Department of Employment. (1998/1999 and earlier years). *Family spending* (Family Expenditure Survey). London: The Stationery Office (HMSO).
Dutton, K. R. (1995). *The perfectible body.* London: Cassell.
Featherstone, M., & Wernick, A. (1995). Introduction. In M. Featherstone & A. Wernick (Eds.), *Images of aging: Cultural representation of later life* (pp. 1–15). London: Routledge.
Foucault, M. (1988). Technologies of the self. In L. H. Martin, H. Gutman, & P. H. Hutton (Eds.), *Technologies of the self: A seminar with Michel Foucault* (pp. 16–49). London: Tavistock Publications.
Furman, F. K. (2000). There are no old Venuses: Older women's responses to their aging bodies. In M. U. Walker (Ed.), *Mother time: Women, aging and ethics* (pp. 7–22). Lanham, MD: Rowman and Littlefield Publishers.
Gannon, L. R. (1999). *Women and aging: Transcending the myths.* London: Routledge.
Gilleard, C., & Higgs, P. (2000). *Cultures of aging: Self, citizen and the body.* London: Prentice-Hall.
Gullette, M. M. (1997). *Declining to decline: Cultural combat and the politics of the midlife.* Charlottesville: University of Virginia Press.
Hansbro, J., & Bridgwood, A. (1997). *Health in England 1996: What people know, what people think, what people do.* London: The Stationery Office.
Holmans, A. (2000). Housing. In A. H. Halsey (with J. Webb) (Ed.), *Twentieth century British social trends* (pp. 469–510). London: Macmillan.
Hurd, L. C. (1999). "We're not old!": Older women's negotiation of aging and oldness. *Journal of Aging Studies, 13,* 419–439.
Levinson, D. (1978). *The seasons of a man's life.* New York: Knopf Publishers.
Levinson, D. (1997). *The seasons of a woman's life.* New York: Ballantine Books.
Lynd, R. S., & Lynd, H. M. (1929). *Middletown: A study in American culture.* New York: Harcourt, Brace.
Marshall, B. L. (1994). *Engendering modernity: Feminism, social theory and social change.* Cambridge, U.K.: Polity Press.
McMullin, J. (1995). Theorizing age and gender relations. In S. Arber & J. Ginn (Eds.), *Connecting gender and aging: A sociological approach* (p. 41). Buckingham, U.K.: Open University Press.
Meyers, D. T. (2000). *Miroir, memoire, mirage: Appearance, aging and women.* In M. U. Walker (Ed.), *Mother time: Women, aging and ethics* (pp. 23–44). Lanham, MD: Rowman and Littlefield Publishers.
Miller, N. (1999). Marking time. In K. Woodward (Ed.), *Figuring age: Women, bodies, generations.* Bloomington: University of Indiana Press.
Minois, G. (1989). *History of old age.* Cambridge, U.K.: Polity Press.
Modern Maturity. (2001). Cosmetic surgery report (March–April), pp. 60–69.
Modern Maturity. (2001). L'Oreal advertisement (January/February), pp. 1–2.
Rowntree, B. S. (1902). *Poverty: A study in town life.* London: Macmillan.
Sheehy, G. (1986). *Passages.* London: HarperCollins.
Sheehy, G. (1996). *New passages.* London: HarperCollins.

Smith, F. B. (1990). *The people's health.* London: Weidenfeld and Nicolson.
Sontag, S. (1979). *On photography.* Harmondsworth, U.K.: Penguin Books.
von Kondratowitz, H.-J. (1991). The medicalisation of old age: Continuity and change in Germany from the late eighteenth to the early twentieth century. In M. Pelling & R. M. Smith (Eds.), *Life, death and the elderly: Historical perspectives.* London: Routledge.
Wetle, T. (1987). Age as a risk factor for inadequate treatment. *Journal of the American Medical Association, 258,* 516.
Wolf, N. (1990). *The beauty myth.* London: Vintage.
Woodward, K. (Ed.). (1999). *Figuring age: Women, bodies, generations.* Bloomington: University of Indiana Press.

11

Body Memories of Aging Women

Marja Saarenheimo

INTRODUCTION

The body has never occupied a major position in gerontological study of autobiographical memory and reminiscence. At most, it has been considered as a topic of content in autobiographical talk or writing. In this chapter, my purpose is to problematize the relationship between body and memory, beyond reducing the body into a specific content of memory. I first focus on the concepts of memory and body and then illustrate the relationship between these concepts in empirical cases drawn from a study on conversational reminiscences of elderly Finnish people. The title of the chapter calls into question the body memories of aging women. The choice of women as subjects is not motivated by an especially gender-sensitive perspective. Rather, it is a practical choice that has to do with the empirical data from which I draw my examples.

In an article published in 1996, Peter Öberg argued that biographical narration as a rule tends to marginalize or even eliminate the bodily aspects of the self. The argument inspired me to take a closer look at my own biographical data involving old people. Going back to the data, I had to agree with Öberg, but only partly. True, there was not much actual talk about the body in the reminiscences of the elderly with whom I had worked. There were memories of illnesses, memories of war injuries, or memories of giving birth, but that was about all. As a topic of conversation, the body always seemed to be in a special state or in special circumstances. Still—the body was constantly there. Perhaps it was not reflected on or talked about, but the "absent body"—as Öberg called it—was constantly present in the conversations, not so much as an object of reminiscence talk, but as a central element of the reminiscing and talking subject.

PREVIOUS CONTEMPLATIONS ABOUT AUTOBIOGRAPHICAL MEMORIES AND THE BODY

In an article written in 1993, Kenneth and Mary Gergen compared memories and accounts of the body in autobiographies written by women and men (Gergen & Gergen, 1993). They analyzed a selection of autobiographies written by 16 famous men and women. According to the Gergens, men scarcely reminisced about their physical being or appearance as they had experienced it in their childhood, youth, or adulthood. For men, a well-functioning body appeared to be merely an instrument for achieving goals in their career. Only for the elderly men, with the appearance of signs of deterioration of the body, did "issues of embodiment [begin] to break through the seamless narrative of career advancement" (Gergen & Gergen, 1993, p. 209).

Women often described their bodily experiences from childhood and adolescence extensively and in a detailed manner in their autobiographies. For the female writers, a close relationship with the body seemed to be a rule and continued all the way from adolescence through the adult years into old age. The Gergens argued that women in general identify their bodies more closely with their selves than do men. The women's bodily relationships with other people can, according to them, be seen as some kind of extensions of the self. Violations of the body, for women, act as threats to their identity; but the sharing of bodily experiences with others strengthens their relationships with others. The Gergens suggested that the aging women continue to "live their bodies" in spite of the body's transformation (Gergen & Gergen, 1993, pp. 210–212).

In some instances, an aging person (be it a woman or a man) prefers to make a clear distinction between her or his body and mind. Statements such as "well, I surely would like to go around and travel a lot, but these feet of mine—they won't obey me" are familiar to most of us working with old people either in elderly care or as researchers. The citation is drawn from an interview with an 87-year-old woman in my own reminiscence study. She seemed to experience her body as a kind of stranger or even as an enemy to the self. Typically, in similar statements, the mind is given the status of the actual self, and the body is interpreted as a stranger one is obliged to live with.

Another common form of distancing the self from the body is expressed in statements like "in my mind I feel as young as I have always been even though my body is getting older." The experience of "an ageless self" has for some time fascinated gerontologists, beginning with Sharon Kaufman, who presented a theory of the continuity of identity in spite of the physical and social changes that come with old age (Kaufman, 1986, pp. 6–7). Kaufman's theory was based on biographical depth interviews with old people. Her intention was to let the old people's own voices be heard in the theorizing about old age. As a result, the statements of the interviewees were transformed into theoretical arguments in a rather straightforward manner. Kaufman did not reflect on the psychological and social functions of the separation between body and mind; neither did she consider the contexts of mind/body dualism in her elderly interviewees' stories.

Peter Öberg, among others, has strongly questioned the notion of an ageless self. He wonders how the self could possibly be ageless or unchangeable "despite the fact that old age like childhood is that period of life when the body changes the most" (Öberg, 1996, p. 702). Öberg argues that the myth of the ageless self is a relic of the Platonic-Christian dualism that gives the mind the status of the true person and the body the status of the mind's prison (Öberg, 1996, p. 702).

EMBODIED SELF, EMBODIED MEMORY

From what has been said earlier, it may be concluded that there are three principal ways or options for relating to the body in autobiographical accounts of elderly people: (1) identification with the body, as described in the Gergens' study of female autobiographers, (2) distancing the self from the body, as defined in the concept of an ageless self, and (3) marginalizing the body, as suggested by Öberg. I argue that these three options exist primarily in the sphere of social construction based on linguistic practices and that they all imply a basically dualistic assumption of an individual mind that is free to choose between different positions in relation to the body. If, however, we assumed that the body and the consciousness were tied together by necessity and had no choice either to keep together with each other or to deny the other, how would this alternative position change our actual empirical observations of autobiographical memories?

The neurologist Antonio Damasio has proposed a theory that connects physical bodily events and the primary emotions to the development of consciousness. In his recent book *The Feeling of What Happens* (2000), Damasio invites readers to contemplate the obvious fact that for each person there only exists one body. In our ordinary world, there does not exist a person without a body. Neither is there a person with two or more bodies. Perhaps we have heard of bodies that are occupied by several personalities. In psychiatry, this kind of experience is called a multiple personality or a dissociative personality disorder. But even the existence of this disorder does not violate the "one body/one person" principle, because at any certain moment only one personality is occupying the body and expressing itself through the body (Damasio, 2000).

The principle of one body/one mind implies that whatever happens in the mind always happens in time and space—more specifically, in relation to a certain moment and a certain part of space where the body happens to be. This situatedness in time and place is the origin for the perspective of an individual being—a perspective that is actualized, first, at the level of what Damasio calls the nuclear self and later in more complicated ways, at the level of what he calls the autobiographical self. The perspective of an individual being is constructed in constant interaction between messages from inside the body and messages from outside the body. This means, among other things, that a pure or objective observation is an impossibility. To be able to experience something, we need information from outside the body, but we also need information on what happens in our body. Only in the interaction between these two kinds of messages are the experiences created. The important thing is—as Damasio argues—that the same kind of process is involved not only when something actually happens to us, but also whenever we are thinking or remembering something. The reason for this, according to Damasio, is that the memory of a thing or an event contains not only the characteristics of the object or sequence of events remembered, but also the bodily emotions involved and the necessary adjustments of bodily movements that were performed during the original experience. It is out of these elements that memories are constructed and reconstructed.

The conception of memory presented by Damasio offers an interesting perspective on the question of the relationship between mind and body in autobiographical memories. From this perspective, the options previously mentioned are in fact mainly narrative options and do not, by any means, characterize the process of the autobiographical remembering. In the process of remembering, consciousness and body are tied together like Siamese twins. Memories as well as talking about memories are thoroughly embodied processes.

There are several common themes in Damasio's theory and in the notions of the French philosopher Maurice Merleau-Ponty (1992), who writes about the lived body as the center of action and the carrier of meanings. According to Merleau-Ponty, one's relationship to one's body is essentially different from all other relationships one might have. This follows partly from the fact that we can never observe our body in its totality. The body is always partially hidden, but it can never be totally absent. In the deepest sense of the word, the body is constantly present. For Merleau-Ponty, too, the body is an essential constituent of the consciousness. The interpretations we give to autobiographical experiences are not given from the standpoint of a freely moving mind, but always from the standpoint of a mind in a body. The mind in a body does not, however, enter the process of meaning construction in a direct manner. Instead, it observes the world through a kind of bodily preunderstanding, which means that the body always carries its own past to new situations.

Analyzing the bodily preunderstanding is difficult because it is not based on verbal and conceptual thinking. Psychoanalytic writers—for example, Levin (1991)—have described the early development of the self with the help of a mirror metaphor. They argue that a child originally recognizes herself or himself in the "gaze" (i.e., the overall feedback) of the parents or carers. Through this mirroring experience, the child joins together messages from inside her or his body and messages from outside and eventually develops a sense of a more-or-less coherent embodied self. Along the same line, it can be argued that intensive bodily changes, for example, in old age, always require a reevaluation of social relations and the self. When radical changes in the body take place, an elderly person is disposed to redefine her or his self by mirroring the "gazes" of other people. In this way, the embodied self is a thoroughly social category even at the preverbal level of meaning making.

SEARCHING FOR THE BODY IN AUTOBIOGRAPHICAL MEMORIES OF ELDERLY WOMEN

In the following, I illustrate interpreting autobiographical reminiscences of elderly women from the perspective of an embodied self (mind in a body), as defined earlier. The conversation extracts are taken from the reminiscence study I conducted a few years ago in Finland (Saarenheimo, 1997). The aim of the study was to explore reminiscence as a conversational and dialogical activity. The data consists of conversations of a group of four elderly men and a group of four elderly women. Both groups gathered together weekly for a period of ten weeks. The sessions took place in a club room of a service center for 1.5 hours at a time. The participants did not know each other prior to the group, although they all lived in the service center apartments. All the group members were first interviewed individually; as the group started, they were simply asked to discuss any memories or contemporary issues that interested them. The conversations were not structured in any way. Although I took part in the group sessions, I did not suggest any themes for discussion. My role was primarily that of a listener, but occasionally I took part in the conversations in a more active manner. All the conversations were tape-recorded and transcribed for interpretation.

In this chapter, my intention is to take a closer look at the women's conversations in order to "search for the body" in the verbal reminiscences. Earlier, I interpreted the same pieces of conversation with an aim of illustrating the variety and the use of different linguistic discoursive and dialogical practices in reconstructing the past to achieve a more satisfying identity (Saarenheimo, 1997).

The extracts presented here are taken from the first reminiscence session in a series of ten sessions. This particular conversation started with general comments about the "social climate" and family traditions of the historical period of the participants' childhood. One of the group members, Rakel (70), concluded:

> We belong to a generation who never received any kind of affection in our childhood. And that's why we ourselves have not been able to show any affection to our children. Because the truth is that if you have not received affection, you are not able to give any affection either.

She continued by sharing a painful experience from the time she was five or six years old:

> I have this memory from my childhood and it is a very bitter one. My father had died and so had the father of my cousin who was two years younger than me. And my mother brought her to our home, for some reason. And I remember that she was sitting on a rock and my mother went to her and put her arms around her shoulders and said "you poor orphan." And I waited for her to come to me, too, and put her arms around *me* and say "*you* poor orphan." Well, she didn't come and she didn't say or do anything.

Rakel presents a short chain of events as well as the concurrent contents of her mind as she recalls these events at the present moment.

It is rather interesting that in the actual story she does not explicitly refer to any emotions such as sorrow or disappointment. These are left to the listeners to infer from the plot and from the details of the narrative. The only explicit verbalization of an emotion is in the beginning of the narrative, where Rakel mentions the *bitter* tone of the memory. "Bitterness" may be thought to offer the listeners a key to the interpretation of the memory. Also, the statement about the *lack of affection* during her childhood and the consequent *inability to show affection* to others acts as an interpretative instruction for the other group members.

Strictly speaking, the actual plot of Rakel's memory consists of successive body positions and actions performed by the "characters" in the story, a meager dialogue, and an inner dialogue of the narrator herself. The cousin is sitting on a rock and Rakel's mother goes to her, puts her arms around her, and utters the words "you poor orphan." We can infer that Rakel herself is standing or sitting at a further distance. This is the only action described. Besides, there is an imaginary action and dialogue taking place in Rakel's mind—one with herself in the place of the cousin. It is probably the tension between the two inner dialogues that "explains" the bitter tone of the memory. Seeing her mother touch and talk to the cousin and the fact that the mother "didn't say or do anything" to Rakel constitute the nuclear contents of the memory. What especially interests us here is the central role of the body in the narrative. One might argue that the entire story is about a body longing to be touched.

Beside illustrating the body/mind relationship, the story also has an apparent cultural dimension. When constructing the meanings for past experiences, the speakers generally make use of existing cultural meaning systems and learned dialogical practices. Rakel's memory follows the structure of a well-formed narrative (see, e.g., Labov, 1972), representing a culturally relevant way of talking about personal experiences. The story has all the distinguishing marks of a "good story": an abstract or prologue, an orientation to the time, place, and characters, a coherent plot, and a coda or evaluative closing remarks that finish the story and place it into a proper moral context.

> So I think . . . I mean because I can still remember this moment so *clearly* even though I was only five or six at that time . . . I think it means that a child like me would have needed a little bit of affection. And so would my own children . . . they would also have needed more affection. But they didn't get it, because I was not able to give them any.

The closing remarks of Rakel's memory could be said to give an explanation and justification to her embodied experiences. The personal experience is placed in a collective context by using a generalized subject "a child like me" and a comparison to her own children. At the same time, the *body longing to be touched* is faded away and replaced by an abstract concept of *affection*.

EMOTIONAL BODY

The history of psychology has witnessed efforts to understand "bodies in action" without any reference to inner experiences and feelings. Perhaps one of the most interesting ones is found in the autobiography of B. F. Skinner. As an example, I quote his description of the end of a relationship with a woman called Neda. According to Skinner, they were having a dinner, when Neda told him that she was going back to her former fiancée.

> It was a reasonable decision, but it hit me very hard. As we walked back to her apartment from the subway, I found myself moving very slowly. It was not a pose; I simply could not move faster. For a week I was in almost physical pain, and one day I bent a wire in the shape of an N, heated it in a Bunsen burner, and branded my left arm. (Skinner, 1979, p. 137)

In his book *Life Histories and Psychobiography*, W. M. Runyan uses Skinner's extract to illustrate "that a behavioral approach to psychobiography is possible, although there may be disagreement about whether this approach illuminates or obscures our understanding of a life" (Runyan, 1982, p. 224). From the viewpoint adopted here, it is interesting how Skinner employs his body to convey his intentions to the readers. Inability to move faster, physical pain, and branding himself with an N-shaped burning hot wire may, for Skinner, represent "behavior," but for any psychologically-minded reader, those bodily states and actions taken toward the body most probably represent strong emotional experiences. In everyday speech, the body is frequently used to convey emotional meanings.

In narrative psychology, it is generally assumed that a central feature of personal narratives is their ability to express emotional experiences. I am arguing here that the power of autobiographical narratives lies not so much in *expressing* emotions as *inviting* or *arousing* emotions in the narrator as well as the audience. While, for example, Skinner may be telling a story of pure bodily states and actions, the reactions of the audience might still be of emotional quality.

We will now move on to consider the group members' reactions to Rakel's story. Anna is an 87-year-old group member who had warned me in the beginning of the group not to expect too much personal disclosure from her. She was especially reluctant to talk about her childhood and her marriage. After listening to Rakel's story, against her original intentions, Anna started to talk intensively about her childhood.

> Yes, that's like . . . *a little bit* like my . . . *exactly* like with me. That's right. My own mother never touched me. . . . I mean I am. . . . I'm not. . . . I don't remember that she *ever* touched me, even once she didn't touch me . . . not even once.

Here the object of remembering is not, as in Rakel's story, a specific event or chain of events. Rather, the object is absent; something that is *not remembered*. We do not know whether Rakel's story activates in Anna an actual memory of the lack of touch or rather an unsuccessful search for memories where her mother would have touched her. The result is, however, that Anna recognizes something familiar in Rakel's story and identifies herself with Rakel as a child who never received any affection from her mother. Anna's way of relating to her childhood experiences is, however, structurally very different from Rakel's. Hers is not a well-formed story, but rather an eruption with numerous repetitions, seemingly loose associations, and uncompleted sentences.

> I know what you mean, I know that if you have not received any kind of affection or love, you are not able to give it to others. . . . I mean I cannot give it to others. I have only one son and then I had a grandson living with me . . . but I'm not the kind of person. . . . I mean I have not been like that (affectionate). . . . but I'm not a *bad* person. I just don't understand. . . . I mean I believe many children, like my grandson . . . he would have needed more hugging and kissing and things like that. . . .
>
> . . . but I never learned (to show affection) . . . but still, I was not *bad*, that much I can say now. And I know that if one has never received affection one is not capable to give it to others.

The French psychoanalyst Julia Kristeva (1984, 1989) has written about the quality of body memories. According to Kristeva, body memories, unlike episodic or semantic memories, are in a way, closely comparable to the actual original experiences. Unlike autobiographical episodic memories, they are not reflected on, but rather lived again. They are not so much thought about as felt and experienced. According to Kristeva (1989), body memories are expressed as moods and affects, bodily emotions and sensations, and also through the paralinguistic elements of speech, such as the rhythmical, melodic, and poetical elements of speech. Because body memories are not so much remembered as relived, they can result in compulsive repetitions of earlier behavior.

According to Kristeva (1984), the linear conception of time fades away in body memories. The past and present melt into one. This is the difference between reflected memories and unreflected memories. Paul Ricoeur (1980) has argued that in episodic memories and especially in the memories organized through a narrative form, there are two opposite temporal movements involved. The story moves in a linear way from the beginning toward the end, but at the same time, the memory itself takes the present moment as its starting point, moving "backwards" (Ricoeur, 1980, p. 176). The sense of an ending characterizes the process of telling the story. In body memories, however, there is no such temporal tension.

In Anna's memory, we can see some of the elements mentioned by Kristeva. The memory narration is repetitive and rhythmical. There is no plot, no linear episodes, but only a repetitive, rhythmical movement. If Rakel's account is a well-formed story, Anna's account could be compared to a piece of poetry, where words and uncompleted sentences signal moods and emotions rather than refer to objects and events. Anna's way of talking is anxious and discontinuous. She talks for a long time and as if she were seeking appropriate expressions for her thoughts and feelings. Once in a while she seems to be reflecting on Rakel's statement about an inability to give affection as a result of her own childhood experiences, and these reflections are followed by a relieved statement: "I am not a bad person." This sentence is repeated in slightly different versions several times during her disclosure, like a kind of refrain in a piece of poetry. One could say that in these moments a conceptual organizing principle is starting to reconstruct Anna's memory. But the bodily elements are still present in a very powerful way. During her disclosure, Anna starts to feel a growing discomfort in her body, and consequently she starts to hyperventilate, which eventually leads to a dramatic situation and a consultation with a nurse.

CONCLUSIONS

In this chapter, my purpose was to conceptually and empirically problematize the relationship between body and memory. The aim was to get beyond the mind/body dualism and consider the autobiographical memory from the perspective of a mind that by necessity is situated in a body. I am using the concepts of "a mind in a body" or an "embodied self" to capture the necessary intertwinement of mind and body.

In analyzing autobiographical memories of elderly people from the perspective of an embodied self, there are, in my view, three separate but interrelated dimensions we should be aware of:

- The mind in the body (or the lived body)—the body as a source of individual perspective and experience.
- The expressive body—the body as a source of social and symbolical interaction.
- The socially constructed body—the meanings attached to the body and the actions upon the body.

Depending on the purpose of the study, it is possible to take one of these dimensions as the main focus of analysis, but in order to gain a fuller understanding of the role of the body in autobiographical memory, it is necessary, to some degree, to take them all into account.

A further aim of this chapter was to illustrate the "search for the body" in empirical data from a reminiscence study. The data in question did not include body as a prominent topic, except in the occasions involving memories of the war or of illnesses. The talk about everyday life events had, however, a strongly embodied nature, if interpreted through the small details of reminiscence conversations. The conversations contained frequent mentions of bodies in action, bodily states joined together with emotions, and paralinguistic elements of speech assumed to signal the body's involvement in memories. The body as a content theme may be marginalized in the autobiographical accounts of elderly people, but the central question is whether we are searching for the body in a relevant direction and using adequate methods.

REFERENCES

Damasio, Antonio. (2000). *The feeling of what happens: Body and emotion in the making of consciousness.* London: Vintage.
Gergen, Kenneth & Gergen, Mary. (1993). Narratives of the gendered body in popular autobiography. In R. Josselson & A. Lieblich (Eds), *The narrative study of lives.* Newbury Park, CA: Sage.
Kaufman, Sharon. (1986). *The ageless self: Sources of meaning in late life.* Madison: University of Wisconsin Press.
Kristeva, Julia. (1984). *Desire in language. A semiotic approach to literature and art.* Oxford: Basil Blackwell.
Kristeva, Julia. (1989). *Black sun: Depression and melancholia.* New York: Columbia University Press.
Labov, William. (1972). *Language in the inner city: Studies in the black English vernacular.* Philadelphia: University of Pennsylvania Press.
Levin, David. (1991). Visions of narcissism: Intersubjectivity and the reversals of reflection. In M. C. Dillon (Ed.), *Merleau-Ponty Vivant* (pp. 47–90). Albany: State University of New York Press.
Merleau-Ponty, Maurice. (1992) *Phenomenology of perception.* London: Routledge.
Öberg, Peter. (1996). The absent body: A social gerontological paradox. *Ageing and Society, 16,* 701–719.
Ricoeur, Paul. (1980). Narrative time. In W. J. T. Mitchell (Ed.), *On narrative.* Chicago: University of Chicago Press.

Runyan, William McKinley. (1982). *Life histories and psychobiography: Explorations in theory and method*. New York: Oxford University Press.

Saarenheimo, Marja. (1997). *Jos etsit kadonnutta aikaa: Vanhuus ja oman elämän muisteleminen*. Tampere, Finland: Vastapaino.

Skinner, B. F. (1979). *The shaping of a behaviorist*. New York: Knopf.

12

The Bodywork of Care

Julia Twigg

INTRODUCTION

The body lies at the heart of carework. *Carework* means working directly on the bodies of older and disabled people. Despite its centrality, such bodywork of care has received relatively little attention within social gerontology. It has largely been allowed to exist at a level below words—an aspect of the work and of the sector that has been passed over in silence within the academic literature, as it has been passed over in policy-oriented accounts also. In this chapter, I want to look at this territory of care, using features of the wider occupational category of "bodywork" to explore central dimensions of the activity.

BODYWORK AS AN OCCUPATIONAL CATEGORY

Bodywork is work that involves working directly on the bodies of others, who thus become the object of the workers' labor. Typically it involves touching, manipulating, and otherwise reviewing the bodies of others. Bodywork forms an element in the work of a wide range of occupational groups: doctors, nurses, physiotherapists, alternative medical practitioners, hairdressers, beauticians, masseurs, and sex workers. The contexts in which they practice and the meaning and status of their work is very varied. However, I have argued elsewhere (Twigg, 2000a) that certain commonalities can be traced across these occupations and that these relate to the bodywork element in their jobs.

In this earlier work, I suggested that bodywork was marked by features that meant that it was recurringly identified as ambivalent work. At times, it is work that verges on areas of the taboo in connection with sexuality or human waste. It is potentially demeaning work, and when undertaken by high-status individuals like doctors, it is typically accompanied by distancing techniques. There is a recurring dematerializing tendency whereby professional status is marked by distance from the bodily, so that as individuals or occupations rise up the ladder of professional status, they move further and further from direct bodywork. Yet at the same time, bodywork can be linked with pleasure and emotional intimacy. Therapies and techniques that rest on it—like massage, aromatherapy, and alternative medicine generally—aim to create a zone of physical well-being and comfort. Bodywork is also gendered work, differentially performed and to some extent received by women.

Last, issues of power and subordination are key. Subordination where it centers on the body takes on a particularly intimate and personal character. Who directs whom become all the more highly charged when the site of struggle is the body. It is because of this that the power dynamics of bodywork can tip either way—into the demeaned and subordinated territory of the sex worker, who performs bodywork at the command of the customer, or the dominant and controlling creator of "docile bodies."

EXPLORING CAREWORK

I want to explore how far and in what ways four of these features of bodywork relate to the character of carework. (In referring to carework, I should clarify that I am talking about work undertaken by paid workers and not by family members.) The features I am going to discuss are the work's

- ambivalent, potentially negative nature;
- body-pleasing, body-pampering character and its potential links to emotional closeness;
- potential as a form of Foucauldian biopower; and

- location on the borders of sexuality, with particular reference to issues around cross-gender tending.

The Bathing Study

The empirical aspects of this chapter derive from a study of the provision of bathing and washing for older and disabled people living at home, published as *Bathing: The Body and Community Care* (Twigg, 2000b). The study was based on qualitative interviews with 30 clients (or their carers, in three cases of dementia) and 38 careworkers and managers. It took place in two localities in England: one a deprived coastal resort, the other a wealthy inner-city borough. Bathing help was provided either by home care services (both local authority and independent sector) or in the London borough, in addition by a voluntary sector specialist bathing service.

THE NEGATIVITIES OF THE BODY

Carework is in its nature negative work, dealing as it does with what can be termed the "negativities of the body," those less attractive features of bodily life that are associated with sickness and old age—incontinence, vomit, sputum, dirt, and decay. These form a central part of the reality of the work. The negative nature of the work is further reinforced by the fact that careworkers deal with a social group—older people—who are themselves often perceived in negative terms. Woodward (1991) and others have argued that culture's response to the aged is marked by denial, fear, and repression, in which anxieties are projected on to the old, who thus come to embody the Other—becoming what Shakespeare (1994) in the context of attitudes to the disabled has termed "dustbins of disavowal." In this, they take on some of the features of Kristeva's Abject, whereby death and decay, like dirt, is feared and rejected, projected into a space of abjection (Kristeva, 1982). These feelings coalesce particularly strongly around the bodies of older people. Many older people internalize a sense of their bodies as no longer pleasant, things that might be distasteful to touch or look at. As one respondent in the bathing study said in relation to her youthful careworkers, "They're so young and beautiful, it must be awful for them to have to handle old, awkward bodies." Evidence from hospital studies support the view that nurses are less willing to touch the bodies of older patients (Montagu, 1986). One respondent in the study described this sense that her body was not something that some staff wanted to touch: "There are people who the old body makes uneasy. They have a sort of thing about touching.... It's in the air. Nobody would *dare* to say anything to you, but you can feel the [pause]—you feel it."

Lawton (1993) argues that modern society has become increasingly intolerant of the unbounded body of sickness and old age. Modern individualistic constructions of selfhood depend on the possession of a stable, bounded, and autonomous body: dirt, decay, incontinence, and smell undermine and disturb this construction, and those who exhibit such features, she argues, are increasingly sidelined and shunned. Öberg (1996) has similarly argued that modern society has become increasingly stringent in its expectations of the body, promoting an antiseptic ideal that is intolerant of bodily odors and secretions, a view endorsed by Classen and his colleagues (1994).

But the reality of carework is that it deals precisely with this unbounded body and with these areas of dirt and decay. This dirty character of the work affects its public status. Carework is in general lowly regarded work; as Bates (1993) and Skeggs (1997) show, among the training options offered to young women it is not highly favored. Careworkers are sometimes reticent about discussing what they actually do. As one worker in Lee-Treweek's study explained, her husband thought it was all about chatting to patients, whereas "he doesn't realise, it's all dirt" (Lee-Treweek, 1998, p. 53). As a result, though it is the bodywork element in the form of personal care that marks the job out as higher in status and pay than just being a cleaner—a status differential that careworkers were otherwise keen to emphasize—they did not foreground this aspect in their accounts of their work. Rather, they preferred to emphasize the "clean" interpersonal and emotional aspects of care, the etherialized, nonbodily elements of the work.

This devaluation of the bodily aspect of the work is part of a wider pattern of evasion and silence. Elias (1978) has argued that Western society since the Middle Ages is marked by a progressive internalization of restraint over the body and its expression, whereby large areas of physiological life are removed from conscious review. In polite terms, they are rendered beneath comment; to refer to them directly is to move into a world of conscious vulgarity, jokes, childishness, or intimacy. Bodywork takes place in areas of life that are now regarded as private. "Personal care" can indeed be defined in terms of those things in relation to the body that adults normally manage for themselves, usually alone. Indeed it is breaching those barriers that makes receiving personal care such a profoundly unwelcome step in the lives of most older people.

This sense of decorum extends to policy writing also. Despite the fact that personal care lies at the heart of long-term care and of the current attempts to maintain frail older people at home that are the aim of policy everywhere, there is remarkably little written on the topic; what there is tends to be abstract and evasive. It is hard to gain from it any real sense of what the work entails. There are parallels here in the treatment of bodywork in nursing. As Lawler (1991) notes, though bed and bodywork comprise the core of nursing practice, nursing texts have traditionally been reticent in their descriptions of it, treating it as "obvious" or in some sense beneath or beyond comment. As a result, she argues, this key element in nursing practice is rendered mute, unspeakable, which has serious consequences for our capacity to conceptualize nursing work—and indeed "care"—more widely. There is silence at the heart of it.

BODY PAMPERING

Bodywork is not necessarily and always negative work. As we have noted in relation to activities like aromatherapy and massage, it also encompasses body pleasing and pampering elements that aim to create a zone of well-being and enjoyment. Though activities like hairdressing are primarily aimed at improving appearance, they also encompass body-pampering, relaxing aspects; as Black and Sharma (2001) show, such elements of pleasure and indulgence are central to the appeal of beauty treatments. How far do such elements enter the world of carework?

In relation to the bathing study, there was evidence of ways in which care did provide forms of sensuous pleasure. Recipients of help described their enjoyment at receiving a bath: the warmth and lightness of the water, the foaminess of the gel. Mrs. Napier explained, "We have nice foamy shower gel, . . . it's lovely like being a baby again." Mrs. Fitzgerald called her bath "the rose of my week." One of the careworkers, describing how she poured water slowly over the client's body, explained: "Water is very very relaxing and it just feels nice, it's a nice sensation to have warm water running on you . . . relaxing and just, you feel good about yourself, feel better in yourself."

Such expressions of pleasure were most strongly associated with the voluntary-sector project that offered a dedicated bathing service, and they were less a feature of home care services where bathing, together with other aspects of personal care, was integrated into a general support service. Partly this was the result of more generous time allocation in the specialist service, which allowed for these body-pampering aspects, but it also reflected the values of the service with its emphasis on enjoyment and pleasure as well as the instrumental matter of getting clean. The voluntary-sector workers also believed that the specialist nature of their work—only providing help with bathing—meant that their relations with the clients were more intimate and warmer, getting away from any sense that the person who cleaned the floor had also come to clean you.

Though these body-pampering aspects were present in the bathing service, in the wider context of carework they are relatively rare. "Care," despite its name, largely adopts a fairly instrumental approach to the body that focuses on a narrow set of issues around physical functioning and hygiene. Indeed the very terminology of "personal hygiene" has a limited, antiseptic quality to it. Such discourses encourage a distant and objectifying approach that is far from body pleasing. A number of older people in the study recounted how their bodies had been pulled and pushed about, particularly in the hospital, and how they had learned to distance themselves from the experience and from their bodies. Furthermore, as a lot of body care turns around dealing with wastes, the experience is often accompanied by unease and embarrassment.

EMOTIONAL CLOSENESS

Work on the body is sometimes seen as creating a zone of emotional closeness. Certainly bodywork professionals like hairdressers and beauty therapists often describe this as part of their work, regarding the physical nature of their tending, particularly the use of touch, as creating a relationship of disclosure and personal warmth (Gimlin, 1996; Furman, 1997; Black & Sharma, 2001). Many alternative medical treatments such as reflexology, chiropractic, rolfing, and other gentler forms of laying on hands use touch in their treatments. Though their aims may be directly physical, the impact is also emotional and psychological, encouraging disclosure and the release of emotion.

Do similar dynamics operate in relation to carework? Does the physical nature of bodycare create a special closeness? Evidence from the bathing study was equivocal. Certainly some careworkers felt that the physical nature of care, particularly the close attention to the person required by help with mobility or the pleasure given in bathing, did create a special bond. But others were uncertain that the body focus as such was the root of this, emphasizing other factors like regularity of contact or their willingness to empathize and listen. Some indeed felt that the physical intimacy of bathing got in the way of the relationship. One careworker, Ros, believed that bathing produced a form of closeness, but not in her view a nice one. It was an enforced thing that went beyond the boundaries with which many people, including herself, felt happy. She interpreted the confidences of care not in terms of closeness but vulnerability. People in the bath are embarrassed, so that they blurt out secrets in an attempt to make up for their sense of unease.

> It's true that when somebody's in the bath, they tell you things that they probably wouldn't when you were having a cup of tea.... I think it's to do with their embarrassment ... if I was sitting in the bath and somebody

was talking to me that would probably be the time when I was feeling more vulnerable and so maybe I might say things that I wouldn't usually want to say.

Similar ambivalence was expressed by the clients. As Sharon, a younger respondent, when asked if the physical closeness of bathing made for a closer relationship with the worker, replied, "No, not really. No, in fact, probably the other way." Her mother, who also received help with bathing, added, "I think bathing is too *personal* to get friends.... Other ways, yeah, but not, not bathing."

Physical contact and especially nakedness are associated with intimacy from our earliest childhood experiences, played out in adulthood through sexual relations, where the physical closeness of sex underscores emotional closeness. But friendship by and large does not operate like this. Though there may be some easing up of bodily formality with growing friendship, there is not the same physical basis of intimacy. This means that the physical closeness of carework is to some degree experienced as discordant when seen in terms of friendship. There is a transgressive quality to its intimacy. Openly to acknowledge pleasure in such touch is to suggest an inappropriate sort of closeness. As a result, clients in general did not associate bodywork with emotional closeness, and indeed sometimes felt uneasy at the idea.

In general, therefore, what people appeared to want in a bathing relationship was a form of intimacy, but one that was bounded in its nature. The closeness of bathing is not the same as the closeness of other forms of friendship; indeed, the two are to a large extent at odds, as the comments of Sharon and her mother show. Personal care is by its nature discordant. It sets up a series of dissonances around closeness, intimacy, distance, boundaries, and roles, and these are played out in the care encounter.

CAREWORK AS THE EXPRESSION OF BIOPOWER

The work of Foucault (1973, 1977) has alerted us to the ways in which power is exercised at the micro level, on and through the bodies of individuals. For Foucault such power has a special name: *biopower*. From the organization of space through architectural forms like the asylum, the penitentiary, and the school through the imposition of modes of bodily comportment in education or military life or in the regime of the clinic to the temporal ordering of the body by means of timetables, bells, and regimes of eating, drinking, and sleeping, the body is surrounded by techniques and technologies of power that serve to monitor, fabricate, constitute, and analyze it. Through the operation of the professional gaze, bodies are made subject to regimes of power/knowledge in which they are rendered knowable, subordinate, and docile. Foucault focused on the fields of medicine, penology, and sexuality, and he did not directly address questions of old age. His work has, however, been extended by Katz and others to encompass the constitution of old age through systems of gerontological knowledge, the operation of institutional and community care policies and the role of social workers and other practitioners in managing and controlling old age (Katz, 1996; Tulle-Winton, 2000). The bodywork element in care needs to be seen in this wider context. Bodywork involves monitoring, surveying, controlling, and disciplining bodies (though also, as we have noted, pleasing and caring for them). There are certain aspects of carework that makes it especially prone to the exercise of such biopower.

First, carework involves nakedness, in a context that is asymmetrical. The client is exposed and subordinated, while the worker is fully clothed and dominant. This creates an asymmetrical relationship of power, one that finds echoes in other practices. Denying prisoners their clothes, interrogating suspects naked, and exposing people's bodily needs to view in a humiliating fashion are common techniques used to subdue and control people, creating a climate of compliance. There are obvious parallels between these situations and that of carework, though the aims and contexts are, of course, different. What this means is that conscious effort needs to be taken to counteract the symbolism and to enact a different social reality in which power relations are not enforced through such bodily practices. Sometimes, however, carework is indeed about domination and compliance; workers may seek to subdue and control clients through such techniques in the interests of getting the job done.

The second theme relates to the use of water. My study of personal care focused on issues around washing and bathing. Water and the imposition of water have long historical links with cultures of coercion. For example, water has been used since the eighteenth century to subdue and control patients in mental institutions through the use of shock immersions, cold-water packing, hosing down, and compulsory baths. These treatments have their own rationales rooted in the principles of hydrotherapy or in ideas of shocking the patient back into reason. But behind them also lies a harsher, more sadistic strand, in which the bodies of patients are disciplined, subdued, controlled, and made subject to the regime of the institution. Something of this remains—in potential at least—in any context where people are taken and *bathed*, in other words, where something is *done to them* and to their bodies.

The process of domination is all the stronger where the control of the body is mediated by machinery. This imposes a further stage of objectification, in which the bodies of individuals are caged, trapped, and made subject to the control of the machine. Community care does not normally deal in such matters, but help with bathing does sometimes involve hoists that raise and lower, straps that tie the limbs, and special baths that have an alienating, technological feel. One respondent's account of being washed down at a day center contained something of this, as she described her unease lying naked on the plastic tray while the hose was moved up and down her body. In other cases, the sense of alienation and objectification was produced not by machinery but by uniforms and gloves. One careworker described the look of panic and fear that came into the face of a client when she and a colleague entered her room wearing strange overalls and pulling on rubber gloves. Such images evoke a visceral sense of fear.

Third, carework involves regimes of control over intimate and personal aspects of life that are normally treated as private. It is part of the nature of biopower that it takes over and regulates the bodies of persons, making them subject to regimes of control in which they are required to get up and dressed, move about, eat, wash, and excrete according to timetables or at the prompting of bells and other signals of authority. Indeed, it is one of the marks of a totalitarian institution that it takes over and controls all aspects of bodily life, driving its authority deep into the physiological existence of the individual. Once again, carework contains something of this. Clients or residents, particularly in institutions, are got up, dressed, and fed at set hours, often artificially early and certainly not at the prompting of their own wishes. They are toileted according to a set timetable rather than at will as in normal circumstances. Their bodily functions are monitored, so that aspects of life that are normally personal and private become publicly noted, recorded in documents and open to review.

Lee-Treweek's analysis of life in a residential home provides a particularly good account of the exercise of biopower in the work of care assistants (Lee-Treweek, 1994,1998). She describes how workers struggle to establish control over the objects of their labor in the form of the bodies and persons of residents. In a context of harsh time constraints, this means organizing, ordering, and disciplining the bodies of residents, containing disruption and mess whether in the form of dirty substances or awkward emotions. In the back bedrooms of the institution, the careworkers labor to produce the end product of the home in the form of what she terms the "lounge standard resident." It is routinized work, based on a production-line approach rather than on a personal response to the individual, in which acts are performed on objects in the quickest, most efficient, and thus most distant way.

Lee-Treweek's account is a harsh one, and it is pertinent to ask how far the exercise of such biopower is characteristic of carework in general. The evidence from my own study of home care workers suggests that while such dynamics are indeed recurringly present, they are not always dominant. They are part of the implicit logic of the situation, but the degree to which they are enacted varies considerably. In particular, careworkers in the study in dealing with the bodies of clients were constrained by the internalization of an ethic of care. This meant that they consciously attempted to mitigate some of the dynamics of biopower, trying as far as they could within time constraints to make space for the client's self-determination, holding back from taking over the situation and of hurrying them. They tried consciously to reduce the element of embarrassment that arose from physical exposure or from bodily mess, averting gaze, avoiding direct language, making jokes, or otherwise distracting the attention of the client. In all this, they responded to the client as a person, not a thing. Their responses were not always perfect, as some critical comments from recipients showed, but they were very far from the cold exercise of biopower described in some of the accounts of institutional life.

My study was of home care, and it is worth asking at this point if there are features of such provision that act differentially to produce this response. Here the setting was clearly significant. Home is space that belongs to the client, whereas the space of institutions belongs to the staff. Home is embued with an ideology of privacy, ownership, and security that is widely endorsed within Western society, so that workers in entering it have in some degree to ask permission and to act on sufferance (Allan & Crow, 1989; Gurney & Means, 1993). Clients in their own homes are on their own territory, which endows them with a form of power that they can to some extent use to resist the domination of workers. It is easier, for example, to say "no" to certain procedures in your own home than on a ward or in an institution.

The second feature of home-based care that militates against the operation of biopower is the fact that it is time-limited in nature. Staff come into the home, engage with the client, perform certain acts, and then leave. As a result they—unlike workers in institutions—are not required to spend hour after hour, day after day in the company of clients who may be confused, boring, or dislikable. There is not the same unremitting exposure. It is easier to relate directly to the client when you know that you will soon escape. Distant, cold, objectifying relationships are most characteristic of situations where workers cannot get away from the client and respond instead by removing themselves psychically in other ways.

Home-based care is also typically performed alone, which supports the development of a one-to-one relationship with the client. In home care, there are no rival attractions from the work group to distract the workers and engage their conversational attention. As a result, personal engagement with the client is common, again reducing the tendency to adopt distancing and objectifying practices.

I should add a note of caution here. My study was based on interviews, which meant that I had to rely on workers' own accounts of their activities, though analyzed in conjunction with those of the recipients. I did not observe practice directly. It may be that the best accounts of the operation of biopower are indeed observational. Much of the impact of Lee-Treweek's account comes from the fact that it is based on participant observation. Such an approach does not rely on accounts of a "caring" workforce that may be self-serving. There is also something about the operation of biopower that is perhaps best captured through observation. Its dynamics work through actions—through stance, gaze, manner—as much as words, which may make it difficult for participants, whether workers or recipients, to articulate its presence fully or openly. Its operation may also be shameful.

There is certainly a need to be cautious in presenting too rosy a picture of home-based care. Home is by its nature hidden from view, and work on domestic violence and other forms of abuse has alerted us to the dangers of assuming that the private sphere is necessarily one of security. Having acknowledged this, however, I would still argue that home-based care contains certain key features that underwrite the autonomy of recipients and that militate against the oppressive exercise of biopower.

ON THE BORDERS OF SEXUALITY

Bodywork is work on the borders of sexuality. Part of the ambiguity of the work comes from the ways in which it transgresses the territory of sex, involving as it does direct physical contact, sometimes in the context of nakedness and physical and psychic closeness. Activities like massage, which belong within the category of bodywork, have traditionally had an ambiguous meaning in Western culture; "legitimate" practitioners in the area have to work to clarify and bracket off these aspects. Such boundary marking is characteristic of a number of bodywork trades. It is clearest to see within medicine, where bodily stance, eye contact, and the deployment of screens and white coats are used as techniques to reorder the potentially sexual meaning of certain activities. The internal examination provides a classic account of these means whereby the sexual connotations of the procedure are symbolically and interactionally overridden. The history of nursing contains similar tensions around the meaning of the work and of the access to the body by nurses (Lawler, 1991; Bashford, 2000); the unstable character of the resolution achieved is carried forward in the fantasy status accorded nurses.

Carework also occurs on the borders of sexuality, and dealing with unwanted sexual advances is one of the minor tasks of carework. For example, sometimes male clients tried it on, as one careworker recounted:

> He was always trying to get us to wash his private parts . . . and I think I did it the first time cos I was quite new, and [the manager] said to me, you never have to do that really. . . . He could do it, and I realised this when he turned the shower on. I thought, if he can do that, then he can do it. He's just trying it on.

Like other forms of sexual harassment, the exact significance of such exchanges lies in their fine grain, and comments that from one person were just part of a flirty, joking relationship could be unpleasant or threatening from another. By and large the careworkers took sexual incidents in their stride.

> "It's just a bit of fun." "We can handle them, can't we?" "We need longer skirts" (laughter). "Cheeky—they just like to egg you on."

Occasionally the experiences were more directly unpleasant; this was usually where the workers felt threatened or where there was an element of nastiness in the comments or actions. Ultimately, however, workers in the study knew that they were safe, in that they were dealing in the main with frail and elderly clients who could offer only a limited sexual threat. As one manager remarked in this context, "They're only old. It doesn't matter." The sexual meaning of the situation was seen as rather different, however, in the small number of cases where the careworker was a man, which leads us to the last theme in relation to bodywork, its gendered character.

CROSS-GENDER TENDING AND THE GENDERED CHARACTER OF CAREWORK

As in so many areas relating to sex and gender, the rules governing cross-gender tending operate asymmetrically, so that the meaning of a man giving intimate care to a woman is different from that of a woman doing the same for a man. There are a number of elements in this: the assumed nature of male sexuality, the differential treatment of male and female bodies, the links between women and motherhood, the presentation of women within culture as inherently more bodily, and the employment status of bodywork.

The great majority of careworkers are female, as indeed are clients. This means that the care system naturally delivers to agencies a pattern of supply and demand that is in accord with the dominant assumptions held by both clients and staff as to what is appropriate. As a result, the norms that govern the area remain largely unarticulated, and the issue rarely emerged directly to view. It was clear, however, that there was a widely shared set of ideas about what was appropriate. Cross-gender tending by women for male clients was regarded as unproblematic except, as we have noted, in those few cases where female careworkers faced sexual expression that was unpleasant or threatening. In these cases, the work was typically transferred to a male worker. Women caring for women was also seen as unproblematic and was regarded as raising no issues of sexuality (interestingly, the only respondent who did question this assumption, in potential at least, was a careworker who had completed a social science degree). Males caring for males was also regarded as acceptable, at least by the agencies. Some of the male clients were less happy with the idea and preferred a woman. This was for a complex of reasons. Many men were accustomed to being cared for by wives, as they had earlier been by mothers, and female careworkers were a natural continuation of that. But there was in addition a sense of unease concerning the potentially homosexual nature of the encounter, an idea reinforced by a belief that carework was not proper work for a man.

The one area of cross-gender tending that was perceived universally as potentially problematic was the situation of male workers giving intimate care to women. This was regarded as breaching a taboo, and in general, it did not happen. Indeed, some agencies had policies forbidding it. Within residential homes and other institutional settings, such cross-gender care does sometimes take place. One male careworker explained that he had done such work in residential homes, but that this was not permitted in home care; he was aware how "accusations can fly, not from my part, but from the woman's side." It is clear that setting was significant here. A male careworker going into a female client's home was perceived as problematic. This was partly because the interchange would be more hidden than in an institutional setting, but it also reflected deeply felt ideas about intimacy and space in relation to the home.

A number of interrelated elements support this asymmetrical pattern of response. The first lies in traditional assumptions about the nature of male sexuality. Hegemonic masculinity constructs men as sexually predatory (Connell, 1995), and limits are thus placed on the free access of men to bodies, female but also to some degree male. The recent discovery of the extent of abuse in children's homes and other institutions has reinforced this traditional account, at a time when masculinity might otherwise be seen to be changing. As a result, agencies are cautious in using male workers in intimate settings; their practice is correspondingly circumscribed.

The second factor concerns the differential treatment of men's and women's bodies within the culture generally. Although there is considerable historical and cultural variance in this, certain patterns do recur. Women's bodies have traditionally been prime sites for the exercise of patriarchy, and visual and physical access to them is often controlled and limited. The rules of modesty operate differentially as between men and women, with women's bodies traditionally more shrouded, hidden from the male phallic gaze. This asymmetry has consequences for how recipients of care view cross-gender tending.

When asked, most female respondents were clear that they did not want a male careworker, and some felt this strongly. Mrs. Bucknell responded, "Oh, no. I wouldn't have a man. No, thank you!" It is important not to assume that current modesty was necessarily a product of prudishness in the past. As Mrs. Elster explained, "I've lost most of my modesty, but I don't like the idea of a man seeing me naked. I'm of the old school. I wasn't a prude. In fact I liked fun and games in my time, but not now, no."

For male clients, however, the meaning was different. They saw help from a woman as a normal part of gendered expectations. For men, being seen and touched by a woman was potentially nice and carried no sense of threat; they often presented it in a slightly flirty, nice-for-me, sort of way. As one manager explained,

> a lot of the men quite enjoy having a woman. And honestly I think, you know, specially a nice young girl come to help them have a bath, they like it. You know, not in any sort of perverted way, just, just in a, you know, they like the attention.

Mr. Wagstaffe, a client, concurred with this sentiment.

Interviewer: Did you find it embarrassing at first or . . .?
Mr. Wagstaffe: Well, not really. I thought it might be more embarrassing for *them* than for me, but they don't seem to mind a bit.
Interviewer: Why did you think it would be more embarrassing for them?
Mr. Wagstaffe: Well, the first girl I had, she was only about eighteen, I think. She was a sort of punk, she'd got bright red hair and earrings in her eyebrows. Sort of girl that a person of my age looks at and thinks Gawd Almighty. But she was absolutely sweet, she was a lovely girl. It turns out that they nearly all live with their boyfriends or something, so I don't bother about it now.

So his response was rooted not in a sense of personal exposure, but in a slightly chivalrous responsibility for the modesty of young women.

Though, as he himself added, "Young ladies in their early twenties these days are rather different from when I was the same age."

The gendered pattern of carework is also a product of the association of women with motherhood and therefore with intimate body care generally. What women traditionally do for babies and children, they continue to do for adults within the family or by extension in employment through occupations like nursing that have their roots historically in home-based body care (Reverby, 1987). As we have noted, for many male clients, being helped by a woman was part of normal gender expectations.

The pattern also has its roots in a wider set of cultural assumptions that present men and women within an asymmetrically valued set of dichotomies in which women are associated with the body, emotion, and the private sphere, while men are associated with mind, rationality, and the public world (Brook, 1999). These dichotomies are used to explain how bodywork is work that belongs "naturally" to women.

Last, the gendered pattern of bodywork is also rooted in questions of status. Bodywork is in general low-status work, and we have noted the recurring dematerializing tendency whereby status within the organizational hierarchy is marked by distance from the body. This is all the more marked where the work involves dealing with more taboo or less attractive aspects of the body such as body wastes. Women are assumed to be "better" at this sort of thing. Ungerson (1983) has suggested that this is because they are perceived to be already polluted and therefore more appropriate to deal with polluting mess. But more persuasive is the idea that such work is generally disliked and demeaned, but that male workers are more successful in avoiding it. Nursing, Williams (1989) argues in her study of nonstandard gender occupations, is work that is deemed below or demeaning for men, and this aspect is closely linked to its bodily character, particularly the bedpan and feces-cleaning aspects. As a result, men within nursing are encouraged and enabled to take the route out of such activity, up the ladder of managerial advance. The glass escalator takes them up and away.

CONCLUSION

In this chapter, I have argued that carework needs to be seen in the wider context of work on the body. Doing this enables us to bring into focus aspects of the work that have traditionally been passed over and obscured. Carework is in many ways "dirty work," and this fact needs to be acknowledged and explored if the status and tensions of the work are to be properly understood. Careworkers deal with aspects of life that society—particularly modern, secular, youth-oriented society—

does not want to dwell upon: death, decay, physical failure, and decline. In coping with them, in tidying them away in private homes or institutions, they help to enable wider society to ignore these disturbing features of life. But in doing so, their own work becomes obscured, hidden from view, rendered unutterable.

Acknowledging and recognizing the centrality of the body also enables us to counteract what can sometimes be an over-etherialized account of "care." This derives in part from current political and philosophical debates concerning an "ethic of care" that place care in a context of wider abstract discourse (Larabee, 1993; Tronto, 1993), but is endorsed also by the more general dematerializing tendency in which bodily life is downplayed and de-emphasized. As a result, workers also prefer to emphasize the emotional and interpersonal elements in their work, rather than the physical and bodily.

REFERENCES

Allan, G., & Crow, G. (Eds.). (1989). *Home and family: Creating the domestic sphere*. London: Macmillan.
Bashford, A. (2000). *Purity and pollution: Gender, embodiment and Victorian medicine*. Basingstoke, U.K.: Macmillan.
Bates, I. (1993). A job which is "right for me"?: Social class, gender and individualisation. In I. Bates & G. Riseborough (Eds.), *Youth and inequality*. Buckingham, U.K.: Open University Press.
Black, P., & Sharma, U. (2001). Men are real, women are made up. *Sociological Review,* 49(1) 100–116.
Brook, B. (1999). *Feminist perspectives on the body*. London: Longman.
Classen, C., Howes, D., & Synott, A. (1994). *Aroma: The cultural history of smell*. London: Routledge.
Connell, R. W. (1995). *Masculinities*. Cambridge, U.K.: Polity.
Elias, N. (1978). *The civilizing process: The history of manners*. Oxford, U.K.: Blackwell.
Foucault, M. (1973). *The birth of the clinic: An archaeology of medical perception*. London: Tavistock.
Foucault, M. (1977). *Discipline and punish: The birth of the prison*. Harmondsworth, U.K.: Allen Lane.
Furman, F. K. (1997). *Facing the mirror: Older women and beauty shop culture*. New York: Routledge.
Gimlin, D. (1996). Pamela's place: Power and negotiation in the hair salon. *Gender and Society,* 10(5), 505–526.
Gurney, C. M., & Means, R. (1993). The meaning of home in later life. In S. Arber & M. Evandriou (Eds.), *Ageing, independence and the life course*. London: Jessica Kingsley.
Katz, S. (1996). *Disciplining old age: The formation of gerontological knowledge*. Charlottesville: University Press of Virginia.
Kristeva, J. (1982). *Powers of horror: An essay on abjection* (L. S. Roudiez, trans.). New York: Columbia University Press.
Larabee, M. J. (Ed) (1993). *An ethic of care: Feminist and interdisciplinary perspectives*. London: Routledge.

Lawler, J. (1991). *Behind the screens: Nursing, somology and the problem of the body.* Melbourne: Churchill Livingstone.

Lawton, J. (1998). Contemporary hospice care: The sequestration of the unbounded body and "dirty dying." *Sociology of Health and Illness, 20*(2), 121–143.

Lee-Treweek, G. (1994). Bedroom abuse: The hidden work in a nursing home. *Generations Review, 4*(1), 2–4.

Lee-Treweek, G. (1998). Women, resistance and care: An ethnographic study of nursing auxiliary work. *Work, Employment and Society, 11*(1), 47–63.

Montagu, A. (1986). *Touching: The human significance of skin* (3rd ed.). New York: Harper and Row.

Öberg, P. (1996). The absent body: A social gerontological paradox. *Ageing and Society, 16*(6), 701–719.

Reverby, S. M. (1987). *Ordered to care: The dilemma of American nursing, 1850–1945.* Cambridge, U.K.: Cambridge University Press.

Shakespeare, T. (1994). Cultural representations of disabled people: Dustbins for disavowal. *Disability and Society, 9*(3), 283–299.

Skeggs, B. (1997). *Formations of class and gender: Becoming respectable.* London: Sage.

Tronto, J. C. (1993). *Moral boundaries: A political argument for an ethic of care.* London: Routledge.

Tulle-Winton, E. (2000). Old bodies. In P. Hancock, B. Hughes, E. Jagger, K. Paterson, R. Russell, E. Tulle-Winton, & M. Tyler (Eds.), *The body, culture and society.* Buckingham, U.K.: Open University.

Twigg, J. (2000a). Carework as a form of bodywork. *Ageing and Society, 20,* 389–411.

Twigg, J. (2000b). *Bathing: The body and community care.* London: Routledge.

Ungerson, C. (1983). Women and caring: Skills, tasks and taboos. In E. Gamarnikow, D. Morgan, J. Purvis, & D. Taylorson (Eds.), *The public and the private.* London: Heinemann.

van der Riet, P. (1997). The body, the person, technologies and nursing. In J. Lawler (Ed.), *The body in nursing.* Melbourne: Churchill Livingstone.

Williams, C. L. (1989). *Gender differences at work: Women and men in nontraditional occupations.* Berkeley: University of California Press.

Woodward, K. (1991). *Aging and its discontents: Freud and other fictions.* Bloomington: Indiana University Press.

13

Going Concerns and Their Bodies

Jaber F. Gubrium and James A. Holstein

INTRODUCTION

Over the past half century, social life has entered the purview of countless social institutions. These institutions comprise discursive environments that provide the interactional resources and opportunities for assembling, altering, and sustaining our selves and identities (Gubrium & Holstein, 2001; Holstein & Gubrium, 2000b). From cradle to grave, schools, correctional facilities, clinics, family courts, support groups, recovery fellowships, and nursing homes, among myriad other institutions, promote particular representations of our inner lives, of who and what we are as individuals. They furnish discourses of subjectivity that are accountably put into practice in the everyday give-and-take of institutional life.

Years ago, sociologist Everett Hughes (1984) coined a useful term for characterizing social institutions. He called them "going concerns." It was his way of capturing the sense in which concerted patterns of interaction were an ongoing, practical matter. For Hughes, going concerns could be as massive and formally structured as government bureaucracies or as modest and loosely organized as a group of friends who get together on Thursday nights to play bridge. Large or small, formal or informal, each represents a continuing commitment to a particular moral order. Each supplies a way of being and conveying who and what we are in relation to the immediate scheme of things. Hughes, of course, was careful not to reify going concerns. He did not view them as static social entities. Rather, he oriented to them as sustained patterns of practical action. For Hughes, there was as much "going" in social institutions as there were "concerns."

The construction of personal selves and identities involves complex interpretive work (see Holstein & Gubrium, 2000b). While our inner lives are inextricably linked to the social circumstances of their production, there are not simple formulas for self-construction. Institutions do not supply complete blueprints for identity, even if they do outline the "conditions of possibility" (Foucault, 1977, 1978) for "institutional selves" (Gubrium & Holstein, 2001). The possible dimensions of our inner lives are nearly limitless, running the gamut from mind to motives, from emotions to attitudes and opinions (Holstein & Gubrium, 2003). Even the physical body figures into their production as the virtual "object" that contains the essence of our being.

Self-construction is typically "embodied." That is, the self and other aspects of inner life are articulated with, tied to, or read from facets of the physical body. The body thus becomes a substantive site of self-realization. In this context, "embodiment" connotes personification. In practice, the body is thus designated as the visible, material manifestation of qualities that are believed to lie within. It provides tangible evidence of invisible interior regions and entities such as the psyche, personality, self-esteem, passion, mental competence, or cognitive impairment, among other personal characteristics.

Bodily features literally objectify inner life when we say things like "he's really got a big head" to signal a person's egoism or she "an empty shell" to designate a sufferer of Alzheimer's disease. From the currently popular interest in body language and tattooing to the well-known connotations of assertive posture and direct eye contact, the body is an omnipresent material mediator of who we are or hope to be. It is a ubiquitous interpretive concern of institutions across the life course.

Since the 1980s, there has been a rush of interest in embodiment, centered especially on the material body. Approaching the body as a social project has swept away the old body-mind duality, situating both body and mind in the interpretive practices by which meaning is assigned to experience. Body and mind are reflexively related surfaces for signifying identity (Elias, 1991; Bourdieu, 1984, 1985; Foucault, 1977, 1978; Garfinkel, 1967; Giddens, 1984, 1991; Turner, 1984, 1992). Images of one inform images of the other, so that one cannot be constituted without reference to the other. A leading sociological question has emerged: How does the body as a material presence serve as surface and resource for the narrative construction of subjectivity?

In this context, institutional understandings of the body are of paramount significance. Different institutions, as we will illustrate, increasingly locate and specify what the body is, was, and could possibly be in highly distinctive ways. The meaning of the body is thus "institutionalized" in the sense that it is subject to institutional mediation. Perhaps more than anyone, Michel Foucault (1977, 1978) drew attention to the way specific discourses associated with the emergence of distinct institutions construct the body and the subject. Citing examples of the modern prison and the medical clinic, Foucault examined conditions and vocabularies for constructing the body in particular ways. Because Foucault worked in a historical register, he understandably had little access to the immediate discursive practices of bodily construction, especially the actual talk and interaction involved. His analyses tended to totalize the ways in which the body might be institutionally constructed. But when we turn to the interactional sites where the body is discursively constituted and used, we see that its articulations are far more "artful" (Garfinkel, 1967) than Foucault often conveyed. Indeed, close examination of the discursive production of the body reveals that its physical presence in our lives is distinctly interactional (Atkinson, 1995; Gubrium & Holstein, 1999).

In our view, the sociological question of how the body is implicated in the construction of inner lives can no longer be answered separately from considering the institutional contexts in which the body becomes relevant. This underscores the importance of the relation between going concerns and their bodies. If we are to understand the meaning of the body in today's world, we cannot simply limit our attention to individual understandings or to situational constructions. We must consider the many and varied institutional environments in which bodies are viewed, assigned meaning, and realized as objects of subjectivity. Carefully attending to the social interaction and discourse of these settings reveals both the variety of embodiments we could or could not be, as well as the everyday discursive practices by which identities are attached to the bodies in question.

Today's range of going concerns for bodily construction was unheard of a century ago. Our forebears were likely to have embodied themselves in relation to localized spiritual and familial contexts. They simply did not encounter and bring their bodies into the presence of the profusion of institutional offerings and interpretive demands that now confront us. Our lives and bodies are now spread across the myriad sites that call for distinctive kinds of bodily production. The social world has become a virtual embodiment enterprise.

This enterprise cuts across the life course. In the following sections, we will illustrate how the body is used to signify the interpretive concerns of manifold and diverse institutions. We will stress how the construction of the body varies across institutions and over time. In our view, the specific categories used to characterize our bodies through time reflect the interpretive orientations, goals, and contingencies of the going concerns we encounter as we grow up and grow old. While we may apprehend many ways of conveying and construing our physical appearances, gestures, and comportment, institutions increasingly inform us of how to select from and apply what we know.

The life course is itself a social construction, shaped by institutions that construct the body and the self in specific relation to time (Holstein & Gubrium, 2000a). Some specialize in early life; some specialize in adulthood. More than ever, there is a proliferation of going concerns focused on later life. Across the life course, our sense of our bodies and our selves through time are institutionally articulated, grounded in the diverse going concerns in which the body and the self and their changes are now being addressed (Holstein & Gubrium, 2000b).

This is not to say that institutions dictate embodiment. Today's going concerns provide distinctive discourses and structures of normative accountability to which participants orient as they view and apprise their own and others' bodies. But participants also bring biographical particulars to the project. What bodies mean within the context of a going concern is certainly guided by institutional imperatives. But the actual everyday process of interpretation and the resulting material realizations of who and what we are are subject to the ongoing practical contingencies of interpretive practice. Both the interactional artfulness and the institutional bases for interpreting the body across the life course are apparent in the following illustrations.

THE CHILD'S SIGNIFYING BODY AT SCHOOL

Consider how the body is used to signify the individual subject and his or her inner life in the context of an educational institution. Cedarview is a residential treatment center for emotionally disturbed children (Buckholdt & Gubrium, 1985). It is privately operated under contract with local public schools and county welfare departments to improve children's learning skills, behavior management, and emotional control. While the average length of stay for children in such facilities has lessened over the years, Cedarview's therapeutic regimen, based on two-year placements at the time, is still typical of some of these institutions.

Cedarview is committed to behavioral programming, centered in part on an elaborate token economy. The children collect tokens for appropriate behaviors, which they can redeem for valued items at a facility store. They also can trade tokens for a variety of privileges, such as participating in extracurricular activities. The token economy is linked with a complex assessment system and treatment regimen in which targeted conduct such as "swearing behavior," "teasing behavior," and "off-task fantasizing" are measured before treatment (called "baselining") and at intervals during and after treatment (called "postbaselining"). The token economy, assessment system, and treatment program are major components of the prevailing therapeutic discourse and the local technology of self-construction.

Staff members are especially interested in the child's body because, in this context, it poignantly signifies the child's therapeutic needs and progress in treatment. It is taken to be a well-articulated surface of signs for the purpose of interpreting children's needy selves. The typical baselining assessment is illustrative. The case considered here centers on Maurice Clay's teasing behavior. Maurice has been referred to Cedarview for an attention deficit disorder with strong emotional overtones.

Maurice is to be baselined while he is in teacher Sally Meath's classroom. Before the children arrive, two staff members, Joe Julian and Francine O'Brien, inform Meath about the assessment and take their places in the observation room at the back of the classroom. All classrooms have observation rooms, outfitted with sound equipment and one-way mirrors. When an observation room is darkened and the classroom is full of light, the one-way mirror is transparent only from inside the observation room. Savvy children, however, reverse this by occasionally cupping their hands around their eyes immediately in front of the mirror, attempting to peek through the glass to see if anyone is watching.

The observer joins the assessment team in the observation room, and together they wait for the children to take their seats and settle down before the baselining begins. Julian and O'Brien are to tally how many times Maurice teases (exhibits "teasing behavior") in a predesignated time period. The following conversation, reconstructed from fieldnotes, soon unfolds. Note the extent to which Maurice's body figures in quantifying the features of Maurice's inner life.

Observer:	Who are you baselining today?
Julian:	Maurice Clay. I'm getting his teasing behavior.
Observer:	What's teasing behavior?
Julian:	Look at these categories [gives rating sheet to the observer]. It's considered teasing if he hits, touches, makes

faces or negative comments, or does any name-calling during work time.

Julian and O'Brien soon turn to the classroom. There is a long pause as they focus their attention on Maurice. Julian eventually expresses his disappointment that "nothin'" has happened and that, instead, Maurice is fantasizing. This prompts the following exchange.

Julian: Damn! I should have done fantasizing this week and teasing last week. He was teasing a lot then, but nothin' now. Just look at him staring into space—that's fantasizing if I ever saw it.
Observer: How do you know what fantasizing is?
Julian: Good point. I guess I really couldn't count staring into space like that. We only count verbal stuff for that. He may be staring into space, but is really thinking about his work. Who knows? So we only count verbal stuff like when he talks about Mr. Greaso, Spiderman, or Super-what's-his-name.

Notice how a possible shift in attention from teasing to fantasizing behavior positions Maurice's body to signify a different self. Concurrently, the institutional discourse of behavior deficits, treatment, and progress is crafted in the colorful terms of what Julian takes to be commonly understood. This gives fantasizing a particular local meaning and attaches it to specific locally recognized signs—talk of superheroes on this occasion signifies attention deficit.

One of the boys in the classroom, Jamie Edwards, approaches the one-way mirror, cups his hands around his eyes, and peers into the observation room. Soon thereafter, Julian and O'Brien designate another rule for interpreting Maurice's body. Of course, the rule—which pertains to physical gestures—continues to take shape in the course of its practical application.

Julian: [Referring to Jamie] There's a little shit. I tried to baseline him last week and got nothin'. He must have known I was in here lookin' at him. He's a real bastard. I know what he's really like from working with him in the cottage [Jamie's dormitory].
O'Brien: Look! Maurice is givin' the finger to Sally [the teacher, who has her back to the classroom]. Can we count that?
Julian: Naw, only if he does it to another kid.

There is a pause in the assessment process as team members chat about Jamie and a few other children, exchanging anecdotes about mischief and misbehavior. The team's attention again turns to Maurice, who now gets out of this seat and stands behind the boy seated to his left, peering over the boy's shoulder at his school work. Interpretive rules again emerge in reflexive response to body observations.

Julian:	Now we may get some action. Come on, touch him or something! If he really gets going, we could see a lot [of teasing behaviors] in a few minutes.
O'Brien:	Can't we count what he's doing?
Julian:	No, not unless he really bothers him, like touches him or makes faces.

It is evident that the significance of Maurice's body and its locally pertinent self-revealing meanings evolve in parallel. The staffers' task at hand is to translate bodily signs into designated behavioral meanings, as institutionally prescribed. But the resulting rules ("only if he does it to another kid," "not unless he really bothers him," etc.) reflexively guide what team members consider themselves to be observing in the very same (baselining) process.

As Maurice heads back to his seat, he ruffles the hair of the boy seated to his left, prompting Julian to comment, "Good! Good! Now we're getting somewhere. Too bad he started so late. [Looks at his watch] Time's almost up." The baselining session ends as other assessments of this kind do, with the knowledge that, had things gone differently, Maurice would have shown up for what he really is. What he is or could possibly be—inside—is read in practice from his bodily gestures and appearances on the outside, in relation to the occasion's going concern.

THE ADULT'S SIGNIFYING BODY IN COURT

Bodies of all ages are used to signify inner lives. As we grow older and become adults, we typically come into the interpretive purview of an amazing number of institutions with a dizzying array of concerns. Jobs bring the body into the domain of employment skills, intelligence, independence, creativity, and attractiveness, among a host of concerns that bear on work performance and public relations. Other going concerns practice embodiment in relation to a lack of skills or even to impairments that makes it difficult to be viewed as a competent adult. In each case, what the body and its signs mean depends on the institutional context in which the body is being read.

Consider, for example, how the body is constructed and used as an interpretive resource for discerning the intentions, predilections, and capabilities of adults who appear in involuntary mental commitment hearings (Holstein, 1993). In most locales, when persons are psychologically troubled and become troublesome to those around them, psychiatric hospitalization provides a remedy for the resulting intrapersonal and interpersonal havoc. Sometimes, however, "patients" do not want to sacrifice their freedom while undergoing evaluation and treatment. In such cases, involuntary commitment procedures may be invoked. These hearings are formal legal proceedings in which judges decide if persons who are deemed mentally ill should be hospitalized because they pose a danger to themselves or others or because they are so gravely disabled that they cannot adequately care for themselves. Candidate patients are typically represented by public defenders (PDs) while attorneys for the state (district attorneys or DAs) argue for commitment. A mental health professional is usually asked to render an opinion about the candidate patient's mental health, and finally, the candidate patient is given the opportunity to speak for himself or herself.

While the candidate patient's mental health is a going concern, it is not necessarily the deciding factor in involuntary commitment cases. Typically, everyone involved in the proceedings concedes that candidate patients are psychologically troubled. But, in practice, decisions revolve around the putative *tenability* or *untenability* of the candidate patient's proposed community living situation as much as they do around the candidate patient's mental health or illness (Holstein, 1993). For example, judges' accounts for their decisions typically address the issue of whether or not the candidate patient has "someplace to go." If an arrangement can be established that is likely to contain, absorb, or tolerate the candidate patient's anticipated erratic, troublesome, havoc-wreaking behavior, judges are likely to order release. In the absence of such tenable community living accommodations, however, commitment is likely.

The decision-making process functionally orients to how well a candidate patient can be matched with a tenable living situation. Concern typically focuses on how manageable or vulnerable a candidate patient might be if released to live in the community. Frequently, the bodies of candidate patients are read for signs of candidate patients' manageability or vulnerability. Candidate patients' "states of mind" are also read from the body in relation to questions of manageability and vulnerability.

Consider, for example, the account for a decision to commit in a case involving Ruth Downey. Downey was a 49-year-old widow with a long history of psychiatric treatment for affective disorders. She had been apprehended by the police and temporarily hospitalized when her neighbors reported that Downey "holed-up" inside her house for weeks and that it appeared that cats and other pets were overrunning the place. After much testimony and due deliberation, the judge in the case decided that he was going to release Mrs. Downey if she would agree to have Jean Knox, Downey's 25-year-old niece, visit her on a daily basis. Knox could then check up on Downey's health, hygiene, and medication compliance. The judge offered the following explanation for his decision.

> I'm going to send Mrs. Downey home. I don't like what's been going on here with the cats and all, but I don't think commitment's the answer right now.... [To the PD:] You're sure that the niece—what is it, Jean Knox—will look in on her everyday? [The PD nods in agreement.] Mrs. Downey doesn't look like she's much trouble to look after. This isn't a big woman. In fact, she's quite petite. I'm confident that her behavior won't get out of hand and there will be someone there to manage her.... This simply doesn't look like a dangerous woman to me. She doesn't have the physical stature to threaten anyone and from the looks of things, she's not going to get so far out of control that her niece can't handle it.

The judge explicitly incorporates a reading of Mrs. Downey's body into his description of a tenable community living situation. Her bodily size and stature—"quite petite"—provide the basis for concluding that Downey would be sufficiently manageable if she just had a little supervision from her niece. But it is not Downey's physical body size alone that impresses the judge. He also infers from her small stature that Downey "doesn't look like she's much trouble to look after." The judge is confident that the behavior of this petite woman "won't get out of hand." He finally concludes that "from the looks of things," Mrs. Downey is not going to get "out of control." In effect, the judge reads Downey's bodily features as signs of her disposition and temperament as much as for her physical capabilities. Either way, the meaning of the body is central to the decision-making in question.

Of course, the body is not always read in ways that promote release. Luis Sanchez, a six-foot, 200-pound Chicano, was ordered to be committed with the explanation that "this is a big guy. We can't just let him go home." The judge's account for his decision also oriented to Sanchez's gender, explicitly noting that "a man's not going to be stopped by his mother's pleading if he gets it into his head that he wants to do something" (Holstein, 1987, p. 148). The combination of Sanchez's being male and being "big" prompted the judge's decision that Sanchez was not going to be manageable in the situation in which he proposed to live.

Repeatedly in commitment hearings, small body size, diminished strength, and physical frailty are cited as features of "manageable" persons—persons who could reasonably be released into the proper living situation. At the same time, however, lack of size, physical frailty, and passive posture and demeanor are also cited as signs of vulnerability, which then provides grounds for commitment. In such cases, if a candidate patient is likely to be physically and/or emotionally vulnerable in a community living situation, commitment is likely. While aspects of both manageability and vulnerability could be read in purely physical terms, it was also common for bodily signs to be cited as indications of inner emotional or dispositional states that were pertinent to the cases at hand, which also figured into decision-making.

It is important to note that the bodily signs that judges chose to read and report in their accounts were far from arbitrary or capricious. Instead, when the bodies of candidate patients were taken into consideration, they were viewed in institutionally relevant terms. That is, body size, structure, comportment, and the like were consistently read in terms of what they said about the manageability or vulnerability of the candidate patient. These were the central "going concerns" of the court. Robust bodies, frail bodies, aging bodies, and many other bodily features were regularly incorporated into commitment decisions. The court's practical and professional agenda directed judges and others to make particular bodily features relevant to their work, while rendering others less significant.

THE SIGNIFYING BODY IN OLD AGE

The aging body, like that of the growing child and the young and middle-aged adult, is a perennial surface of signs for signifying identity. For some, the body comes center stage in later life, as the leading questions deal with how the disintegrating body reveals personhood. Institutions such as rehabilitation hospitals, nursing homes, adult day care centers, and caregiver support groups are ubiquitous venues for linking the self and the body in old age.

The nursing home provides an increasingly commonplace institutional venue for self-construction, bringing the body and the self into focus as interpretive projects. While there is both therapeutic and palliative interest in the condition of the body as a physiological entity, the body also is monitored for what it can reveal about a gamut of related psychological states. These range from the nursing home resident's personal identity to family caregivers' lingering sense of responsibility after institutionalization and more.

Before an individual is placed in a nursing home, the home may be a relatively distant discursive anchor for linking the body and the self (Gubrium & Holstein, 1999). Still, it can cast an interpretive shadow on personal meaning. For example, in an in-depth home interview with the adult daughter of a frail, elderly mother, the daughter links the mother's future with thoughts of when "it's time," which refers to time for institutional care. In the following extract from the interview transcript, the nursing home serves as a device for making meaningful linkages with the mother's deteriorating body.

> When ya think ahead—I try not to think too far ahead—ya can't help feeling what might happen to her [the mother]. She's getting pretty frail. You can see for yourself. And she's becoming a real burden to me. She's my mother, of course, and ya can take a lot because of that, you know what I mean? What makes me nervous, though, is thinking about what's ahead, you know, when it's time [for nursing home placement] and after that. Everyone keeps telling me not to get myself all riled up and sick caring for her and I know—better than anyone, don't ya know—what that can mean. Ya think too, about what those places are like. Sure, they take care of 'em, but do they *really* take care of 'em? She's declining, but she might decline all that much faster if I put her in one of them. When I think about her becoming a bunch of bones there in one of those beds, with three others in the same room, it's frightening. They say they decline fast in those places, don't they?

Note how the nursing home is considered a potentially useful resource, given the difficulty of continued home care. But it is also presented as a source of anxiety centered on what it signifies about the bodies and selves of anyone living there. According to the daughter, because of what "they say" about "those places," the nursing home might turn the mother into a "bunch of bones," bereft of who she is to the daughter. This can be taken literally or figuratively, as in a skeletal self, so to speak. It descriptively anchors the daughter's description of her mother's body in ways that are widely recognized by those familiar with nursing homes. The daughter's anxiety is admittedly drawn from what the nursing facility represents in this regard. She infers a dire future from what "they" say about "those places," implicating the broader discourse of contemporary frailty and aging.

The nursing home continues to be a basis for forming meaningful linkages between bodily signs and aspects of inner life after one becomes a resident. For example, as repugnant as the term "vegetable" might be to some, it can come alive and reflexively construct the identity of its users as nonvegetables, as they might be. In the following conversation between two elderly, wheelchair-bound, African-American nursing home residents, the identity indexed by bed location serves as a basis for humorously interpreting more than the selves of others.

Muriel: Don't know how you stand it, girl. Why you go over there, down there by those rooms? I saw you lookin' in there.

Ruby: What you mean? I was just passin'. That Miss Casey, the one just over yonder, couple doors over there? Oh my, she is a bag of bones. Oh, wee! She's just in there in bed and she's on her back. You be hardly knowin' she's alive. They got her hooked up to all kinds of stuff. Her mouth's hangin' open, like that. [Imitates Casey] Oh, wee!

Muriel: That one's a vegetable. Sweet Jesus, I don't know why they keep 'em alive. What good are they? The bags of bones they have in the place, it gives me the chills when I see 'em. I don't know how you can stand it, Ruby. Why do you look there, girl?

Ruby: Who you talkin' to?

Muriel: You, girl. [Chiding Ruby] You thinkin' of bein' one of them there vegetables? You look like you gettin' pretty skinny. I'll get me one of those pills that knock me dead before I get like that!

Ruby: I'm no vegetable! Look at you, girl. That nappy hair look like ol' dried up corn silk. You better watch out, in a place like this here I can see you in one of those beds down there, like ol' Miss Casey. I be comin' down that hall and look in there and there you is, mouth open like this [imitates Casey], like an ol' dried up melon, oozin' and bruisin'.

Muriel: Now look at you, Ruby. You already a bag of bones. You *all* skin and bones! You no vegetable, you a skeleton!

Ruby: Oh, wee! What you talkin' about, girl? You got no behind!

Muriel: I'm leavin' this ol' place tomorrow. This here is bonetown. Ain't gonna be one of them vegetables like you Ruby. You gonna look at 'em so much, you gonna be one of 'em. [Laughing] You turnin' green already!

As the women banter and laugh about the "bags of bones," Muriel describes how chilling it is to wheel past "the vegetables," asserting that she would take a suicide pill before she would let herself come to that. Joking with each other, their own bodies become a complex surface of related signs. Note, in particular, how these residents use and cleverly embellish what they know about their neighbor "Miss Casey," to concretely describe what they themselves could become. With wit and sarcasm, the two women present their own bodies and selves, discursively constructing them out of both locally relevant and broadly recognized linkages. Using the institution's own terms, they indicate who and what they themselves could become "in a place like this here."

Talk of nursing home life can conjure up the body even after a resident has died or otherwise left a facility. This is especially poignant when the body appears in retrospect to have been "near perfect" despite an illness. It is widely known that cognitively incapacitating illnesses such as Alzheimer's disease do not necessarily result in visible bodily markings. Still, family members wonder how a loved one can "look so good" and, at the same time, have completely lost his or her mind, to become the "shell of a former self." A surprisingly supple body is especially unsettling in the context of the nursing home, because residents' bodies are assumed to be frail. "Body talk" in this context typically deploys the discourse of decline and decrepitude.

Consider how this could unfold in support groups for the caregivers of Alzheimer's disease sufferers (Gubrium, 1986). Some participants, mostly wives and adult daughters, "made it a point" to keep attending group meetings even after their husbands or parents had died, because they felt others benefited from their experience. Especially pertinent here are the wives of now deceased husbands. The husbands had previously been placed in nursing homes because of their worsening dementia, which made it too difficult to care for them at home.

During a meeting of one of the groups, an animated exchange emerged around the irony of how dementia sufferers sometimes "looked" despite their cognitive impairment. The received wisdom was that Alzheimer's dementia may develop full-blown in a relatively healthy body. Nonetheless, the exchange soon settled on the "unfairness" of death in such cases, the reasoning being that it is not fair for individuals to be taken by death when they "look so good" and are "so healthy."

This led to a discussion of nursing homes and the so-called vegetables one typically encounters in these facilities. Even the floor plan of one of the homes under discussion was made discursively relevant and used to elaborate upon bodily descriptions. When one of the participants mentioned the unit with the "living dead," several other participants jumped in to contrast the bodily condition of their demented spouses.

Here, we quote the spouse of a former resident named Andy, who lived in a nursing home for years before his death. Andy's wife constructs her account of "what Andy looked like," using what the nursing home resident's body typically signifies to underscore the unfairness of Andy's death. We should note that the irony mentioned in these contrasts is especially striking when participants talk about the bodies of their demented spouses and parents in relation to the nursing home as opposed to other social contexts.

I'm not saying I haven't accepted it. Andy's gone. I know that and I think I've accepted that. [Elaborates] He lived a good life for an 81-year-old man. But when you think about it—if you just looked at him in that room of his at Parkview [nursing home] or saw him walking down the hall—you'd think, what's he doing in here? He doesn't belong in here, right? That's that damned Alzheimer's. Ya look around and ya see this one next door [in the adjacent room] and ya see a vegetable. He's in bed and looks, well, dead. No color. And on the other side—Mrs. Korski, I think her name was—was she ever bad off. When I went in there, I couldn't believe she was alive! But she lived a long time like that. It's a shame really, when you think about it. [Draws comparisons with residents on another unit] Andy wasn't even in that there skilled care area, either. Now that's a doozy. Those are the one's really dyin'! Gosh, what a sight that is. I'd go through there to get to the smoking room and wonder why I didn't faint. I couldn't imagine those people were still alive. [Elaborates] It just didn't seem right that Andy was in that place. It really makes me wonder. I could write a book about it, I guess. And Andy goes [dies], just like that. [Snaps her fingers] You can't say that was really fair, was it? Like in comparison? [Pause] To this day, I can't understand it, but I think I've made my peace with it.

The nursing home, of course, is not a discursive template that designates exactly what will be said about bodies considered and described in relation to it. It is not as if the personal meaning of the body is specified wholesale in institutional terms. The biographical particulars that enter into talk and interaction also bear on how the body figures into the construction of the selves in question. As we saw in the preceding extracts, the nursing home can be used to signify the elderly body both fairly and unfairly, both sadly and humorously, depending on the working discursive context. At the same time, once the nursing home is made topical, it provides a discourse of its own—a going concern—for the embodiment of the elderly self. While the discourse itself is not definitive, it nonetheless serves to provide the narrative contours for who and what people are or can be, as their bodies grow old.

CONCLUSION

Such are the bodies of going concerns in contemporary life. While we have provided illustrations from institutions that deal with problem bodies and selves, the argument applies to other, more benign concerns as well. If some institutions that gaze upon our bodies and our selves concentrate on damaged identities, many other going concerns train participants in how to embody successful selves. From the varied self-improvement programs touted in the mass media to the "weekend warriors" of conscious-raising masculinity groups, self-improvement movements not only draw interpretive inspiration from the body but in turn view the body as signifying all things positive and glorious for the selves in tow. Today's going concerns and their bodies not only construct who and what we are through time, they also specify our physical hopes and moral horizons. They use both sound and unsound bodies to signify the range of human beings we can be in contemporary life.

The primary lesson of our argument is that the body is no longer just a surface for individual and interpersonal designation. It has become an interpretive enterprise. Sometimes institutions concerned with reading the body do so for profit. Peddlers of bodily "treatments" and rehabilitated physiques—and their contained selves—abound. What else, after all, are Charles Atlas, Vic Tanny, and Richard Simmons than cheerleaders for the body and self-esteem building industries? Other concerns with bodily signs are less profit-oriented. Some, for example, have spiritual motives. This is typical of "recovery" movements such as Alcoholics Anonymous and Narcotics Anonymous. Whether the motive is bound to profits, spirituality, or something else, we have become quite enterprising in our concern with the body. It is this enterprise, we argue, that now significantly bears upon the construction of our bodies and our selves. Organizations and institutions construct our bodies, over and above what we as individuals have perennially contributed to the process.

REFERENCES

Atkinson, Paul. (1995). *Medical talk and medical work*. London: Sage.
Bourdieu, Pierre. (1984). *Distinction: A social critique of the judgment of taste*. London: Routledge.
Bourdieu, Pierre. (1985). The social space and the genesis of groups. *Theory and Society, 14*, 723–744.
Buckholdt, David R., & Gubrium, Jaber F. (1985). *Caretakers: Treating emotionally disturbed children*. Lanham, MD: University Press of America.
Elias, Norbert. (1991). *The symbol theory*. London: Sage.
Foucault, Michel. (1977). *Discipline and punish*. New York: Vintage.
Foucault, Michel. (1978). *The history of sexuality*, vol. 1. New York: Vintage.
Garfinkel, Harold. (1967). *Studies in ethnomethodology*. Englewood Cliffs, NJ: Prentice-Hall.
Giddens, Anthony. (1984). *The constitution of society*. Berkeley: University of California Press.
Giddens, Anthony. (1991). *Modernity and self-identity*. Stanford, CA: Stanford University Press.
Gubrium, Jaber F. (1986). *Oldtimers and Alzheimer's: The descriptive organization of senility*. New York: JAI/Elsevier.
Gubrium, Jaber F., & Holstein, James A. (1999). The nursing home as a discursive anchor for the aging body. *Ageing and Society, 19*, 519–538.
Gubrium, Jaber F., & Holstein, James A. (Eds.). (2001). *Institutional selves: Troubled identities in a postmodern world*. New York: Oxford University Press.
Holstein, James A. (1987). Producing gender effects on involuntary mental hospitalization. *Social Problems, 34*, 141–155.
Holstein, James A. (1993). *Court-Ordered insanity: Interpretive practice and involuntary commitment*. Hawthorne, NY: Aldine de Gruyter.
Holstein, James A., & Gubrium, Jaber F. (2000a). *Constructing the life course*. Walnut Creek, CA: Alta Mira.

Holstein, James A., & Gubrium, Jaber F. (2000b). *The self we live by: Narrative identity in a postmodern world*. New York: Oxford University Press.

Holstein, James A., & Gubrium, Jaber F. (2003). *Inner lives and social worlds.* New York: Oxford University Press.

Hughes, Everett. (1984). Going concerns: The study of American institutions. In *The sociological eye: Selected papers* (pp. 52–64). New Brunswick, NJ: Transaction Books.

Turner, Bryan S. (1984). *The body and society*. Oxford: Blackwell.

Turner, Bryan S. (1992). *Regulating bodies*. London: Routledge.

14

Dis-Membered Bodies—Re-Membered Selves: The Discourse of the Institutionalized Old

Haim Hazan

PRELIMINARY CONSIDERATIONS

The cultural site of the aging body in contemporary society has occupied scant attention in socioanthropological discourse (Turner, 1995; Featherstone, Hepworth & Turner, 1991; Gergen & Gergen, 1993; Furman, 1997; Öberg, 1996; Gubrium & Holstein, 1999). Compared to the deluge of research on the malfunctioning aging body, the embodiment of the category of the wrinkled, cracked experience of late-life personhood is a widely neglected matter. The alleged "invisibility" of the aged in Western society (Myerhoff, 1978) coupled with the blurring of age-group differences in today's consumer culture (Hareven, 1995) could offer a cogent explanation for this lacuna. Fig-leaf standards of political correctness inspired by the spirit of the time of antiaging healing might be adduced in support of the avoidance of the ignoble decaying body—a corporeal symbol negating premises and promises of modernity and displaying flamboyant, albeit virtual, postmodern transitional bodies (Featherstone, 1995; Blaikie, 1999).

The habitus of the postmodern renders the body social of the aged invisible, as the "mask of aging" (Featherstone, Hepworth, & Turner, 1991) is not admitted to the masquerade of unigenerationally interchangeable selves. The effervescence of media-spun signs locates and locks visual somatic imagery within aesthetic conventions of genderized youthfully embodied discourse. Between and betwixt the interstices of that youth-riddled culture, the aging image is suppressed and disembodied, claiming recondite presence of nostalgic flavor (Blaikie, 1999). The question of the symbolic whereabouts of the aged is further amplified since the discrepancy between the growing ubiquity of the old and the dearth in their representation spells a cultural bias that calls for elucidation.

This chapter converges these two foci of interest—the representational site of the aged and the cultural properties reflected by it—into one ethnographically inspired account. I would like to suggest that: (1) the concrete site of the elderly could be spotted in those enclaves designed and designated for the unadulterated carriers of the cultural tag of old and (2) that such sequestrated territories for the category of the old not only set boundaries between inside and outside in terms of social inclusion and exclusion (Hazan, 1994), but also are a reflection and reification of the ocucentric norm prevailing in contemporary global culture. These two propositions require some elaboration.

Practices of separation and exclusion are performed where social identities are severely eroded to the extent of symbolic extinction. Those afflicted by that process are often confined to community-cum-organization hybrid facilities generally referred to as total institutions. Since Goffman's revolutionary exploration of the characteristics of such organizations (Goffman, 1961), the concept has captured the sociological imagination of post-1960s sociologists who realized the critical potential embedded in breaking down the walls between the socially concealed and the culturally exposed. Foucault's work expounded the societal underpinnings that constitute practices of institutional surveillance under the watchful gaze of pastoral agents (Foucault, 1972, 1980). However, the concept has fallen out of sociological grace as the ethos of antipsychiatry (Szasz, 1962) waned as inmates turned into residents, clients, and citizens. In other words, while the walls of incarceration remain, their impregnability weakens, and the line dividing those inside from those outside becomes finer and blurred. Hence, the current political agenda in the postcolonial is concerned with the struggle for citizenship among transmigrant workers, repressed minorities, and fourth world nationals rather than with the condition of those confined to mental health institutions, prisons, or old age homes. Indeed, most ethnographies of institutional facilities for the aged do not tend to draw on the theory of total institutions but invoke themes of meaning seeking (Savishinsky, 1991), of the management of near-death experience (Hockey, 1990), of situational anchorage (Gubrium, 1993), and of the predicament of professional caregiving (Foner, 1994). The institution as a recognizable social entity has lost its academic viability and visibility; likewise its subjects are deemed to be constituted under the same social gaze as those of any other agency subjected to extra institutional forces.

Invisibility of the old is not just a function of ageism or a consequence of structural dependency (Hockey & James, 1993; Bytheway, 1995; Gilleard & Higgs, 2000). It could be construed as a prime representation of the position of the old in a society dominated by yardsticks of the visibly "proper." While the ambit of culturally permissible youthlike images expands, the scope of legitimate depictions of the abominable unsightly end of life constricts, and figurative allusions to that tabooed zone turn into figures of speech consigning it to a disturbing discourse of visibility versus invisibility.

THE DISCOURSE OF IN/VISIBILITY

The reduction of the old into corporeal attributes not only restricts the language about aging to physiological determinants, but also introduces a split within the Western cultural "paradigm" of the indivisibility of body and soul. It confines the old to a category of social treatment such as medicine or the social welfare system, where bodies are separated from selves. It is intriguing to observe that protest against the social abandonment of the old often invokes the "invisibility" (e.g., Myerhoff, 1984) of the elderly. Put under the social gaze, it is really a case of over-visibility, as the old in fact exist only as long as they are being seen (*être vue*, in the words of Sartre). Indeed, it is the separation of bodies from selves that makes the aged only too visible. The old, the patient, and the defendant all share the over-visibility of a subject objectified and a person-cum-personal. Still, it is visibility rather than audibility that becomes a banner against discrimination and inadvertently reinforces it.

Old age is presented by and to middle-aged society through the aforementioned "mask of aging." The subject of aging is masked, concealed behind specular stereotypes, objectified through medical and gerontological discourses. The public self-presentation of the elderly, often made to conform to its social image, further reenforces this image. Featherstone, Turner, and Hepworth's (1991) important concept of the "mask of aging" recapitulates much of the conceptualization already suggested in the sociology of aging (e.g., Hazan, 1994; Gubrium, 1993). It proposes that the image of the elderly is part of the regimes of modernity whose other inmates are the sick (most recently and blatantly, the HIV/AIDS patient), the insane, the primitive, and, ultimately, the "other" in all of its embodiments. The sociology of aging, itself a powerful image-maker, is also part of this scopic regime. It is part of the ocular centrism of contemporary society and sociology, which gives prominence to the image and privileges sight over sound (Jay, 1988a, 1988b). The ocularcentric gaze of the sociology of aging, even when self-reflexive, has tended to emphasize the visual: either the hypervisibility of the "mask" of aging or its complementary opposite, namely, the social "invisibility" of the elderly (e.g., Eckert, 1980; Myerhoff, 1982; Unruh, 1983).

Masking is often a repressive act. Woodward (1991), for example, argues that the repression of aging is connected to the visible oppression of old people in our society. Following Germain Greer's contention, in her recent book *The Change*, that old age generates angst, Woodward proposes that aging is not only seen as a general catastrophe, but is also particularly associated with women, reflecting a Western "gerontophobia" of the aging body, regarded as bad, and split off from the youthful body, which is regarded as good. While the image of the elderly should be deconstructed and unmasked, the attempt may prove self-defeating. Invoking both hypervisibility and invisibility as a banner against ageism may be self-subversive, as it carries the risk of inadvertently strengthening that which it seeks to criticize. Conjuring up images, even in a critical manner, already reproduces them.

Caught up in that discourse of in/visibility, the category of the old faces three options of managing its cultural presence: (1) to claim a self-conscious identity as coculture (Orbe, 1988) integrated within the intergenerational social fabric, (2) to disappear as an identifiable cultural entity by negating age as a criterion for social belonging (Kaufman, 1986), or (3) to succumb to the recognized ageist position of separation and subordination through wearing the mask of aging with all its expected consequences. This third possibility of assumed visibility turned invisibility might easily reverse the fortunes of those complying with it and turn the tide from tolerable appearances to intolerable presence.

When such critical transformation occurs, the visible presence of the old in an ocucentric public sphere is discarded, voluntarily or otherwise, to geographies of exclusion (Sibley, 1995), namely, to the unknown land of total institutions. The enforced invisibility wielded by that relocation seems to serve a dual purpose: to distance and veil the living icons of death and to resolve the irreconcilable, that is, to remove from the public gaze blatant testimonies to the incongruity between body and self—a discrepancy that in ocucentric culture is rendered problematic. The total institution therefore functions as a symbolic device for restoring representational order by eliminating potentially subversive discourses.

Those committed to institutional life are deemed to subscribe to proverbial models of restricted freedom and curtailment of choice and power. However, once the mask of aging is removed and the tension of straddling inner self and outer appearances dissipates, residents might find themselves in a new domain of dialogue between body and mind. This is to say that the constitutive forces of the specular no longer operate to subjugate the self to the discourse of visibility. The construction of subjectivity under such a nascent condition could be framed in different terms of personhood liberated from accountability to perpetual pressure of embodiment.

SITE AND SIGHT

The ethnographic account is a longitudinal report of three phases in the organizational life of one old age home. Changes in managerial policy and the allocation of resources espoused to transitions in the macrosocial map of aging determine the thrust of the process hereafter described. The momentum of that dynamic might spell the gradual abandonment of the imperative of embodiment and of the regime of the corporeal. But before entering the field of that particular institution, let us begin with an illustration of the cultural properties of old age homes in a contemporary modern-cum-postmodern epoch.

On the outskirts of an Israeli suburb of Tel-Aviv, two facilities for long-term eldercare emerge. The first, a publicly administered nursing home for the physically and mentally incapacitated, is a somber-looking building, set apart from its surroundings, girded by intimidating walls, and frequently entered by ambulances and vehicles of staff and visitors. The other facility, a privately owned old age home for both the able-bodied and the infirm, is situated within walking distance from the first but looks entirely different. Its exterior resembles a "Lego" design encircled by pastel-colored stripes with chalet-styled red roofs overlooking slide-like flights of stairs leading to a bustling shopping mall. As one of the local papers named it, "Grandpa's Lunar Park" gives the impression of a theme park of and for the elderly, an enticing simulation of old age to be visited, viewed, and enjoyed like any other type of funland of consumerism, with supermarkets, department stores, fast-food restaurants, and brand-name shops galore. Mobile residents are indeed regular buyers and baskers indistinguishable in the crowd of funseekers.

The two institutions seemingly have very little in common, as the former territory is a reflection of modern care conceptions of segregation and exclusion, while the latter draws on postmodern traits of high consumerism and ageless habitus. Moreover, the nursing home renders its inmates invisible, whereas the old age home allows its "holiday-makers" a pronounced spectral presence. In effect, they blend in with the other pilgrims to that temple of contemporary urban living in the very same spirit of the time from which the invisible aged body is banished, as is the case for the inmates of the adjacent institution.

On the face of it, two modes of aging persona are embodied in the two settings. The first is embedded in a structuralist positioning of the elderly in the forbidden ground of modernity, a taboo area populated by contaminating antibodies to the project of incessant upward progress. The second, however, seems to be anchored in a postmodern experience of blurred boundaries, hybridity, and dissolved cultural codes (Bauman, 1992). Although it would seem seductive to consider the two cases as a double reflection of two consecutive epochs in one spatiotemporal space (Giddens, 1991), this is not the case.

The hyper-reality of a childlike amusement park juxtaposed to the prison-like walls of an old time facility of incarceration are both made of the same macrosociological bodily mold. The old age home-cum-mall dissolves the aging corporeal presence into the absence of nonrepresentation, of simulacra, while the concealing of the nursing home captives from the public gaze is achieved by means of wrapping bodies in fig leaves of social conscience. In either case, the aged body is made to be neither specular nor audible, and in both it is rendered nonexistent.

OCULARCENTRIC MONISM

I would like to take up this interpretation to further pursue the general argument at the outset of this chapter. Sociocultural discourse on the site of the body reverberates three images, the duality of the body-mind dichotomy, the holistic indivisibility, and the monistic approach. Out of these options, only one has become a predominant symbolic capital pervading the fabric of everyday life in late modernity. Between the Cartesian view of the divide between senses and soul and the undifferentiated whole of the bio-psycho-social, the monistic agenda of being prevails. Monism is indeed an old-fashioned idea contested and defied by the great traditions of the major religions, whose theological dogmas separate the terminally visceral from the eternally spiritual, usually by iconic representations of celestially inspired martyred bodies. However, a close unadulterated look at the public sphere allocated to the mind-body problem in our society would reveal a decisive cultural bias toward the body supreme. This implies that phenotypical properties set a consumerists' iconography consisting of self-referent, body-riddled signifiers turned signifieds and vice versa. The surge of sociological preoccupation with the status of the body as social scripture, coupled with the prominent standing of embodiment in popular culture, attest to the contention that in a secular, bureaucratic, yet fragmented society, the index of bodily parameters serves as a nonreflexive common denominator for legitimizing the distribution and mobilization of resources and images, which are in and of themselves bodily anchored.

Thus, unless synchronized and validated by bodily signs, declared experience could be misconstrued, rendered unintelligible, or simply effaced. This proposition questions both the dualistic and the holistic discourses as templates for the construction of culturally endorsed identities and draws on a whole gamut of currently fashionable provinces of knowledge and consciousness, such as postcolonialism, feminism, queer theory, and cinematic and other visual media studies—all gradually substituting voices for gaze and selves for body. Tension between ocular tropes and personal identity could then erupt under socially unleashed conditions, such as anorexia, self-mutilation, and other practices, regulating the body as a malleable entity to befit culturally embodied desires, relationships, and identities. The disembodied self thus remains a squashed option reserved for selected enclaves of mind over matter, such as knowledge-producing communities and other markets of mentally engineered commodities.

The monistic proposition could be put to the test when a dualistic model of mind versus body challenges standard modes of action and calls for decisions and resolutions that throw into relief the dilemma of the incongruity between the two. When the body is presented as the self—"Our Bodies Ourselves"—it enjoys social exposure and thus occupies transparent spaces such as physical fitness rooms, the beach, and other public places governed by the cultural assumption of expected correspondence between appearance and selfhood. However, when such imagined rapport can no longer be taken for granted, a split is introduced into the monistic code, and the situation is charged with potential rupture. Thus, when reason is branded pathological, the recalcitrant mind together with its enchained body is concealed from the public eye and is confined to a mental institution; when bodily functions are not informed by cognitive competence, we might be looking at institutional arrangements for the retarded; when soul is designed and designated to overrule body, monastic living is in order; and when either body or mind—sometimes both—no longer conform to rules of acceptable monistic conduct, they are consigned to institutions for the old. In other words, total institutions may be, as Goffman suggested, social mechanisms for the mortification of self, but their apparent presence shields society from encountering the possibility of the mind-body schism. Old age homes, being such veiling devices, provide a geography of exclusion in which infirm bodies may coexist with alert minds and degenerated minds may dwell within relatively fit bodies, until both finally merge at the end of a joint death trajectory. Before that terminal unification, a cessation of representational relations could take place, that is, the monistic nexus is broken. The result is that under the guise of institutional sanctuary, the mask of aging can be removed, and bed and body work is unrelated to the business of identity constitution. This double life of inmates is well studied and documented in the literature on total institutions and seemingly reflects both the struggle to preserve a sense of selfhood and the focused effort of staff to reduce inmates to manageable objects of care.

It is, therefore, in the interest of the institutional framework to encourage the cleavage between mind and body as two discrete sets of signification. This severance of identities is often accentuated by the composition of the workforce recruited to tend to the institutionalized aged. Employment opportunities in the era of extensive labor migration brings many "foreign workers" to seek menial jobs in the caring for the old. Their cultural position as strangers in the Simmelian sense allows them to have physical contact with other bodies on that ground only, with both minds suspended from the arena of mutual recognition. The worker's self-image is set outside the institutions, as is the inmate's identity. Such interaction between dismembered selves is situationally conditioned and thus might generate a miniscule body-dominated juncture of communication. The strict present-bound capsules of this ephemeral relationship forestalls the possibility of introducing past identities and prospective planning into the context of contact, hence preventing the reciprocal production of memories. Not sharing a common language helps reinforce that rendezvous of de-memorized bodies—both literal, neither metaphorical.

A DISEMBODIED GENEALOGY OF ONE INSTITUTION

This conjectural analysis offers a glimpse into recent lives of the institutionalized aged. As implied at the outset of this discussion, a better understanding of the disjointed narrative of being in a home could be gained by tracing some evolutionary paths leading to the dissolution and disappearance of aged bodies in the two institutional settings hitherto described. To pursue this exercise of unfolding a sociologically imagined yarn of vanishing bodies, a three-phased research project was inadvertently carried out.

The first study (Hazan, 1992) was an ethnography of an Israeli old age home run by the Trades Union, admitting and accommodating only able-bodied and mentally alert residents. Lack of facilities for caring for the incapacitated compelled those with deteriorating competences to seek alternative living arrangements. This exigency was fostered and wielded by staff as an administrative instrument for managing the life in the home by putting residents to everyday tests of functioning. Residents were thus expected to publicly display acceptable measures of physical and mental capacities under the watchful eye of staff, whose clout made staying at the home a strenuous ordeal. Excepted were residents whose standing in the Israeli cultural and political milieu exonerated them from being accountable for their condition, for such criteria did not apply to their presence in the institution. Those residents, however, not only approved of that managerial policy, but took special initiatives to promote and enforce handicap cleansing. They berated the management for being too lenient with the physically weak and the feebleminded. Selfhood was deemed by them to be a vibrant spirit contained in a flesh-and-blood vessel, a stance furnished by their own social- and self-image as immortal icons at the pantheon of nation-builders.

The rest of the inmates, however, had to yield to this double pressure of bodily-minded staff and mind-geared fellow residents and hence were engaged in a constant game of staging rituals of bodily control and performances of independence alongside faked impressions of intellectual pursuits. Temporary hitches in the management of daily routine were hidden either by self-imposed confinement to the room or through the unobtrusive aid of friends and spouses.

The evident aftermath of participating in this game of "now you see me, now you don't" was an effervescent atmosphere of intrigue, playfulness, role reversals, and mutant appearances. Bodies and spirits were mixed, fused, disentangled, split, synergized, and unified. This carnival-like scene was propelled and stimulated by the common joy of risk-taking engendered by the constraint turned liberation of having to subscribe to limits and chances set by a regime that divorced discounted consciousness of self from the acclaimed masquerading of its false image.

Risk is not always fun. The burden of constantly gambling with one's fate would often turn into untoward events such as deep depression, renunciation of institutional order, and suicide. Thus, when impending betrayal of the body threatened to subvert the frontal show of good demeanor, residents would resort to desperate measures marking irreversible returning to the backstage of the shambles of their eroded subjectivity.

The question then arises as to the constituents of the remains of defendable selfhood within that context of a depleted armour of effective impressions and strongholds of self-esteem. This problem was partially addressed in the second stage of the research, as undertaken by a graduate student who, under my guidance, studied the very same home 13 years later.

The institution changed as management and the elite cohort of public figures died out. The stringent policy of good functioning was very much mitigated due to the increased availability of other long-term care facilities. Under these altered circumstances, residents reconciled themselves to the possibility of relocation and hence devoted a great deal of their socializing time to a certain style of dwelling on the past. Personal reminiscences were not exchanged, nor were shared experiences recounted. Rather, an invocation of popular adages and statements, aphorisms and proverbial teachings, prompted body-based gatherings and casual chatting mainly around mealtimes and the queue for the local infirmary. Universal wisdom encapsulated in common clichés such as "all that glitters is not gold," "too many cooks spoil the broth," "out of sight, out of mind," "absence makes the heart grow fonder," and the like were continuously hurled around. Situations, incidents, relationships with kith and kin, social positions, and cultural images were all reflected upon in terms of instructive lessons drawn from general truisms embedded in time immemorial. This immutable symbolic capital governed ethnic and national stereotypes as well as individual declarations of character and belonging. In that sense, the discourse of decontextualization and a temporality rendered both subjectivity and corporeality irrelevant to the here and now of life in the home. As a lessening of external pressures of survival also entailed very little risk-taking in conducting daily interactions, residents immersed themselves into a global program of rules and meanings from which personal body and mind, jointly or separately, were expunged.

Stereotypical labeling remains a means of communication among residents in a later—third stage—period of research currently conducted by a Ph.D. student also under my supervision. The home has been renovated, and a nursing ward for the incapacitated was incorporated into the array of services it offers. Awareness of being on the verge of the last frontier is espoused to reassurance of secured treatment and guaranteed care. Since the average age of residents has sharply increased compared to the second term of study, susceptibility to illness, distress, and pain has risen accordingly. The ravaged body cannot be ignored, and its agonizing presence has to be reckoned with. The body thus reclaims prominence, not as a symbol of tormented self, but as a signifier of the presence of others, such as "the fat man" and "the red-headed woman." Withdrawal into one's being, to the abandonment of any will or force of habit, spells a failure to acknowledge other residents by personal address of name or title. However, the body and its treacherous senses occupy another terrain alienated, embattled, hostile, and mainly dissociated from any identification with mind, thoughts, and feelings. Residents refer to their bodies as estranged entities dispossessed of personal attributes and denied subjectivity. Some assigned and consigned the body to a disappearing mundane world, whereas they themselves presumably existed in a far removed realm of inner self or transcendence. In other words, when the stakes are down and risk-taking can no longer bring any redemption or even relief in the form of a further lease on life, the body becomes a superfluous irritant. Debunked of its metaphorical values, robbed of its functioning capacities, and deprived of its negotiable properties, biopower can no longer colonize the mind.

DISCUSSION

From the point of view of the bystander or even the participant observer, the output of this process is somewhat frustrating. The object of interest and inquiry seems to be out of reach, and since its voice lacks resonance and its gaze is not deflected, there is a tendency to accord it silence and invisibility. It is the interplay between the audible and the visible that engenders dualistic permutations of body and mind. However, the career of that relationship as follows in the annals of the home is underpinned by a dwindling tension between the two and leads toward an obliteration of the body and a monistic domination of the mind. This marks a reversal of codes from reported embodied experiences to their disembodied counterpart. The fact that such transformation takes place behind institutional walls presents the home as a mirror image of society at large and hence as a yardstick by which the position of the body at the core of culture could be reassessed.

The muffled sound of the mind-body problem as echoed from the closed chamber of institutional life merely resonates the illegitimacy of the visible aging body in particular and the hegemony of bodily monism in general. Both the Disneyland-like home and the jail-like institution camouflage that body and make a case for revisiting the discourse of the mind-body problem as an emergent property of commonplace practices masking the old.

When the body is covered, it no longer restrains the mind whose presence must be eclipsed. Thus, the reversal of the monistic fortunes from body to mind is performed and perfected in hidden niches of society symbolized by invisible territories. The psychotherapist clinic, the theater and cinema audience who are shrouded in darkness, and the image of the academic ivory tower are just a few examples of the contrast between the dazzling exposure of the monistic body versus the underground existence of the mind.

This leads us to a brief oxymoronic postscript. The old age home as a sanctuary for the unbounded mind is a refuge for those whose mental agility is deemed to grow dim. The juxtaposition between sheltered living and agency free of the external impositions of social structure puts an interesting complexion of the whole issue of settings for practicing the nexus of power-knowledge. In a way, it could be posed as a test case for the dilemma of the sources of subjectivity in Western, so-called individualistic society (Morris, 1991) and for the plausibility of realizing and recognizing self or selves within a socially disengaged context. To offer a more understated, less presumptuous interpretation, the arena of old age homes merely sets the scene for yet another escape attempt from the ravages of the tyranny of the embodiment. As the somatic being is vanishing anyway, its suppression is merely a presumptive measure before succumbing to the final strike of departure from the secularly shaped body (Mellor & Shilling, 1997). The removal from the body social discharges the self of the responsibility to accommodate within its spectrum different stokes of meanings and constraints, thereby reverting from the postmodern experience of multiple selves to the old-fashioned pattern of a unitary re-membered personhood.

REFERENCES

Bauman, Z. (1992). *Mortality, immortality and other life strategies.* Cambridge, U.K.: Polity Press.
Blaikie, A. (1999). *Ageing and popular culture.* Cambridge, U.K.: Cambridge University Press.
Bytheway, B. (1995). *Ageism.* Buckingham, U.K.: Open University Press.
Eckert, J. K. (1980). *The unseen elderly.* San Diego: Campanile Press.
Featherstone, M. (1995). Post-bodies, ageing and virtual reality. In M. Featherstone & M. Wernick (Eds.), *Images of aging.* London: Routledge.
Featherstone, M., Hepworth, M., & Turner, B. S. (Eds.). (1991). *The body: Social process and cultural theory*: London: Sage.
Foner, N. (1994). *The caregiving dilemma: Work in an American nursing home.* Berkeley: University of California Press.
Foucault, M. (1961). *Madness and civilization.* London: Tavistock.
Foucault, M. (1972) (1965). *The archeology of knowledge.* Trans. A. M. Sheridan Smith. London: Tavistock.
Foucault, M. (1980). *Power/knowledge: Selected interviews and other writings, 1927–1977.* Brighton, U.K.: Harvester Press.
Furman, F. K. (1997). *Facing the mirror: Older women and beauty shop culture.* New York: Routledge.
Gergen, M. M., & Gergen, K. J. (1993). Narratives of the gendered body in popular autobiography. In R. Josselson & A. Leiblich (Eds.), *The narrative study of lives*, vol. 1. Newbury Park, CA: Sage.

Giddens, A. (1991). *Modernity and self-identity: Self and society in the late modern age*. Cambridge, U.K.: Polity Press.
Gilleard, C., & Higgs, P. (2000). *Cultures of ageing: Self, citizen and the body*. Essex, U.K.: Prentice Hall.
Goffman, E. (1961). *Asylums*. New York: Doubleday.
Gubrium, J. F. (1993). *Speaking of life: Horizons of meaning for nursing home residents*. New York: Aldine de Gruyter.
Gubrium, J. F., & Holstein, J. A. (1999). The nursing home as a discursive anchor for the ageing body. *Ageing and Society, 19*, 519–538.
Hareven, T. K. (1995). Changing images of ageing and the social construction of the life course. In M. Featherstone & A. Wernick (Eds.), *Images of aging*. London: Routledge.
Hazan, H. (1992). *Managing change in old age: The control of meaning in an institutional setting*. Albany: State University of New York Press.
Hazan, H. (1994). *Old age: Constructions and deconstructions*. Cambridge, U.K.: Cambridge University Press.
Hockey, J. (1990). *Experiences of death*. Edinburgh: Edinburgh University Press.
Hockey, J., & James, A. (1993). *Growing up and growing old: Ageing and dependency in the life course*. London: Sage.
Jay, M. (1988a). The rise of hermeneutics and the crisis of ocularcentrism. *Poetics Today, 9*(2), 307–326.
Jay, M. (1988b). Scopic regimes of modernity. In H. Foster (Ed.), *Vision and visuality* (pp. 3–23). Seattle: Bay Press.
Kaufman, S. (1986). *The ageless self: Sources of meaning in later life*. Madison: University of Wisconsin Press.
Mellor, P. A., & Shilling, C. (1997). *Re-forming the body: Religion, community and modernity*. London: Sage.
Morris, B. (1991). *Western conceptions of the individual*. Oxford: Berg.
Myerhoff, B. (1978). *Number our days*. New York: Dutton.
Myerhoff, B. (1982). Life history among the elderly: Performance, visibility and re-membering. In J. Ruby (Ed.), *A crack in the mirror: Reflexive perspectives in anthropology* (pp. 99–120). Philadelphia: University of Pennsylvania Press.
Myerhoff, B. (1984). Rites and signs of ripening: The intertwining of ritual, time and growing older. In D. L. Kertzer and J. Keith (Eds.), *Age and anthropological theory* (pp. 305–330). Ithaca, NY: Cornell University Press.
Öberg, P. (1996). The absent body: A social gerontological paradox. *Ageing and Society, 16*, 701–719.
Orbe, M. P. (1988). *Constructing co-cultural theory: An explication of culture, power and communication*. Thousand Oaks, CA: Sage.
Savishinsky, J. (1991). *The ends of time: Life and work in a nursing home*. New York: Bergin and Garvey.
Sibley, D. (1995). *Geographies of exclusion*. London: Routledge.
Szasz, T. S. (1962). *The myth of mental illness*. London: Secker and Warburg.
Turner, B. (1995). Ageing and identity: Some reflections of the somatization of the self. In M. Featherstone & A. Wernick (Eds.), *Images of aging* (pp. 245–262). London: Routledge.
Unruh, D. R. (1983). *Invisible lives: Social worlds of the aged*. Beverly Hills, CA: Sage.
Woodward, K. (1991). *Aging and its discontents*. Bloomington: Indiana University Press.

Index

Activity theory, 5
Adult development theory, 3
Age segregation: future prospect of, 10; in housing, 46, 104–5; in retirement, 96–97, 100; in total institutions, 208
Age-graded culture: counterculture model in, 96; in Western society, modernity paradigm of, 107. *See also* Subcultural aging
Ageing and Society (journal): aim of, 60–61; authors and disciplines represented in, 61–63; overview of articles in, 63–74
Ageism, 8, 45–56, 60; of adolescents and young adults, 65–66; and bodily demeanor and functions, 47; and capitalist industrial and economic management, 46–47; concept and definitions, 45–47; in critical theory, 46, 48–49; cultural dimension of aging and, 47; decline model and, 68; functional versus structural focus on, 46–47; in gerontological literature and research, 64–69, 72, 73, 99; globalization and, 50–53; individual, 65–66; institutionalized, 46–47, 65; migrants and, 53; and nationality and citizenship linkage, 49–50, 53–55; older people's reactions to, 66; and other forms of discrimination, 49; practitioners and, 66–69; and social welfare, 47–51; structural dependency paradigm and, 68; and transnational organizations' agendas, 51–53

Ageless self: concept of, 162–63; and pure consciousness, 40
Ageless Self, The (Kaufmann), 106
Agency: food choice as expression of, 148–49; and organized social activities, 78–82, 83–84, 92
Age-stratification paradigm (Riley), 7, 9
Aging: chronological versus physiological, 78–79; crisis construction of, 51; and discourses of health and illness, 146–49; gender and class as factors in, 78–80; and gerontophobia, 8; global, 52–53; and physiological aging process, 78–79; scientific management of, 27; secularist approach to, 35; theological and cultural ideals of, 38; and wisdom, 38–39. *See also* Subcultural aging
Aging body: and age redefined as beauty, 151, 152; and body-mind dualism, 162–64; disembodied and suppressed image of, 207–8; disregard/disrespect for, 152, 154; as gendered site, 149; and health-promoting lifestyle, 146–49; and institutional embodiment, 200–204; and "mask of aging," 208; modern manipulation of, 142–45; negativities of, carework and, 175–77; and ocucentric monism, 212–14; and patterns of symptomatology, 147; representational and cultural site of, 207–11; and self-identity, 47; as source of discrimination, 47
Aging women. *See* Women aging
Aging and Popular Culture (Blaikie), 48
Alzheimer's disease sufferers, 202–3
Ameliorative gerontology, 7
American Journal of Sociology, 95
Andrews, Molly, 72
Anti-aging movement, 27, 207–9
Autobiographical narratives: and body memories, 169–70; and cultural meaning systems, 167; emotional arousal and, 168–70; in gerontological research, 36–37; mind-body dualism in, 162–64; theoretical and practical value of, 28. *See also* Body memories

Bartky, Sandra, 150
Bathing: The Body and Community Care (study), 175, 177–79, 182–83
Beauty Myth, The (Wolf), 151
Behavioral programming, 195; and child's signifying body, 194–97
Berlin Aging Study, 14
Birth cohorts, and collective identity, 79
Björnheden, John, 112, 113–14, 116, 117–19, 120
Blaikie, Andrew, 48
Body, material: of children in behavioral program, 194–97; in elderly reminiscences, 161–71; institutional embodiment of, 192–95, 197–204; and one body/one person principle, 164–65; as site of social text, 153–54. *See also* Aging body
Body images: impact of photography and cinema on, 142, 144; and intragenerational modes of cultural transmission, 142–44
Body memories: of aging Finnish women, 162, 165–71; and concept of ageless self, 163; and Damasio's conception of memory, 164–65; and identification with the body, 162, 163; and marginalization of the body, 163
Body-mind dualism, 209, 212, 213–18; aging body and, 162–64; and bodily monism, 213–14, 217; and concept of ageless self, 162–63; embodiment and, 192–93
Body-mind relationship, in autobiographical memory, 164–65
Bodywork: ambivalence toward, 174; boundary marking in, 183; devaluation of bodily aspect of, 175–76; gender and power dynamics in, 174; in nursing practice, 177; as occupation, 173–74. *See also* Carework

Branting, Hjalmar, 115, 114, 115
British Household Panel Survey (BHPS), 84–92; data and methods, 84–85
British old-age pensioners, political mobilization of, 125
Burgess, Ernest, 5
Bus Pass Bandits (Britain), 102

Capitalist societies: gendered power relations in, 149, 150; and global social policy, 51; institutional ageism in, 46–47; medicalized consumer culture in, 35
Carework, 174–88; and asymmetrical nakedness, 180; and body pampering, 177–78; and client characteristics, 182; dynamics of biopower in, 179–83; gendered character of, 184–87; home-based, 182–83, 185; implications of water use in, 180; negative nature of, 175–77; and physical closeness, 178–79; regimes of control in, 181; sexuality and, 184
Child development, and mirroring experience, 165
Child's institutionalized body, 194–97
Chronological age, and social activities, 79
Citizenship: and break with nationality, 49–50, 53–55; post-national model of, 54–55; and social policy on aging, 49–50
Class: and cultures of aging, 155–56; inequalities, and status of aging body, 79–80, 155
Cole, Thomas R., 25, 48–49
Consumer culture: and age-group differences, 207; cosmetics industry in, 142, 143–44, 151; gray market in, 104; and lifestyle enclaves of older people, 104–5; medical, 35; teenage, 104
Continuity theory, 3
Cosmetic surgery, 144–45, 152
Cosmopolitanism, and national citizenship, 55

Court proceedings, adult's signifying body in, 197–200
Criminality, in old age, 102–3
Critical theory, ageism and, 46, 48–49
Cultural conservatism, generation-based, 105
"Culture of Aging" research program, 130
Cumming, Elaine, 3–4

Damasio, Antonio, 164–65
Developing countries, sociogerontological approach in, 14
Developmental psychology, 2–3, 8
Disengagement theory, 3–4, 5

Elder abuse and neglect, policies against, 69
Elder subcultures. *See* Subcultural aging
Embodiment: and bodily pre-understanding, 165; of children in treatment facilities, 194–97; in institutional contexts, 192–95, 197–204; of self-construction, 192–93; of successful selves, 204–5
Employment, ageism in, 65
Erasmus, 33
Erikson, Erik, 3
Erlander, Tage, 124
Eth-elders, American concept of, 135
Europe, aging and gerontology in, 7–8

Feeling of What Happens, The (Damasio), 164
Foucault, Michel, 140–41, 179–80, 193, 208
Fourth Age, 106; maintaining sense of self in, 103; marginalization in, 100–101
Freud, Sigmund, 3
Functionalism, in gerontological research, 5–6, 73

Gaunt, David, 130
Geertz, Clifford, 37
Gellners, Ernest, 136

Gender: and ageism, 49; culturally-informed research approach to, 149; and embodiment issues, 162; and health talk, 147; and inequalities of income and health, 155; in social gerontological research, 139–40; and social organizational membership, 78–80, 85–87. *See also* Women aging

German gerontology: dichotomizations of old age in, 17*Tab*; old age concepts in, 16–18; sociology's challenge to, 15; and user-dominated contexts, 19–21; and welfare regime changes, 22

Gerontological knowledge, 13–23; diffusion and extension of, 15–16; and dynamics of models and concepts, 16–18; and increase in user-dominated contexts, 19–21; practical, perspectives on, 20–21; trivialization and hierarchizations of, 18–19; and utilization contexts, 18–21

Gerontology: as academic discipline, 59; and ageism, 6, 64–69, 72, 73, 99; and continuity versus change theories, 3, 4, 9; and developing countries, 14; developmental paradigm in, 3; and disengagement theory, 3–4, 5; diversification in, 22; early focus in, 5–6; emergence and institutionalization of, 2–3, 6–7; and emphasis on disability and impoverishment, 100; and focus on applied issues, 7; functionalism in, 5–6; and future research, 9–10; growth and differentiation in, 14–16; humanistic, rationale for, 27–40; humanistic educational ideal and, 26; intellectual autobiography in, 25; interdisciplinary, 6–7, 8, 14–15; limitations and low status of, 1–2; as multidisciplinary science, 6–7; mythology of scientific management of, 27; narrative turn in, 36–37; positioning of, 58–74; postmodern religious humanism and, 25–40; practical and user-dominated contexts in, 22–23; and psychology and sociology, 2, 3–5; researchers' relationship with research subjects in, 69–71; and role theory, 5–6; scientific status of, 3–5; and selectivity theory, 6; and small-scale modeling, 6; and sociology, 2, 3–5, 7, 9, 15; spirituality and religion in, 25–40; successful aging as focus in, 6; terminology of agelessness in, 72; theoretical dilemmas in, 6–7; us/them distinction in, 70–71, 73; women's aging research in, 139–40

Gerontophobia, in modern society, 8
Gibson, H. B., 72
Globalization: and ageist agendas, 50–53; and development of hybrid identities, 52–53; and international law, 52; and social welfare restrictions, 51
Greer, Germaine, 210
Growing Old (Cumming and Henry), 3–4

Hall, Stanley, 2
Handbook of Humanities and Aging, 27–28
Hansson, Per Albin, 112, 113, 114, 116, 118, 119, 121, 122, 125
Havighurst, Robert, 5
Hayden, Jacqueline, 151
Health: gender and class inequalities in, 79–80, 155; and questions of morality, 106; resources, 87, 88
Health care: in capitalist consumer culture, 35; and discriminatory medical frameworks, 68. *See also* Carework; Medicine
Henry, William, 3–4
Home care workers, and power dynamics, 182–83, 185
Hughes, Everett, 191
Humanism: and dialogical rationality, 31–32; postmodern attack on, 29–32; rhetoric and, 30, 32

Humanism, religious: co-existence of religion and science in, 32; humanistic educational ideal in, 26, 29, 31, 32, 33; and humanistic gerontology, 27–28, 35–40; and humanistic knowledge, 33; and individual's search for meaning, 36–37; and postmodern anti-humanism, 29–32; and postmodern Western culture, 28; rationale for, 25–40; and Renaissance humanism, 29, 30–31; and secularism, 34–35, 36

Identity: body as site of, 153–54; cultural options for, 210; food choice as expression of, 148; globalization's impact on, 52–53; institutionalization's impact on, 207–17, 214; and social organization membership, 81–82, 82, 84. *See also* Self and identity
Implicit theory of aging, 5
Institutionalized aged, 207–18; and discourse of in/visibility, 209–11; disembodiment of, 207–17; monism and, 212–14; severance of identities of, 214; signifying body of, 200–204
Institutions: embodiment and, 193–94, 204–5; gerontological, increase in, 14; as going concerns, 191–92; life course and, 194; signifying body in, 194–205. *See also specific institution*
Interdisciplinary research, 6–7, 8, 14–15
International Association of Gerontology, objectives of, 59

Journey of Life: A Cultural History of Aging in America, The (Cole), 26

Language, formative power of, 30, 32
Left Socialist Party (Sweden), 113
Life course: and age-stratification paradigm, 9; as institutionally articulated, 194

Life Histories and Psychobiography (Runyan), 168
Life stages, transitions and rebellion in, 102–3
Life stories, of American elders, 28. *See also* Autobiographical narratives
Lifestyle: aging as context for, 153–54; enclaves, 104–5; health-promoting, 146–49; notion, and postmodern theories of self and identity, 105–6
Lindhagen, Carl, 124
Lundstedt, Gunnar, 116, 122

Marginalization: of the body, and myth of "ageless self," 163; of Fourth Agers, 100–101; and production of social categories, 132; social, and imagined community, 106
Marsden, George, 34
Mask of aging concept, 209–11, 214
Mature Imagination, The (Biggs), 48
Medicine: geriatric, dichotomy between normal and abnormal aging in, 152–53; model of decline in, 68; surveillance, 147, 148
Memory, as embodied process, 164–65. *See also* Body memories
Merleau-Ponty, Maurice, 165
Midlife: and implicit theory of aging, 5; research, 63, 73; transition to retirement in, 102. *See also* Retirement
Migrants, and citizenship struggles, 208
Möller, Gustav, 117, 119, 121, 123, 124, 125
Morality, in postmodern culture, 28

Narrative: and elderly reminiscence, 162, 165–71; revival of, 28
Nationality, and emergence of older people as social group, 49–50
Neugarten, Bernice, 5
Nursing: carework in, 177; gendered aspect of, 187

Nursing homes: cultural properties of, 211–12; as venues for self-construction, 200–204

Old age: competing and overlapping concepts of, 16–18; crisis of meaning in, 28; and discourse of visibility versus invisibility, 209–11; diversity in, 96–97; intact versus decrepit, 16; and "mask of aging," 209–11, 214; in public domain, 18; segregation and fragmentation in, 97, 100, 105, 106. See also Aging; Subcultural aging
Old-age home. See Residential care facility(ies)

Parsons, Talcott, 3–4
Patriarchal societies, gendered power relations in, 149, 150
Pensioners: diversity and segregation among, 96–97, 100; politics of, 105; social system status of, 99–100. See also Swedish pensioners' movement
Pensions, global discourse on, 51
Pettersson, Karl, 121–22
Phychological well-being, and social group activities, 82
Physiological aging, and gender and class inequalities in health, 79–80
Political action, age-based, 68–69. See also Swedish pensioners' movement
Postmodern culture, morality and spirituality in, 28; resistance to images of bodily aging in, 151
Postmodern theory: humanism and, 29–32; old-age research in, 8–9; of self and identity, 105–6
Poststructuralism, subjective experience of aging in, 153
Privatization, ageism and, 51–52
Protagoras, 30–31

Racism, and ageism, 49
Religion: and human quest for self-knowledge, 38; and humanistic gerontology, 27–28, 35, 35–40; and physical decline, 38–40; as poetic invention, 32; popular interest in, 34; and religious group membership, 83. See also Humanism, religious
Reminiscence study of aging Finnish women, 162, 165–71; body's central role in, 167; group members' reactions in, 168–70; verbalization of emotion in, 167. See also Women aging
Renaissance humanism, 29, 30–31
Residential care facility(ies): ageism and alienation in, 68; carework and power dynamics in, 181; cultural properties of, 211–12; Israeli, ethnography of, 215–17; as veiling devices, 213–14
Retirement: age-cohort differences in, 100; and crisis construction of aging, 51; and role theory, 82; segregation and fragmentation in, 97, 100; twentieth-century processes of, 46
Riesman, David, 95–96
Riley, Mathilda White, 7
Role theory, 5–6, 82
Ronström, Owe, 129
Runyan, W. M., 168

Sacred texts, aging in, 38
Scientific management of aging, 26–27, 35
Scientism, 35, 36
Scienza Nuova (Vico), 32
Secularism: negative versus positive concept of, 34–35; in scholarship and society, 34
Selective optimization model, 6
Selectivity theory, 3, 6
Self and identity: and discontinuity of aging body, 47; and emergence of mature identity, 48; and external value frameworks, 29; impact of aging body on, 47; postmodern theories of, 105–6; religion and, 38

Self-construction: embodiment of, 165, 192–93; institutions and, 192, 200–204
Self-fulfillment and agency, and organized social activities, 78–82, 83–84, 92
Senescence: The Second Half of Life (Hall), 2, 3
Skinner, B. F., 168
Smith, Huston, 39, 40
Sociability, and organizational membership, 82, 83–84
Social categorization: ethnically-based, 133–34; problem-driven, 132
Social Democratic Workers Party (Sweden), 114–15
Social gerontology. *See* Gerontology
Social institutions. *See* Institutions
Social marginalization, and notions of "imagined community," 106
Social movements: and competing concepts of age, 18; and concept of ageism, 46. *See also* Swedish pensioners' movement
Social organization, and age-stratification paradigm, 7, 9
Social organizational membership: age and gender differences in, 80, 85–88; and age-related change in type of organization, 89–90; benefits of, 82–83; and class, education, and material resources, 80–81, 87–89, 90; and health resources, 87, 88; of older single men, 81–82; and organization type, 82–84; overall levels of, age and, 91; and perpetuation of bases of inequality, 92; as sources of self-identity and self-esteem, 81–82, 90–91, 92; UK study of, 77–84; and widowhood, 81, 89, 90, 91
Social policy on aging: citizenship and, 49–50; and marginalization and discrimination, 68, 129–30
Social sciences: autonomization of knowledge production in, 22; gerontology and, 2, 3–5, 7, 9, 15
Social welfare system: ageism in, 47–51; globalization and privatization impacts on, 51–52; pensioners' dependent status in, 99–100; Swedish, ethnicity and age in, 133–36. *See also* Swedish pensioners' movement
Soul of the American University: From Protestant Establishment to Established Nonbelief, The (Marsden), 34
Spirituality. *See* Religion
Stage theory, 6
Ström, Albin, 113
Ström, Fredrik, 117, 118
Structured dependency paradigm, 46, 68
Subcultural aging, 95–108; and classification of values, 106; and cultures of consolation, 105–6; and decline narratives of biological essentialism, 107; early research on, 97–98; imagined community and biographical continuity in, 106; potential for unity or division in, 100–102; and postmodern theory, 105; power relations and subversive inclinations in, 103; repertoires of resistance in, 102–3; research status of, 98–99; and sociologically-imposed classifications, 100; and vocabularies of motive, 106
Subculture, defined, 99
Swedish older immigrants: age and ethnicity categorical frames in, 134–35; health and care systems and, 135–36; immigrants' language in, 131; official immigration policies and, 130–31; as problematic social category, 132–34; social technological research perspective on, 131; study of, 129–36
Swedish pensioners' movement, 111–26; British Beveridge Plan and, 123; left-wing politics in, 112–16; local poor-law administration in, 111–12, 116–19
Swedish People's Pensioners National League/Organization, 116–21, 122–23

Swedish Social Democratic Party, 112–13, 119–20, 121, 122, 123, 124
Swedish welfare policies, ethnicity and age in, 133–36

Taylor, Charles, 29, 36
Tel-Aviv study of eldercare facilities, 211–12
Third Age cultures: compared to youth cultures, 97–98; concept of, 100; consumerism in, 104–5; economic status of, 97; and marginalization of the very old, 100–101; self-fulfillment and agency in, 78; segregation in, 104–5. *See also* Subcultural aging
Total institutions: double life of inmates in, 214; and representational order, 210–11; separation and exclusion practices of, 208; theory of, 208–9
Transnational organizations and communities, 50–56; and global social policy, 51–53; and nature of citizenship, 54; and older adult employment strategies, 52
Trettondal-Eriksson, Edvin, 116

United Kingdom (UK): age discrimination legislation in, 52; social organizational membership study in, 77–84
University education, secularism in, 34
Us/them dichotomy, 70–71, 73

Vico, Giambattista, 32

Western culture: age-gradedness in, 107; body and its negativities in, 176; and paradigm of indivisibility of body and soul, 209; and religious humanism, 28. *See also* Consumer culture
Widowhood, and social organizational activity, 78, 79, 81, 89, 90, 91
Wolf, Naomi, 150, 151
Women aging, 139–57; and antiaging cosmetic surgery, 144–45; and bodily-focused technologies of self-care, 141–49, 150; and body memories, 162, 165–71; and body-mind relationship, 162–63; and class/gender inequalities, 155; and cohort changes, 79–80; and discourses and paradoxes of resistance, 149–52; and discourses of subjectivity and agency, 148–49; and Foucault's technologies of the self, 140–41, 149–50; and gendered power relationships, 149, 150–52; media and, 142–43, 144; and physical culture technologies, 145–46; research approaches to, 139–40; and sharing of discursive practice, 144, 146; and social structure, 140–57; and systems of production, 150, 155–56; and technologies of signification, 149, 152–54
World Trade Organization's General Agreement on Trade in Services, 51–52

Youth culture, 151; compared to Third Age cultures, 97–98; and youth rebellions of 1960s, 99

About the Contributors

LARS ANDERSSON is Research Director at the Stockholm Gerontology Research Center, Associate Professor of Gerontology at the Karolinska Institute, Stockholm, and President of the Swedish Gerontological Society. He has edited *Socialgerontologi* (in Swedish) (2002) and contributed chapters in several books, the latest being *Family Care of the Elderly* (1992), *Encyclopedia of Human Development* (1993), *The Social Networks of Older People* (1996), and *Work and Caring for the Elderly* (1999). He has published extensively in scholarly journals.

SARA ARBER is professor and Head of the School of Human Sciences and the Department of Sociology at the University of Surrey, United Kingdom, and codirector of the Centre for Research on Ageing and Gender (CRAG). She is coauthor of *The Myth of Generational Conflict: Family and State in Ageing Societies* (with Claudine Attias-Donfut, 2000) and *Women, Work and Pensions* (with Jay Ginn and Debra Street, 2001). Her book with Jay Ginn, *Connecting Gender and Ageing* (1995), won the Age Concern prize for the best book on aging in 1996.

About the Contributors

ANDREW BLAIKIE is professor of historical sociology, Department of Sociology and Anthropology, University of Aberdeen. His books include *Ageing and Popular Culture* (1999). He has contributed numerous chapters, the latest in *Sociological Review* (2001) and *Cultures and the Everyday* (2002).

BILL BYTHEWAY is senior research fellow, School of Health and Social Welfare, The Open University. He is the editor of *Ageing and Society*. His books include *Ageism* (1995) and *Understanding Care, Welfare and Community* (editor) (2001). He has contributed a chapter (together with Julia Johnson) in *Researching Ageing and Later Life: The Practice of Social Gerontology* (2002).

THOMAS R. COLE is Painter Distinguished Professor and Graduate Program Director at the Institute for the Medical Humanities, University of Texas Medical Branch, Galveston. His primary work lies in the field of humanistic gerontology. He is the author of *The Journey of Life: A Cultural History of Aging in America* (1991), senior editor of *Handbook of Humanities and Aging* (1992, 2nd ed. 1999), and senior editor of a newsletter, *Aging and the Human Spirit*.

SVEIN OLAV DAATLAND is Senior Research Fellow at NOVA (Norwegian Social Research), Oslo. He is the editor of *Aldring & Livsløp* and has published extensively in gerontology, including Nordic and international comparative studies. His latest edited books are *Aldring og samfunn* (with Per Erik Solem, 2000) and *Framtidens boformer for eldre* (1999).

KATE DAVIDSON is lecturer and researcher at the University of Surrey. She is Honorary Secretary of the British Society of Gerontology and Codirector of the Centre for Research on Ageing and Gender (CRAG). She has published on widowhood, late-life marriage, and the health and social relationships of older people.

DAVID GAUNT is professor of history and head of planning at the Baltic and East European Graduate School, University College of South Stockholm. He has written widely on the history of family and working life. His recent research is about the history of religious and ethnic minorities in Eastern Europe. His latest publication is the chapter on kinship in *The History of the European Family* (2001).

CHRIS GILLEARD is Director of Psychology for a large mental health NHS Trust serving South West London and Visiting Reader at the Joint Faculty of Health and Social Care Sciences, St. George's

Hospital Medical School, London. He is the coauthor of the recently published book *Cultures of Ageing: Self, Citizen and the Body* (2000) and is currently working on a follow-up, tentatively called *Contexts of Ageing*. He has published a variety of papers on aspects of age and ageing, ranging from biomedical and psychological themes to economic and sociological ones.

JABER F. GUBRIUM is professor of sociology at the University of Florida. His research focuses on the descriptive organization of personal identity, family, the life course, aging, and adaptations to illness. He is the editor of *Journal of Aging Studies* and author of several books, including *Living and Dying at Murrey Manor* (1975), *Caretakers* (1979), *Describing Care* (1982), *Oldtimers and Alzheimer's* (1986), *Speaking of Life* (1993), and (with J. Holstein) *The New Language of Qualitative Method* (1997).

HAIM HAZAN is professor of sociology and social anthropology at Tel Aviv University, Israel. He is the author of numerous articles and several books on aging, community, and nationalism. His latest books are *From First Principles: An Experiment in Aging* (1996) and *Simulated Dreams* (2001).

JAMES A. HOLSTEIN is professor of sociology at Marquette University. He has studied people processing and social control settings, including courts, clinics, schools, and mental health agencies. He is the editor of *Social Problems*, and his books include *Court-Ordered Insanity* (1993), *Dispute Domains and Welfare Claims* (1996), *Reconsidering Social Constructionism* (1993), *Social Problems in Everyday Life* (1997), and (with J. Gubrium) *The Self We Live By: Narrative Identity in a Postmodern World* (2000).

KIM PERREN is research fellow at the Centre for Research on Ageing and Gender (CRAG) in the Department of Sociology, University of Surrey. Her research focuses on secondary analysis of large-scale and longitudinal data sets addressing issues associated with the life course and older people's health and social relationships.

CHRIS PHILLIPSON is professor of applied social studies and social gerontology, dean of postgrauduate affairs, and director of the Centre for Social Gerontology at Keele University. He has published a number of books and articles, including *Reconstructing Old Age* (1998). His latest book (with Miriam Bernard, Judith Phillips, and Jim Ogg, 2001) is *The Family and Community Life of Older People: Social Networks and Social Support in Urban Areas*. He is presently conducting research on issues relating to social exclusion and poverty in old age.

About the Contributors

OWE RONSTRÖM is Associate Professor (docent), Lecturer in Ethnology at Gotland University College, Visby, Sweden. Among recent publications are *Music, Media and Multiculture* (with Dan Lundberg and Krister Malm, 2000) and articles on heritage politics, ethnic humor, and aging.

MARJA SAARENHEIMO, Ph.D., is Research Coordinator, Tampere School of Public Health, Finland. She is the editor of *Gerontologia*. Recent publications include *Jos etsit kadonnutta aikaa—vanhuus ja oman elämän muisteleminen* (1997) and a chapter in *Experiencing Ageing* (1994).

JULIA TWIGG is Professor at the School of Social Policy, Sociology and Social Research, University of Kent. Her books include *Bathing: The Body and Community Care* (2000). She is currently working on a book on the body in social policy.

HANS-JOACHIM VON KONDRATOWITZ is Senior Researcher at Deutsches Zentrum für Altersfragen (DZA) and Privatdozent at Freie Universität Berlin. His publications include *Gerontologie und sozialgeschichte* (with C. Conrad, 1982), *Alltag und alter* (with G. Göckenjan, 1988), *Zur kulturgeschichte des alters* (with C. Conrad, 1993), and *Konjunkturen des Alters* (2000).